VINDICATING
ANDREW JACKSON

American Presidential Elections

MICHAEL NELSON

JOHN M. MCCARDELL, JR.

VINDICATING ANDREW JACKSON

THE 1828 ELECTION AND
THE RISE OF THE
TWO-PARTY SYSTEM
DONALD B. COLE

UNIVERSITY PRESS OF KANSAS

Published by the University Press of Kansas (Lawrence, Kansas 66045), which was organized by the Kansas Board of Regents and is operated and funded by Emporia State University, Fort Hays State University, Kansas State University, Pittsburg State University, the University of Kansas, and Wichita State University

Library of Congress Cataloging-in-Publication Data

Cole, Donald B.
Vindicating Andrew Jackson : the 1828 election and the rise of the two-party system / Donald B. Cole.
p. cm. — (American presidential elections)
Includes bibliographical references and index.
ISBN 978-0-7006-1661-9 (cloth : alk. paper)
1. Presidents—United States—Election—1828. 2. Political campaigns—United States—History—19th century. 3. Jackson, Andrew, 1767–1845, 4. Adams, John Wuincy, 1767–1848.
5. Political parties—United States—History—19th century.
6. Policical culture—United States—History—19th century.
7. United States—Politics and government—1825–1829
I. Title.
E380.C655 2009
973.5´5—dc22   2009015244

British Library Cataloguing-in-Publication Data is available.

Printed in the United States of America

10 9 8 7 6 5 4 3 2 1

The paper used in this publication is recycled and contains 30 percent postconsumer waste. It is acid free and meets the minimum requirements of the American National Standard for Permanence of Paper for Printed Library Materials Z39.48-1992.

For Tootie

CONTENTS

Illustration sections follow pages 19, 29, and 60

It has been called many things.

It has been called the "era of the common man." Constitutional revisions in almost every state had brought the vision of universal white manhood suffrage close to reality. That very term, of course, had limitations, but the boundaries enclosed a more spacious territory, with more room for more participants, than ever before.

It has been called the "era of the transportation revolution." All across America there appeared canals, turnpikes, bridges, and then railroads, binding a loose federation of states into a closer Union. A restless population, in pursuit of the main chance, became more easily mobile. A growing economy linked city and country, supply and demand, and served larger, more distant markets.

It has been called the "era of sectionalism." Separate states began to detect interests in common with their near neighbors, interests at variance with other regional clusters. "North," "South," and "West" became more clearly identifiable. Balancing the demands of state, section, and nation taxed the skills of America's ablest political leaders.

It has been called the "era of reform." A dynamic social order could be unsettling. Debt, drink, and crime seemed out of control. Old ways could seem inadequate, even irrelevant. New ways needed to be found to deal with what seemed monstrous sources of disequilibrium. Root causes needed to be identified and then either remade or slain.

It has been called, simply, the "middle period." Before it came the Jeffersonian age, with the last of the Revolutionary generation defining and securing the meaning of what had been their lifelong struggle. After it would come first the threat, and then the reality, of disunion. The years 1828–1860 sought balance, equilibrium, neither accelerating the coming of the future nor retreating into an unrecoverable and largely mythic past.

And it has been called, perhaps most appropriately, the "age of Jackson." "Old Hickory," the "hero of New Orleans," a bold opportunist and a patriotic traditionalist, burst onto the national political scene in the presidential election of 1824. His defeat, termed by his supporters a "corrupt bargain," launched a new political era, initiated new political practices, fostered new forms of political organization, and, four years later, was avenged in a landslide. The stern, gaunt, imposing figure of Andrew Jackson would tower over the new political generation ushered in by his victory.

Andrew Jackson has been called a "symbol for an age." In Donald Cole's vigorous narrative of the election of 1828, readers will see why. The age was very much one of ambiguity, and to tame it—never mind ultimately to symbolize it—a leader needed to be poised, like the mythical figure Janus, for whom the month of January is named, with one face looking backward, mindful of the known past, and the other looking forward, facing an unknown future. Harnessing the forces of change and tradition, of aspiration and memory, of possibility and experience, Andrew Jackson, and the party he helped found, would define the nation's political agenda, reinvigorate the executive office, and lay down markers clearly evident to supporters and opponents alike.

But these views are all retrospective. They reflect a knowledge of how the story turned out. They impart an ahistorical element of inevitability. Donald Cole wisely avoids such omniscience. As his story unfolds we are reminded of the unpredictability of events, the uncertainty of outcomes. We are reintroduced to a colorful cast of characters, some familiar, others less well known. We learn that on the state level, much of the most interesting and consequential political debate and decision making occurred. We discover, perhaps not to our surprise, that the campaign of 1828 had more to do with personalities than with issues. Finally, we are swept into office with the "Jacksonian Democrats" and witness, in appointments, attitudes, and decorum, just what that term had come to mean.

Most scholars agree that the 1828 election did indeed bring about a reconstitution and reorientation of American political culture. In this volume we learn just how profound those changes were. We see clearly their sources. And we find ourselves persuaded that new men, for new times, are taking their places on a redesigned political stage.

One hundred eighty years have passed since Andrew Jackson was elected president, yet his election and Barack Obama's have much in common. The recent election campaign seemed intolerably long, but the 1828 campaign, which began when John Quincy Adams named Henry Clay secretary of state, was even longer. In both 1828 and 2008 the incumbent president was the son of a former president, and his party had lost control of Congress. Participants on each side hurled dirty, unfair charges toward their opponents, maintaining that Adams had been a pimp, that Jackson was a murderer and an adulterer, that Obama had consorted with traitors, and that John McCain had had an affair. McCain, seventy-two, wore the scars of a melanoma and was called too old, while Jackson, sixty-one, carried two bullets in his body and looked too old. Adams and Obama were dismissed as weak, intellectual elitists who had been educated at Harvard. Jackson and McCain were war heroes with tempers difficult to control. When each election was over, the public knew that something historic had taken place. In 1828, for the first time, Americans elected a man who did not come from the Massachusetts or the Virginia aristocracy, and in 2008 they chose a man whose father was black. And there were more similarities to come. The inauguration in 1829 attracted an enormous, unmanageable mob; in January 2009 the crowd broke all records but was unusually manageable.

Yet the two elections were also quite different. The comparisons depict an Obama similar to Adams and a McCain much like Jackson, but Obama won and Adams lost. In 1828 the incumbent was running for reelection; in 2008 he was not. In the earlier election Americans had put the financial panic of 1819 behind them; in 2008 a worldwide recession was under way. In Jackson's day, the new president was relatively free from international troubles; in Obama's day, the president faces global financial and climatic concerns. Most important, Obama came into office calling for change but may, as of this writing, have to settle for economic recovery. Jackson came in calling for a return to traditional republican ideals and brought in new concepts of political parties and the presidency.

It is this balance of similarities and differences that helps the historian overcome the main hazard in writing about an election—that the reader already knows who won. Since we cannot hide the outcome, we must compensate by raising other questions and by putting our readers in the shoes of earlier Americans who did not already know the outcome. To accomplish this, I have brought part of the story down from the upper level of national party politics to the state and local levels. Americans in 2008 did the same thing when they agonized over whether states such as Pennsylvania, Ohio, and Florida would go to Obama or McCain. I have devoted two chapters to the election in six states—New Hampshire, New York, Pennsylvania, Ohio, Kentucky, and Virginia. I believe these are "representative" states, in that they offer a good social, economic, and political cross section of the United States at the time. I do not, however, contend that they were key states on which the outcome of the election depended, as were Ohio, Pennsylvania, and Florida in 2008.

In writing this book I have incurred debts to a number of persons. Two of them—Thomas M. Coens, assistant research professor at the University of Tennessee and assistant editor of the Andrew Jackson Papers, and Mark Cheathem, associate professor of history at Cumberland University—cheerfully and skillfully found the time to read and evaluate my first draft. Another, William N. Copely, reference librarian at the New Hampshire Historical Society, provided a picture of Isaac Hill and pertinent information about election returns, gazetteers, and campaign books. Director of the University Press of Kansas Fred Woodward and the editors of this series, Michael Nelson and John McCardell, carefully edited and improved the second draft. William C. Cook, a member of the Advisory Board of the Papers of Andrew Jackson, provided fresh insights into the smear campaign waged against Jackson. Jacqueline Thomas and everyone else at the Phillips Exeter Academy library have been my friends for many years. They sent away for books, copied articles from the Internet, and showed a warm interest in what I was doing. Staff members at the University of New Hampshire library were uniformly helpful and courteous. My friend and neighbor Dr. James Tucker rushed over at a moment's notice to rescue me from disasters on the computer. Friend and colleague Robert Brownell helped edit my introductory chapter and was kind enough to ask about the book when he really wanted to talk about the 2008 election. I am also grateful to several libraries that granted me permission to quote from documents in their collections:

the Princeton University Library, the New-York Historical Society, and the New York Public Library.

But above all there was my family, who gave me love and support. Suz and Jeff helped write this preface. Most of my children live far away, but none could escape my panicky calls for technical support. The book is dedicated to Tootie, who contributed to it in many ways while continuing to do the more important work of caring for the family.

The presidential election of 1828 has long been one of the best known and most compelling stories in American history. As the story was first told, the hero of New Orleans and man of the people, Andrew Jackson, came out of the West in 1824 to run for president. In a four-man election he won a plurality of the popular and electoral vote, but because of some questionable political maneuvering by his opponents, he lost the runoff election in the House of Representatives to John Quincy Adams. Four years later Jackson mounted a hard-hitting, democratic campaign filled with mudslinging on both sides and won an overwhelming victory. The people responded by storming Washington for Jackson's inauguration and staging a rowdy celebration that left the White House in shambles.[1]

Since that time the story has been amplified, and the election of 1828 has taken on great proportions. Historians and biographers have described Jackson as the leader of the common man in the election and have given him credit for the rise of democracy in America. Political scientists have designated the election as the start of a new American political system.[2]

The story has been oversimplified and overdramatized, but it need not detract from the significance of what actually took place. The election of 1828 contributed greatly to the rise of democracy and mass political parties, the hallmarks of American politics. Politicians on both sides used partisan campaign techniques on a scale never seen before, laid the groundwork for the Democratic and Whig parties, got Americans into the habit of coming out to vote for president in large numbers, and elevated a new type of American to the presidency.

The election also cast a long shadow. Andrew Jackson became president just as the last of the founding fathers were passing from the scene. With power now in their hands, the Jackson Democrats and their Whig opponents had the opportunity to shape the world the founding fathers had given them. For the next three decades they set the political agenda and molded the American political culture at a time when it was most malleable. In the terms of political scientist Stephen Skowronek, the election of Jackson—midway between those of Jefferson and

Lincoln—brought about the second major reconstruction of American political life.[3]

Through the use of the spoils system the Democrats and the Whigs established a lasting two-party system and brought into the government a more representative group of officials than in the past. The Democrats sought to reduce the power of the government but quickly strengthened the office of the president, who became the tribune of the people and the head of the party as well as the chief executive. Jackson showed the possibilities of these new roles when he vetoed the bill to recharter the Bank of the United States.

The election of 1828 did much to bring democracy to America, but what sort of democracy? During his eight years in office Jackson moved thousands of Native Americans across the Mississippi River, where they would live apart from American citizens. In the social quarrel about Margaret Eaton, the promiscuous wife of Secretary of War John Eaton, the new president won a Pyrrhic victory over the women who dominated the society of Washington, lessening the political power they had begun to assert. And in response to abolitionism Jackson's party used legislation, court decisions, mob riots, and control of the mails to keep black Americans in their place.

The election of 1828, then, offers an opportunity to examine a decisive moment in the rise of American democracy. And since democracy plays such a large role in this book, it seems best to start with a definition (adapted from one I used in a book on Amos Kendall, author of the bank veto and a key figure in the 1828 election and the rise of American democracy): *Democracy* is a constantly changing political culture based on ideals that men and women have had to fight for and that have never been fully achieved. It has its roots in an egalitarian society in which the mass of the people enjoys what historian Gordon S. Wood has called "a rough equality of condition." It depends on a political system that provides organizations and procedures that enable the people to express their opinions, elect a government, and ensure that their will is carried out. In many ways democracy is like the republicanism that Americans talked and wrote so much about during the Revolution and afterward (we still call our government a republic), but unlike republicanism, which places limits on the power of the government and the people in order to protect liberty, democracy assumes that the majority can rule and expects it to do so.[4]

In the mid-1820s the United States had a rudimentary egalitarian society, but it denied suffrage to large blocs of people and lacked a political system on which democracy could depend. To understand how the election of 1828 affected democracy we go back to the spring of 1825, when the campaign began.

THE SPRING OF 1825

In the spring of 1825, fifty years since the minutemen had stood their ground at Lexington and Concord, Americans were taking stock of their young republic. They were unusually pleased with themselves—some foreign travelers thought excessively so. Americans had won their independence, had written federal and state constitutions, and were becoming the world's first large-scale democracy.

They had doubled the physical size of their nation and more than quadrupled its population. Instead of 2.5 million British colonists, most of them within a day's ride of the Atlantic Ocean, there were now more than 11 million Americans, more than a third of them living west of the Appalachian Mountains. The thirteen original colonies had grown into a nation of twenty-four states and three territories reaching west to the big bend in the Missouri River. And the expansion showed no signs of letting up, for the Louisiana Purchase had brought the United States to the crest of the Rockies—within striking distance of the Pacific Ocean.

It was a banner year for the movement westward. On February 12, 1825, U.S. government agents started opening up land in western Georgia by signing a treaty under which a portion of the Creek Indians agreed to move west. On July 4 woodsmen would start clearing the way for a National Road running from the Ohio River at Wheeling, Virginia, across the new states of Ohio, Indiana, and Illinois. And on October 26 the state of New York would celebrate the opening of the Erie Canal, connecting the Atlantic Ocean with the Great Lakes.

Americans bragged that they made more money and lived better than their counterparts in Europe. In foreign affairs they had negotiated successful treaties, fought off a British attack at New Orleans (though not one at Washington), and warned the powers of Europe not to tamper with the Americas. The United States was the world's great new nation.

And Europeans agreed. The German poet Heinrich Heine exclaimed admiringly, "This is America indeed! / This is a new world, really new!"[1] British foreign secretary George Canning, describing his role in keeping the European Holy Alliance away from America, boasted that he had "called the New World into existence to redress the balance of the Old."[2] Scholars Alexis de Tocqueville and Gustave Beaumont would soon come to the United States ostensibly to examine the Americans' new prisons but really to find out about their new democracy.

Despite these paeans to newness, Americans in 1825 were preoccupied with the past. As they celebrated the fiftieth anniversary of the Revolution, they not only reveled in American greatness but also mourned the deaths of the Revolutionary heroes and founding fathers. There was a steady drumbeat of anniversaries and funerals as the old heroes, one by one, passed away—Daniel Boone in 1820, John Stark of New Hampshire in 1822, John Taylor of Virginia in 1824. In 1820 only thirteen of the eighty-three signers of the Declaration of Independence or the Constitution still lived. On the Fourth of July 1826, the almost simultaneous deaths of Thomas Jefferson and John Adams would reduce the number to five. The election of 1828 would be carried on amidst a somber national mood of memory, emotion, nostalgia, and, most of all, introspection.[3]

Looking to the past, Americans firmly believed that the Revolution and the rise of the United States were epochal events brought on by divine providence. To commemorate these events they turned to a wide range of the arts. Congress commissioned painter (and Revolutionary War veteran) John Trumbull to prepare four massive murals (twelve by eighteen feet) for the Rotunda of the Capitol building. The paintings, which depicted the signing of the Declaration of Independence, the surrender of Burgoyne at Saratoga, the surrender of Cornwallis at Yorktown, and the resignation of George Washington from his command, were installed in 1826. Five years later divinity school student Samuel Francis Smith would write the words for "America," and in 1832 Congress would call on Horatio Greenough to carve a statue of Washington for the Rotunda.

Historians also told the nation's story. By 1825 David Ramsay, Mercy Otis Warren, and Jedidiah Morse had written histories of the Revolution, and hardly a state was without its own published history. Jeremy Belknap's *History of New Hampshire* (1792) and Benjamin Trumbull's *Complete History of Connecticut* (1818) are still classics. As yet no one had written a definitive history of the entire nation, but George Bancroft would soon give up schoolmastering and start his *History of the United States.*[4]

One of the more popular sources of American history was the story of Natty Bumppo, the hero of James Fenimore Cooper's five *Leatherstocking Tales,* three of which appeared between 1822 and 1827. Cooper follows his hero as a young man (modeled, some say, on Daniel Boone) through the French and Indian Wars (*The Deerslayer, The Last of the Mohicans,* and *The Pathfinder*) to the settlement of upstate New York (*The Pioneers*) and on to the West (*The Prairie*), where the old man dies.

Perhaps even more influential than the histories were the orations, for Americans prized oratory and were accustomed to being moved by the spoken word. In December 1820, 1,500 people squeezed inside the First Church of Plymouth to hear Daniel Webster give his oration on the 200th anniversary of the landing of the Pilgrims. With his giant head and massive body, his black, piercing eyes, and his powerful yet melodious speaking voice, Webster had no peer as an orator. His young friend George Ticknor, already a professor at Harvard, was so moved by the address that he feared his "temples would burst with the gush of blood."[5]

In the late spring of 1825 Webster gave another oration, this time to celebrate the fiftieth anniversary of the Battle of Bunker Hill. As he completed his address he called on Americans to build a nation "upon which the world may gaze with admiration."[6] Webster's orations and Bancroft's history—both based on American faith in divine providence—helped lay the foundation for the view, still powerful today, that the United States is a special, exceptional nation. Bancroft's most recent biographer refers to his ten-volume history as a "multivolume sermon."[7]

Stirred again, Ticknor reported that the oration "brought tears into the eyes of many."[8] One of them was the Marquis de Lafayette, now sixty-eight, who had returned to America to join in the celebration of the Revolution. After landing in New York in August 1824, Lafayette set out on an emotional tour that took him through every state in the Union. Congress received him in the Capitol, which had been restored after the British attack, and Andrew Jackson entertained him at his Tennessee plantation, the Hermitage. The tour, Charles Sumner later remarked, "belong[ed] to the poetry of history."[9]

Webster had reflected this mood at Bunker Hill when he turned to the handful of Revolutionary veterans seated near him and said gently, "Venerable Men! You have come down to us from a former generation," then added sadly, "But alas! You are not all here. Time and the sword have thinned your ranks." Then, speaking to the entire audience, he uttered a challenge: "The great trust now descends to new hands. . . . We can win no laurels in a war for independence. Earlier and worthier hands have gathered them all. . . . But there remains to us a great duty of defense and preservation. . . . Let us see whether we also, in our day and generation, may not perform something worthy to be remembered."[10]

Webster spoke for most Americans, who, steeped in national pride, wondered whether they were capable of carrying on for men "worthier" than they. His generation would not be the last to take on such a burden—especially in troubled times. Long after the Civil War, southerners persisted in glorifying Robert E. Lee and his lieutenants. In our own time Americans have showered praise on the "greatest generation," which survived the Depression and won World War II. And, as best-seller lists demonstrate, Americans have not ceased looking back longingly at the founding fathers.

The common thread running through all these memories and celebrations was devotion to the republican ideals that had stirred the revolutionaries of 1775. Republicanism was based on the central theme of individual liberty versus institutional power. Like the founding fathers, Americans believed that all white men had the right to be free from the control (power) of any person or government. To achieve this goal they had to act with personal and civic virtue and support a virtuous government. Most Americans in 1825 believed in simplicity, a rural, agrarian way of life, and the preeminence of the community over the individual, local government over national authority, and individual liberty over central power. They looked suspiciously at capitalism and the individualism that went with it. They feared the corruption of city life, commerce, and monarchical power. And they longed for a farmer-hero like George Washington who would, like the Roman hero Cincinnatus, give up his plow and defend his people. Trumbull's art and Webster's orations drew heavily on republican themes, while Cooper's *Leatherstocking Tales* portrayed Natty Bumppo as a free, virtuous, republican man of nature, resisting the gross materialism of a new age.[11]

The best expression of republicanism in the North was the writing of Jeremy Belknap. In the final paragraph of his *History of New Hampshire,* which was republished in 1813, Belknap gives his readers a "picture of a happy society." It would be, he wrote,

> a land well fenced and cultivated. . . . The inhabitants mostly hus-bandmen; their wives and daughters domestic manufacturers; a suit-able proportion of handicraft workmen; and two or three traders; a physician and lawyer, each of whom should have a farm for his sup-port. A clergyman of any denomination . . . a man of good under-standing . . . not a metaphysical, nor a polemic, but a serious and practical preacher. A school master who should . . . teach his pupils to govern themselves. A social library. . . . A club of sensible men, seek-ing mutual improvement. . . . No intriguing politician, horse jockey, gambler, or sot.[12]

Even better known and more influential were the opinions of the "Old Republicans" of the South. Their spokesman was John Taylor of Caroline County, Virginia, who, between 1814 and 1823, published four volumes warning of the dangers of social and economic change. The United States, he argued, could maintain its republican ideals only if it remained a predominantly farming society, with a clear separation of power between the people and their governments and between the states and the federal government. He warned that capitalism, with its system of banking and paper money, would break down the separation of powers and corrupt the republic. Slavery was necessary, he insisted, to provide a barrier against capitalism and to allow poor southern whites to maintain their status as free republican farmers who did not have to do the bidding of anyone.

Starting with the American Revolution, this republican vision had blended with the individualistic, free-labor, egalitarian concepts that came with the war and with independence. Most of the Tories—an im-portant element in the old ruling class—were soon gone or out of power, and less elegant men were taking their place. Aristocratic ways of dress, recreation, and even dueling in defense of honor were going out of favor. Hierarchy and deference were in retreat. The spirit of democracy was in the air.[13]

Fascinated by reports of the democratic New World, British and other European travelers were coming to America to see for themselves. One of them, William Cobbett of Surrey, England, came twice, and on returning from his second visit in 1818 he painted a vivid picture of American democracy. Few Americans, he wrote, were "very much raised in men's estimation, above the general mass." Great wealth did "very little indeed in the way of purchasing even the outward signs of respect."[14]

Americans found many outlets for this democratic feeling. In the parades and festivals celebrating the founding of the new nation, artisans and common laborers, women and blacks marched with more powerful Americans, waving banners to make their opinions known. In salons and at afternoon teas women tried to goad men into seeing the world as they did. A new print culture spawned by an explosion of newspapers made it possible for Americans to see beyond their local spheres, absorb new ideas, and take part in shaping their society. America was becoming a participatory, republican-democratic society in which a wide range of groups found ways to express themselves.[15]

Despite this egalitarianism the original states had been surprisingly cautious in granting the most important mode of expression—the right to vote. Although all thirteen state constitutions granted suffrage to a large segment of adult white males, eight of them tacked on substantial property and taxpaying requirements. As a result only about 60 percent of adult white men were eligible to vote.[16]

By 1825, however, the rising tide of democracy had swept away almost all the restrictions, and only three of the twenty-four states still had property requirements. One of the last great debates over the issue came at the New York convention of 1821, when the old Federalist chancellor James Kent, dismayed by the change, warned that it would lead to "corruption, injustice, violence, and tyranny." Taxpaying requirements for voting remained in thirteen states, but most were worded so that relatively few men were actually kept from voting. It is safe to say that by 1825 almost all adult white males were eligible to vote in state and federal elections.

Women and black Americans were treated less well. None of the original states, except New Jersey, granted suffrage to women, and even there the right applied only to wealthy widows and was soon removed. Ten of the thirteen states gave free blacks who owned property the right to vote, but by 1825 free blacks could vote in only eight of the twenty-four states, and the number continued to drop. Democracy had grown for white men but had declined for women and blacks.

The broadening of male suffrage greatly increased voting, but many obstacles still stood in the way. One was the difficulty of getting to the polls. In New England, where voting took place in small towns, the problem was not great, but in other states, where voting was by counties, it was a serious deterrent. The states dealt with this problem by creating voting districts or townships within counties and by continually creating more counties. In Ohio, for example, the number of counties grew from nine in 1803 to twenty-eight in 1809 and sixty-four by 1825.

Other obstacles were slowly—often too slowly—disappearing. One was the underrepresentation of certain counties in state legislatures, which was a constant source of friction in the western counties of Virginia, North Carolina, and Louisiana. Virginians held a constitutional convention in 1829 to deal with this question but made little change. In other states rapidly growing cities such as Providence, Philadelphia, and Baltimore were also underrepresented.

A third obstacle existed in states where the governor or a special council rather than the voters had the power to choose many of the state and local officials. New York abolished its council of appointment in 1821, but a similar effort to strip this power from the governor of Pennsylvania fell short in 1825.

At first the percentage of adult white males who exercised the right to vote in state elections was low, but the fierce political battles between Federalists and Republicans in the late 1790s soon brought more voters to the polls. In Massachusetts, for example, the vote doubled and by 1808 had reached 70 percent of eligible voters. The same was true in Pennsylvania, where turnout rose from a low of 25 percent to 70 percent in 1808. Up to 1825 the median highest recorded turnout in each state was a respectable 69 percent, even though several states lagged far behind. In Virginia, where property qualifications were still restrictive, the highest turnout was barely one out of four.[17]

The voting percentage in presidential elections was consistently low, partly because many state legislatures, which had the authority to decide how presidential electors were chosen, kept the power in their own hands rather than give it to the people. In the decisive election of 1800 the people voted for the electors in only five of the sixteen states, and in 1812 in only nine of eighteen. But popular pressure forced a change. By 1824 the number had risen to eighteen out of twenty-four. Even New York—where Martin Van Buren's powerful state party preferred to keep the voting right in the legislature, which it controlled—was forced to give in a year later.[18]

Even in states where the people were allowed to vote for electors, the turnout for presidential elections was low—31 percent of eligible voters in 1800, 37 percent in 1808, and 26 percent in 1824.[19] One reason was that at this early stage, national economic issues such as the tariff did not affect enough voters to draw them to the polls. A second reason was sectionalism, which encouraged people to vote for candidates from their own section of the country; if there was no such candidate, they tended not to vote at all. And in years when there was no doubt about the presidential outcome, as in 1820, there was little incentive for anyone anywhere to vote for president.

A third reason for the low turnout was the general (winner-take-all) system of counting the votes of the states. This arrangement was favored by the large states because it increased their influence. Under this system, which was in effect in almost all the states, voters who favored a certain candidate had no incentive to vote if the rest of the state was against him. This general system is still in effect today in all states except for Maine and Nebraska.

After overcoming the many obstacles to voting and making their way to polling stations, voters still had difficulty voting freely. Voting was ordinarily viva voce, and even the increased use of printed ballots did not entirely solve the secrecy problem. Ballots were usually prepared by the candidates and were so distinctive in shape and color that onlookers could easily tell how an individual was voting. This interfered with free voting. Based on a study of congressional investigations of contested elections, Richard Franklin Bensel concluded that violence and drunkenness were common at the polls. Political party men frequently attacked their opponents and bribed bystanders with liquor to get their votes. Congressional investigating committees generally refused to take any action unless conditions at the polling stations were worse than a man of average courage could stand.[20]

Despite the many obstacles and limitations, the democratic surge that historians once attributed to Andrew Jackson and the election of 1828 was already well under way before the campaign had even begun. Americans had come out of the Revolution believing in democracy and had found many formal and informal ways of putting it into operation. Nearly all adult white males had the right to vote, and in many states increasing numbers were beginning to take advantage of that right. George Bancroft, who would become America's first great historian, was exaggerating when he said in 1826 that "the government [was] a democracy, a determined, uncompromising democracy," but that is what white male Americans believed.[21] The task of defining democracy and making it work was only beginning.

Much of this task would lie in the hands of political parties, which held an anomalous position in the political culture of colonial and early republican America. From the earliest days down to the 1820s politics was a vital part of American life. The battles between British governors and their legislatures, between landed gentry and tenants, between Patriots and Tories, and between Federalists and Anti-Federalists were early examples of American politics. After the establishment of the national government in 1789 the struggle continued, this time between Federalists and Republicans.

But Americans had been slow to accept politicians and political parties, in part because of the doctrines of republicanism. Immersed in the republican ideal of political harmony, they believed that virtuous candidates should rise up freely from the people and serve the common good without the aid of parties or politicians. They disapproved of parties, saying they were organized by selfish politicians with selfish interests. In 1784 Jeremy Belknap pointedly remarked that in his ideal society there would be no room for "intriguing politician[s]." While running for Congress in upstate New York in 1802, James Fenimore Cooper's father William Cooper, perhaps hypocritically, denounced his opponent for engaging in politics, which he called "'the art of Hook and Snivey' (trickery and deceit)."[22]

A second reason for the slow growth of political parties was what Daniel Walker Howe has dubbed the "tyranny of distance."[23] Political parties depended on the ability of groups of men to meet frequently, and with the rough transportation and communications systems of early America, this was well nigh impossible.

Trapped by republican idealism and medieval systems of communication and transportation, Americans made do with an ad hoc political system in which national parties were not fully developed. Although 1789 to 1815 has been called the era of the first American party system, that system fell far short of modern American politics, and after the War of 1812 the Federalist party disappeared. America then entered what has been called the Era of Good Feelings, in which a majority of the voters thought of themselves as Republicans.

At about the same time Americans rejected one of the few national political institutions that had been developed during the first party system—the congressional caucus. Ever since 1796, Republican members of Congress had held a caucus in the winter of every fourth year to nominate a presidential candidate. First the small states turned against the caucus, saying that it violated their constitutional rights by giving the large states more votes. When Van Buren arranged a caucus in 1824, which nominated Secretary of the Treasury William H. Crawford, only a minority of Republican congressmen attended. It never met again.

Ironically, the start of the Era of Good Feelings, when parties were supposedly superfluous, coincided with revolutions in transportation and communication that encouraged the growth of a new theory of political parties. The transportation revolution came in many forms. New toll roads allowed travelers to go from New York to Boston in half the previous time. The advent of the steamboat did even better—cutting the trip from New York to Albany from a week to half a day and the upriver ordeal from New Orleans to Louisville from three months to one or two weeks. The economic impact of the Erie Canal exceeded all expectations. Between 1820 and 1850 the combined populations of Rochester, Buffalo, and Syracuse rose from about 5,000 to 100,000; the cost of shipping goods from New York to Buffalo plummeted; and the migration of New England Yankees to northern Ohio, Indiana, and Illinois increased at a rapid pace. A comparable stimulus to westward movement was the National Road (built between 1811 and 1838), which eventually ran from Baltimore to Vandalia, Illinois. In the long run, however, the most influential development was the railroad. The first steam railroad, the Baltimore and Ohio, was chartered in 1828 and put into operation in 1830.[24]

The communications revolution was just as dramatic and had an even greater effect on political parties. The increase in the number of newspapers, on which parties depended to disseminate their doctrines, was spectacular, rising from about ninety in 1789 to about eight hundred in 1829. But this increase would have meant little without the expansion of the U.S. Post Office, which was designed primarily to transport newspapers rather than private correspondence. The seventy-five local post offices in existence in 1790 had multiplied to about 6,500 by 1825. That same year there was a post office for every 1,542 Americans, compared with one for every 43,084 in 1790.[25] After his visit to America in 1831 and 1832, Alexis de Tocqueville would conclude that Americans on the frontier received more news and information than did people in the middle of France.

Hand in hand with these two revolutions was the spread of capitalism. By 1825 urban financial centers and state banks—both essential to capitalism—were becoming increasingly available. A handful of state banks in the 1790s had multiplied into more than three hundred by 1825, and after doing away with the First Bank of the United States in 1811, the federal government set up the Second Bank five years later. With populations approaching 200,000 each, New York and Philadelphia were becoming major centers of national and international commerce; New Orleans and Cincinnati offered thriving markets in the West.

The rise of businesses that crossed state lines brought the national government into the economy. Republicans, who had come into power as states' rights agrarians in 1801, warmed up to nationalist, capitalist ways by purchasing Louisiana, establishing the National Road and the Second Bank of the United States, and supporting protective tariffs. People began to call them National Republicans. John Marshall's Supreme Court endorsed the Second Bank in 1819 in *McCulloch v. Maryland* and five years later encouraged the spread of steamboat companies by ruling against a state monopoly in *Gibbons v. Ogden.*

The first great American industry, textile manufacturing, was already emerging. Encouraged by the success of small cotton mills in Rhode Island and southern Massachusetts, Boston Associates in 1813 had raised $400,000 and built the first American factory that put the entire process of manufacturing cotton under one roof. This venture was so successful that by 1825 Lowell, Massachusetts, was built—a new town devoted exclusively to cotton and woolen manufacturing. Between 1820 and 1825 the number of cotton spindles in the United States jumped from 200,000 to 800,000. Supporting the new industry was an enormous expansion in the growth of cotton and the raising of sheep. Between 1815 and 1826 southern planters increased their annual production of cotton from 210,000 to 730,000 bales, while farmers in states such as New York, Pennsylvania, Ohio, and Kentucky added greatly to their flocks of sheep.[26]

The transportation and communications revolutions and the emergence of a national capitalist economy with national issues stimulated the rise of national political parties. Capitalism, with its individualism and private interests, convinced many Americans that republican political harmony was no longer attainable. The republican assumption that candidates would spring up freely among the people no longer seemed to apply. New-style party politicians, such as Martin Van Buren in New York, Stephen Simpson in Pennsylvania, Isaac Hill in New Hampshire, and Amos Kendall in Kentucky, began to form state parties and argue that parties were a positive good. Only parties, they insisted, could keep selfish economic, sectional, and political interests in check.

By 1825 the central committees in a few state parties had become so powerful that the public had begun to use regal terms to describe them, such as Van Buren's Albany Regency in New York and Hill's Concord Regency in New Hampshire. In addition, there were Thomas Ritchie's Richmond Junto and John Overton's Nashville Junto. The new concept of parties was becoming more and more acceptable, but with one important caveat. The public, still loyal to republican views, insisted that parties be based on republican principles, not partisan interests. So the election campaign of 1828 began with a paradox: politicians were busy forming political parties, while at the same time denying that they believed in parties.[27]

The transformation of the economy had important sectional and political implications. Before the economic changes New England had been a Federalist stronghold relying on commerce and opposed to high tariffs. At the Hartford Convention in the winter of 1814–1815 delegates from the New England states had denounced the War of 1812 and adopted states' rights resolutions designed to weaken the central government. But now that New England had become a manufacturing region, it had abandoned states' rights and come out in favor of tariff protection. The South, in contrast, had once been sympathetic toward nationalist programs, including the tariff and the War of 1812. Now, with its rapidly growing dependence on cotton growing, it had swung toward an extreme states' rights position in opposing protective tariffs.

The expansion of American economic interests led to more intensive political conflicts that had to be settled on a national basis. All this greatly strengthened the importance of the national government, which alone could pass laws concerning tariffs, internal improvements, banking regulations, land policy, and bankruptcy that affected the entire economy. In this setting, political parties could serve as useful organizations, defending principles and passing legislation that could reduce sectionalism and unite the country. There were no national parties in 1825, but the need for them was growing.

Accompanying the rise of political parties was the emergence of evangelicalism. The religious revivals of the Second Great Awakening, which had begun at Cane Ridge, Kentucky, in 1801, were now in full swing. In 1825 the most famous revival preacher of the era, Charles Grandison

Finney, was starting his ministry in western New York. The surge of evangelicalism had much in common with the rise of democracy, capitalism, and political parties. As a form of individual self-expression, evangelicalism offered those who lacked political power a chance to participate in American society. Like capitalism and political parties, evangelicalism took advantage of the transportation and communications revolutions. The rapid expansion of roads, canals, post offices, newspapers, and other forms of communication and transportation spread the evangelical word just as it transported manufactures, publicized political messages, and reported financial information.

The religious fervor greatly increased membership in the Baptist and Methodist churches at the expense of the established Congregational, Presbyterian, and Episcopal denominations. It also contributed to the emergence of a series of reform groups that appeared, one after another, between 1816 and 1828—the American Colonization Society, American Bible Society, American Sunday School Union, American Tract Society, American Home Missionary Society, American Temperance Society, and American Peace Society. Sabbatarianism was revived; abolitionism, labor reform, and other humanitarian movements were just ahead. Out of these movements came political techniques such as holding conventions and petitioning the government, which influenced the development of political parties.[28]

Within this setting two events took place that sparked economic and political conflicts and stimulated the rise of state and local parties. The expansion of the economy in the three years after the War of 1812 created a financial bubble—particularly in the West, where prices rose 30 percent and the number of banks more than quintupled. In 1819 the bubble burst. Startled by a sudden drop in the European demand for corn, wheat, and cotton and an abrupt reversal of the favorable American balance of trade, directors of the Bank of the United States and many of the new state banks began to call in their loans. The contraction started a sharp economic panic. Prices fell precipitately—30 percent in Cincinnati—workers lost their jobs, dozens of banks closed, and farmers faced the danger of losing their land.

The panic of 1819 shook American confidence in the new capitalist economy, arousing resentment among speculators, disappointed investors, laid-off workers, and farmers facing foreclosure. It triggered a shift from politics built on personal factions to politics based on social and economic issues. In Kentucky a protest movement led by the populist

Relief party gained control of the legislature and passed legislation to help protect debtors from foreclosure. Relief parties sprang up in almost a dozen other states.

The panic threatened the political order in many communities. In the small milling and manufacturing town of Dayton, Ohio, failure of the town bank led to the formation of a new party that demanded republican moral and economic reforms and quickly overthrew the old Presbyterian-Federalist leadership. In the neighborhoods of Philadelphia, Pittsburgh, and Harrisburg, the panic united poor workers and farmers against the business-oriented New School party, which controlled Pennsylvania's state government. And in Boston the panic strengthened the hand of the "middling interests" made up of mechanics, shopkeepers, and day laborers in their efforts to overturn the established Federalist party. Although the movement failed, it reshaped politics in the city.[29]

While the panic was at its worst, another crisis was reshaping American politics. On February 13, 1819, James Tallmadge, a congressman from the De Witt Clinton wing of the New York Republican party, introduced an amendment to a bill for Missouri's admission to statehood. His amendment prohibited the further introduction of slaves into Missouri and called for the gradual emancipation of slave children born after the state was admitted. The proposal threatened to stop the spread of slavery and, like the panic, caught most Americans by surprise.

Ever since the acceptance of slavery in the Constitution there had been a truce in the dispute over the subject. Northerners were free to abolish slavery in their own states but would not interfere with it in the South. Influential southerners seemed embarrassed by slavery and resigned to its eventual disappearance. Only three years before Tallmadge spoke, northern and southern men of substance had joined in forming the American Colonization Society, which proposed giving slaves their freedom and transporting them to Africa.

But the invention of the cotton gin and the rise of the textile industry had turned cotton into a precious commodity, sending cotton planters into Alabama and Mississippi and increasing the demand for slaves. Between 1810 and 1830 the number of slaves in the United States would double, and attitudes toward slavery would harden.

Tallmadge's amendment opened a passionate congressional debate over the power of the central government to stop the extension of slavery. The debate was cut short in March by the adjournment of Congress but was renewed in December when two prominent New Yorkers, Federalist senator Rufus King and another follower of Clinton, Congressman John W. Taylor, led the charge against permitting slavery in Missouri. Their efforts were blocked by Speaker of the House Henry Clay, who engineered the famous Missouri Compromise. Congress admitted Missouri with no restriction on slavery (in effect, making it a slave state) and Maine (which was being separated from Massachusetts) without slavery, and it prohibited the spread of slavery into the Louisiana Purchase north and west of Missouri.

Many southerners were convinced that a combination of northern Federalists (or former Federalists) and Clintonian Republicans was out to abolish slavery. Within a few months two other events increased tension in the South. In 1821 Benjamin Lundy founded the antislavery newspaper the *Genius of Universal Emancipation* in Ohio, and a year later a free black, Denmark Vesey, planned a slave revolt in Charleston, South Carolina. The plot was discovered and put down before it got started, but southerners were alarmed. One cried out that "the unreflecting zeal of the North and East" had stirred up Vesey "in his hellish efforts."[30] Others warned that a government with the power to decide on slavery in Missouri could also claim the right to abolish slavery entirely.

In the spring of 1825 two complementary forces were at work in America. The republican writings of Belknap and Taylor, the reaction against capitalism and political parties, the southern defensiveness about slavery, and the mood of introspection over the passing of the founding fathers all encouraged Americans to stick to the doctrines of classical republicanism. At the same time the spectacular expansion of capitalism, the pride in economic growth, the removal of obstacles to voting, and the new attitude toward political parties were turning Americans toward a more democratic republicanism. The sudden resentment and fear aroused by the panic of 1819 and the abrupt polarizing of attitudes toward slavery demonstrated the power of the two forces. These forces would have to be reckoned with in the election of 1828.

Men, of course, would also have to be reckoned with, especially the handful of political figures who were about to assume leadership of the generation succeeding the founding fathers. First in 1825 was the new president, John Quincy Adams of Massachusetts, the son of former president John Adams. The new President Adams was a scholarly man who had begun his political career as a Federalist but then shifted over to the Republican side. As secretary of state he had acquired Florida, arranged to have the Spanish give up Oregon, and helped Monroe write the Monroe Doctrine.[31]

When Adams took office on March 4, however, the public was more interested in how he had got there than what he had accomplished. In the election of 1824 Senator Andrew Jackson of Tennessee had won a plurality of the popular and electoral vote, but since he had not won a majority of the electoral vote, the election was sent to the House of Representatives. There on February 9, 1825, the members of the House had to choose among the three candidates with the most electoral votes—Jackson; Adams, who had come in second; and Secretary of the Treasury William Harris Crawford of Georgia, who was third. Speaker of the House Henry Clay of Kentucky, in fourth place, was not eligible, but he was in a position to affect the outcome of the election through his influence over the three states he had carried in November.

In the House election each of the twenty-four state delegations had one vote, and a majority, or thirteen votes, was needed to be elected. After much maneuvering, Adams barely won the thirteen required votes, leaving seven for Jackson and four for Crawford. His thirteen votes included three states—Illinois, Indiana, and Louisiana—that had voted for Jackson in the original election and two—New York and Maryland—in which the decisive votes were cast by Federalists won over by Daniel Webster. According to Webster, Adams had promised to appoint Federalists to office in return. But the Jacksonians laid the blame for their loss on the delegates of the three states won by Clay—Kentucky, Missouri, and Ohio. In all three Jackson had come in second to Clay in the original election but, at Clay's direction, they went over to Adams in the House election. Had any one of these eight delegations voted for Jackson or Crawford instead of for Adams, the latter would not have had a majority, and the outcome would have been uncertain. Van Buren thought that Crawford might have won as a compromise candidate on a later ballot.

When Adams immediately appointed Clay secretary of state, the Jackson men were outraged and accused the two of having made a "corrupt bargain." The Jacksonians were angry because the secretary of state was considered the heir apparent to the presidency. They also thought it dishonorable that Adams and Clay, who had once been enemies, were now plotting to gain power. The accusation was never proved and was somewhat unfair, since the two men agreed on most economic issues and

Henry Clay deserves credit for organizing the Adams (later Whig) party.

John Quincy Adams was accused of winning the election of 1824 by making a bargain with Henry Clay.

Daniel Webster, known as "godlike" because of his oratory, worked to get Federalists into the Adams party.

Andrew Jackson became the first presidential candidate to participate actively in his election campaign.

John C. Calhoun. Early in the campaign he attacked President Adams in the "Onslow"–"Patrick Henry" debate; at the end he attacked the North for its tariff policy.

Martin Van Buren went to the Senate in 1821 to restore the old Virginia–New York political alliance, and succeeded.

thus had every reason to join forces. It would, however, continue to dog Adams and Clay throughout the coming campaign.

Soon after Adams took office Clay and others suggested that it would be good politics to remove officeholders who had opposed Adams during the campaign and replace them with his friends. The new president was not naïve or ignorant about politics. He noted in his diary that several of these opposition officials had been particularly "noisy and clamorous" and that an "opposition" was already forming "under the banners of General Jackson." But he was also the cold, puritanical, stubborn son of President John Adams, the most moral of the founding fathers, and he could not bring himself to put politics ahead of morality and duty. He promptly told Clay that such removals would seem "harsh and odious" and insisted that he would reappoint everyone except for those about whom there was a valid "complaint." Adams wrote smugly in his diary that Clay "did not press the subject any further."[32]

Clay, the witty, ebullient, always political antithesis of Adams, was upset not only by Adams's stubbornness but also by the charge of bargain and corruption surrounding the two of them. He was so disturbed that he had already tried, unwisely, to defend his honor by challenging his chief accuser, Congressman George Kremer of Pennsylvania, to a duel. It soon became clear, however, that Kremer was such an odd, inconsequential figure that he was not worthy of a duel. Embarrassed and frustrated, Clay had to withdraw his challenge.[33]

Two months later Clay was still uneasy as he left for his estate in Lexington, Kentucky. Even though he would be traveling through two states—Ohio and Kentucky—in which he was extremely popular, he had no idea what sort of reception he would receive. He knew that he had violated one of the democratic rules of the day—that congressmen must obey the instructions of their state legislatures. The Kentucky legislature had specifically told Clay and the other Kentucky congressmen to vote for Jackson, not Adams, in the House election. He was therefore much relieved when he received boisterous, adulatory receptions during his stops at Ohio and Kentucky towns on his way down the Ohio River.

Congressman Daniel Webster of Massachusetts was also concerned about Adams's position on patronage. One of the last of the old Federalists, and already famed for his Plymouth oration and his appearances before the Supreme Court, he intended to hold Adams to his promise of appointing Federalists to office.[34] He and Adams did not care much for each other. Adams distrusted Webster, and Webster was suspicious of

Adams for having deserted the Federalist party early in his career. Now forty-three, Webster was in the process of reinventing himself. No longer able to campaign as a Federalist, he had no alternative but to move into the Adams camp. He was also rethinking his position on the tariff. As spokesman for the Boston shipping interests, Webster had opposed tariffs and had recently voted against the protective tariff bill of 1824. But Webster knew that Boston money was being shifted from commerce to manufacturing and realized that he might have to look at the tariff from a different point of view.

On the opposite political side, the defeated Andrew Jackson was also treated well as he made his way to the Hermitage. To this point the chronology of Jackson's life had been almost identical to that of Adams. They both were born in 1767, played minor roles in the Revolution, practiced law, achieved fame during the War of 1812 (Adams at the Peace of Ghent and Jackson at New Orleans), shared credit for adding Florida to the Union, and decided to run for president in the early 1820s.

But no two men could have been more different. While Adams had been raised with great care as the oldest son of a Yankee president, Jackson was the son of a poor Carolina woman whose husband had died before Andrew was born. Adams, an intellectual, had been trained and educated in Europe and at Harvard; Jackson had very little education. Adams was a diplomat, Jackson a military hero. The stubborn yet self-controlled Adams took out his fears and disappointments in his diary; Jackson, noted for his volcanic temper, had killed a man in a duel. Even their appearances were different: Adams was stocky and balding; Jackson was tall and angular, with a mass of gray hair that flew off in all directions.

On the surface Jackson had taken his defeat with good grace. Well disposed toward Adams, whom he liked personally, the Old Hero had greeted the president-elect graciously and held himself above the fray, as candidates were supposed to do in a republican world. Privately, though, he was furious. Always quick to smell a conspiracy, he had braced himself for bad news as the vote in the House approached. "Intrigue skulk[ed]" around him, he wrote, as a "coalition" led by the cabinet laid plans to defeat him. When Clay accepted Adams's offer to be secretary of state, Jackson wrote that rumors of "intrigue" and "corruption" filled the air.[35] And he showed no hesitation in putting the blame on Henry Clay.

Jackson had hated Clay for years. In addition to being Jackson's main rival for the western vote, Clay had gone out of his way to attack the general for his behavior in the first Seminole War. In the spring of 1818 Jackson had invaded Spanish Florida, capturing St. Marks and Pensacola and executing two British subjects, Alexander Arbuthnot and Robert Ambrister. Jackson's aggressive behavior (he had interpreted President James Monroe's orders for the Florida campaign very loosely) prompted a debate in both houses of Congress the following winter. Clay's two-hour speech denouncing Jackson was particularly devastating. He not only portrayed Jackson as a frontier bully run amuck but also compared him with military tyrants such as Alexander, Caesar, and Napoleon.

Even though republican protocol would not allow him to say so, Jackson was already running for president—and running on old-fashioned republican principles. Two weeks before Adams took over, the Old Hero told friends that Clay, the "Judas of the West," and Adams had abandoned their republican ideals. Aware that his opponents were calling him a dangerous "military chieftain," he wrote two contradictory letters—one denying the charge, and the other stating that if defending the rights of his country meant being a "military chieftain," then he was one. After arriving home on April 13, he was honored by a public dinner at the Nashville Inn, where he compared himself to George Washington and stated that he would "neither . . . seek nor decline" the presidency. John Overton and his Nashville Junto were stoutly behind him, and the *Nashville Gazette* had already announced that he was a candidate.[36]

Another political figure heading home after the election was John C. Calhoun of backcountry South Carolina. A tall, slender, serious, somewhat humorless man with a finely chiseled face and dark, tousled hair, Calhoun had risen rapidly in American politics. Since arriving in Congress in 1811 he had won a reputation as a staunch American nationalist. He had joined Clay and other War Hawks in leading the cry for the War of 1812, and after the war he had backed federal internal improvements, the Bank of the United States, and protective tariffs. Although his speeches were not as powerful as Webster's or as lively as Clay's, they were superior in logic and intellectual depth. His career was already intertwined with those of Clay and Webster, and within a few years the three would commonly be known as the Great Triumvirate.

After eight years as secretary of war, Calhoun had run for president in 1824. He had expected strong support in his native South and had many friends in Pennsylvania, but he soon ran into difficulties. Jackson had overtaken him in Pennsylvania, and Calhoun's nationalist economic views had become unpopular in the South, where high tariffs were running up the costs of growing cotton and supporting slaves. Facing reality, he backed out of the race and settled for vice president. Like Webster, but moving in the opposite direction, Calhoun began to shift toward the states' rights position, for which he would become famous.

As vice president Calhoun was nominally a member of the Adams administration, but he was already reconsidering his allegiance. A southern slave owner, he had much in common with Old Hickory, and during his eight years as secretary of war he had worked well with the general. Calhoun still aspired to the presidency and, at only forty-three years old, could afford to wait. Since Clay seemed to be in line to run as Adams's successor, Calhoun's best chance would be to serve under Jackson and then succeed him. On arriving home he wrote that the "voice of the people should prevail," not the "Pretorian Band" that had just "sold" the election to Adams. Calhoun was moving away from the Adams administration.[37]

As Senator Martin Van Buren headed back to Albany, New York, he neither expected nor received the sort of receptions lavished on Clay, Jackson, and Calhoun. The short, stout, amiable son of a Dutch tavern keeper, Van Buren never made enemies and was more interested in organizing a political party than in seeking public attention. For the past ten years he and his Bucktail Republican faction had been working doggedly to wrest control of New York from the Clintonian faction. The Clintonians had gained the upper hand in 1817–1818 when Clinton was elected governor and succeeded in pushing through his bill for the Erie Canal—a bill so popular that Van Buren had to give it his last-minute support.

In 1820 Clinton was reelected, but the Bucktails dominated the legislature and the all-powerful council of appointment. Van Buren and the Bucktails were now the strongest political party in New York and the strongest advocates of the new positive view of political parties. With their newfound power the Bucktails elected Van Buren to the U.S. Senate in 1821 and took over the governor's office in 1822. In the Senate Van Buren became the leader of the Radical Republicans of the North, the counterpart of the states' rights Old Republicans of the South. Together the two groups backed Treasury Secretary Crawford for president. Departing from the spirit of the Era of Good Feelings, Van Buren sought to reunite the Republicans of the North and South and return to the old party system of Republicans versus Federalists.

In the election of 1824 Van Buren and the Bucktails began to overreach. Trying too hard to guarantee that New York's votes would go to Crawford, they fought a protracted defensive battle to keep the choice of electors in the hands of the legislature, which they controlled. They won the battle, but their undemocratic position antagonized the voters and strengthened the Clintonians (now called the People's party). Then the Bucktails foolishly went out of their way to humiliate Clinton by removing him from the canal board.

Both moves backfired. In the fall of 1824 Clinton, the People's party candidate, was elected governor, and the Bucktails lost control of the legislature. When the legislature met a few weeks later to choose presidential electors, no one could predict the outcome. Van Buren was backing Crawford, Clinton favored Jackson, and large numbers of New Yorkers, many of whom had migrated from New England, preferred Adams. After much political maneuvering the great majority of New York's electoral votes went to Adams. On his way to Washington after the election, Van Buren later confessed that he was "as completely broken down a politician as my bitterest enemies could desire."[38] He felt no better when Crawford lost badly in the presidential election in the House of Representatives.

There was also another group of men who would have to be reckoned with in the campaign. These men were socially inferior and less well known than the six political leaders; they were at much earlier stages of their careers and had much less lofty goals. They were all journalists, a growing class of men in American politics. The rapid rise in the number of newspapers had greatly improved the social status of their editors. Once scorned by Adams and men like him as boorish, ink-stained wretches, many editors had become organizers of political parties. Six of them would emerge as decisive figures in the presidential campaign.

On April 4, while still in Washington, Henry Clay had written to a new friend thanking him for a newspaper article attacking Jackson. That friend was Charles Hammond, the well-educated, ruthless, short-tempered son of a prosperous, slave-owning planter who lived near Wheeling, Virginia. Hammond, aged thirty-one, had moved to Belmont County in eastern Ohio in 1810 and had become a successful Federalist lawyer, legislator, and newspaper man. In 1822 he moved again, across the state to Cincinnati to become editor of the *Liberty Hall and Cincinnati Gazette,* one of the most influential newspapers in the West.

Hammond soon crossed paths with Clay, who was working in Kentucky and Ohio foreclosing on property for the Bank of the United States.

Even though the two men were on opposite sides in one of the lawsuits, they came to respect each other. A month after the April letter Clay wrote again to give his new friend a little advice. He urged Hammond, who was thinking of getting out of politics, to remain involved because he wrote well and was a good politician, even if he did occasionally lose his temper.

Across and down the river in Frankfort, Kentucky, Amos Kendall was the editor and owner of another influential western newspaper, the *Argus of Western America*. Kendall was a strange, reclusive, gaunt, frail man in his mid-thirties, with prematurely white hair. He had grown up on a small farm in Dunstable, Massachusetts, and had worked his way through Dartmouth College, graduating first in his class. Traveling to Kentucky in 1814 to seek his fortune, he had tried his hand at teaching school, practicing law, and running a post office before finding his niche as a newspaperman and politician. In the spring of 1825 he and Governor Joseph Desha were at the head of the Kentucky Relief party, which had won a great victory in the 1824 state election.

While most members of the Relief party were beginning to line up behind Andrew Jackson, Kendall was having a hard time making up his mind because he felt an obligation to the Clay family. His first year in Kentucky he had tutored the Clay children, and Clay's wife Lucretia had done her best to introduce him to Lexington society. Kendall had written articles for Clay and had supported him for president in the election of 1824.[39]

A third westerner, Duff Green of Missouri, was having less difficulty taking sides. Born near Lexington, Kentucky, in 1791 and educated almost entirely at home, Green had served in the War of 1812, married the daughter of Governor Ninian Edwards of Illinois, and moved with his family to the Missouri Territory. There, like Kendall, he became the proverbial jack-of-all-trades: a land speculator, mail contractor, merchant, and lawyer. He was active in the state constitutional convention, where he vigorously defended slavery as a source of liberty for white men, and in the state legislature, where he supported relief measures. After buying the *St. Louis Enquirer* he backed Calhoun in the 1824 election, shifting to Jackson only after Calhoun dropped out.

A tough, aggressive man who did not take slights lightly, "Rough Green," as he was called, made enemies easily and was often drawn into brawls. In one he drew a pistol and would have killed his opponent had the gun not misfired. Always on the move, Green went west to live in

Duff Green was a jack-of-all-trades who moved from the Missouri frontier to Washington and became the central editor in the Jackson campaign.

Amos Kendall. A strange, gaunt, reclusive man, he rivaled Van Buren as President Jackson's most influential adviser.

*Thurlow Weed. A self-made
newspaper man in New York,
he rose to become the leading
political figure in the Whig party.*

*Isaac Hill. A harsh, crippled
man, the newspaper editor
threatened to take power away
from the Adams party in New
Hampshire. Courtesy of the
New Hampshire Historical
Society.*

Jefferson City early in 1825 but was looking east, just in case an offer came from Calhoun or Jackson.[40]

Far to the east, in New Hampshire, the best known and most feared party leader in the state was Isaac Hill. The glowering, irascible Hill had persevered through a difficult childhood. Both his father and grandfather had been insane, and Hill himself had suffered an injury that left him crippled for life. Apprenticed at age fourteen to a New Hampshire printer, he had saved enough money by 1809 to establish the *New-Hampshire Patriot* in Concord, the new state capital. During the next ten years he built a powerful political machine and led the state Republican party in a successful battle against the once-entrenched Federalists. After the demise of the Federalists in 1816, the Republican party gradually split into factions. Although Hill's faction was the strongest, he lost ground in 1824 when he backed Crawford for president and was now trying to decide which candidate to support in the next election.

Another of the rising newspaper men was Thurlow Weed, who spent his early years in Catskill, New York, on the Hudson River, twenty miles south of Van Buren's early home in Kinderhook. Sent out as an apprentice at the age of eight, he worked for printers in many parts of the state—Albany, Syracuse, New York City—before settling down in 1825 as editor and part owner of the *Rochester Telegraph*. As a member of the People's party, he had helped Clinton win the governor's seat in 1824 and was himself elected to the state assembly. There he engineered a secret deal between the Clay and Adams men that enabled Adams to win a majority of the state electoral votes. The tall, broad-shouldered, good-natured but shrewd Weed, who preferred Clinton to Van Buren, was becoming one of the leading political figures in western New York and a potential threat to Van Buren's plans for regaining power in the state.[41]

For several decades the most controversial newspaper editor in Pennsylvania was the mercurial infighter John Binns, who was known less for what he stood for than for what he hated. Born in Ireland in 1772, he had moved to London, joined the underground United Irishmen, and spent two years in jail before fleeing to America. There he settled in Philadelphia, founded the *Democratic Press,* and joined Jacobins like William Duane in fighting the Federalists. He soon split with the Jacobins, however, and for many years carried on a vicious fight with Duane. In 1823 he refused to join the Jackson movement and spent the rest of his career passionately opposed to the Old Hero, whom he considered a murderer.

First a Crawford man, Binns went over to Adams in 1825 when Clay awarded him the federal printing contract.

In the spring of 1825 these six powerful, well-known political leaders and six aspiring newspaper men, representing (except for Calhoun) a broad band of states from New England west to Missouri, had maneuvered themselves into key positions for the coming election. How they responded to the republican and democratic forces in forming political parties would go a long way toward determining the outcome of the election and ultimately the future of the country.

2

TAKING SIDES, 1825–1826

The political calendar of the early republic imposed a rigid institutional cycle on presidential politics. The president and the new Congress both took office on March 4, but Congress did not convene until the first Monday in December, some nine months later. This first, or "long," session of Congress went on until late spring or early summer and was the session in which most major laws were passed. Then came another hiatus, followed by the second, or "short," session, running from December to March 4. Tied to this calendar, party politics centered on Washington during the winter and then moved back to the states for the rest of the year. Congressional and state elections were held in March and April or between July and October. The presidential election took place in the states during a two-week stretch between the end of October and the middle of November every four years.

The calendar gave John Quincy Adams nine months to get his administration in order before Congress descended on him in December. Of primary importance was the thorny problem of appointments. If Adams acted as a party man and appointed only those who had backed him or Henry Clay, he would please Clay but would antagonize supporters of Jackson, Crawford, and Calhoun. If he followed his own antiparty instincts and appointed candidates of all political persuasions, he would discourage the party men who had backed him in the election. There was also the problem of the Federalists. With the decline of Federalism, Delaware and Massachusetts were now the only states with anything resembling a Federalist party, leaving thousands of Federalists looking for a new party. Appointing Federalists would satisfy Webster and help carry states such as Delaware, Pennsylvania, and Maryland, but it would anger the large numbers of Republicans who hated Federalists.

In his inaugural address Adams followed his own instincts. He began by paying tribute to the founding fathers and reminding Americans that this was their fifty-year jubilee. He combined democratic ideology ("the will of the people") with republican words such as "purity" and "virtuous." Settling in to his main theme, he strongly denounced "the collisions of party spirit," especially those based on the "adverse interests" of geography and way of life. This display of nonpartisanship led many to believe that he planned to ignore old party distinctions and bring Federalists into the government.[1]

Adams's cabinet choices sent a similar antiparty message, even though no Federalists were included. Among the selections were two Calhoun men, Secretary of the Navy Samuel Southard of New Jersey and Postmaster General John McLean of Ohio; a Crawford man, Secretary of War James Barbour of Virginia; and Attorney General William Wirt of Virginia, who had ties with the Richmond Junto, the most powerful political organization in the state. Rounding out the cabinet were Clay and Secretary of the Treasury Richard Rush of Pennsylvania. The inclusion of three holdovers from the antiparty Monroe administration—Wirt, McLean, and Southard—reinforced the impression that Adams hoped to maintain the Era of Good Feelings.

In making other appointments Adams continued to reach out toward men of all parties. He asked De Witt Clinton to be minister to Great Britain, but Clinton, already thinking about running for the presidency, was not willing to leave the country. Overtures were also made to Clintonian General Jacob Brown, Calhounite Beaufort T. Watts, Jacksonian Samuel R. Overton, and Van Buren's close friend Louis McLane of Delaware. Another Calhoun man, Joel Poinsett of South Carolina, was named minister to Mexico.

Most important, he appointed Federalists. Soon after his inauguration Adams convinced Rufus King of New York, who had already been minister to Great Britain, to return for a second tour of duty. Republicans were shocked, for Adams could not have picked a more famous or more controversial Federalist. One of the last of the founding fathers (only three survived him), King had been a member of the constitutional convention, had served a dozen years in the Senate, and had been the last Federalist to run for president. Large groups opposed his appointment. Southerners detested King for his attacks on slavery in the Missouri debate. Irish Americans hated him because he had used his diplomatic position to block the migration of Irish rebels to the United States. Republicans in general attacked him for his vigorous opposition to the War of 1812. In the minds of many King personified the worst sort of Federalism.

More Federalist appointments followed, and in a number of the northern states amalgamation parties began to appear, uniting Federalists and Republicans in favor of the Adams administration. Members of the Federalist establishment such as Webster and Isaac Parker of Massachusetts and Philadelphia editor Robert Walsh were delighted, but committed Republicans were furious. They pointed out that Adams's father had been a High Federalist and that John Quincy Adams himself had started out as one. The president, they predicted, was going to restore old-time Federalism.

The appointment of one Federalist, Alfred Conkling, as judge of the Northern District in New York outraged Lieutenant Governor James Tallmadge, the congressman whose amendment had instigated the debate over Missouri. On hearing the news he blurted out to his friend Thurlow Weed, "Will [Adams] succeed to keep old friends and buy up old enemies?"[2] Tallmadge, who had helped the People's party defeat Van Buren's Bucktails in 1824, and Weed, who had secured a majority of New York electoral votes for Adams, considered themselves "old friends" of the president. Assuming that Adams would reward them, Weed traveled to Washington, hoping to bring back a postmastership for himself and a foreign mission for Tallmadge. At first all went well. He had dinner with a very warm and friendly Henry Clay, attended a wedding at the home of John McLean, and watched a nude President Adams taking his morning swim in the Potomac. But when Weed met the president he found him cold and distant and came away empty-handed.

Next to patronage, the most contentious issue facing Adams was the Treaty of Indian Springs, in which a minority group of Creek Indians, led by Chief William McIntosh, had ceded land in western Georgia to the United States. When warriors from the main body of Creeks assassinated McIntosh and rejected the treaty, Adams declared the Creek cession invalid and refused to authorize a state survey of the land. He ordered U.S. armed forces, already in Georgia, to be ready to use force to stop the survey.

Adams's defense of Indian rights led to a showdown between the president and the governor of Georgia, George M. Troup, a belligerent states' rights Crawford man. Troup, who had a difficult reelection campaign coming up in the fall, took two unusually extreme positions. He not only announced that the federal government had no right to interfere in a controversy between an Indian tribe and a state government but also accused Adams of favoring the abolition of slavery. According to Troup's somewhat twisted logic, Adams's sympathetic treatment of the Creeks gave proof of a similar attitude toward slaves. This argument was too much even for sensitive slaveholding southerners such as John Randolph of Virginia, who had no patience with Troup's "demented Rant," and John C. Calhoun, who called him "wicked" for trying to combine the slave and Indian questions.[3]

The quarrel had implications for the next presidential election. The Georgia Creeks were only a small part of the thousands of Indians—Cherokees, Chickasaws, Choctaws, Seminoles, and other Creeks—who stood in the way of white settlers in the Old Southwest. Now that cotton had become a vital international commodity, Indian land was much in demand. Feeling was so intense that the Adams administration became alarmed. In November 1825 Clay warned his Ohio friend Charles Hammond that if the Creeks persisted in their refusal, there would be no way to stop the "agitation" in Congress about Indian removal, and Secretary of War Barbour told Adams that unless the president reversed course, he would not carry Georgia in the next election.[4]

Adams insisted that he had no interest in how Georgia voted, but he prudently took steps to ease the crisis. When the administration began to negotiate with the Creeks, Troup, who was soon reelected, postponed his survey. In January 1826 the Creeks ceded a large part of their land, but the conflict was renewed when Troup demanded the remainder of the Creek land and made plans for another survey. Again there were threats of force on both sides, and the struggle went on until November 1827, when the Creeks gave in and ceded the rest of their territory.

The rise of state amalgamation parties, Adams's appointment of Federalists, and his handling of the Georgia Indian affair played a large part in determining the future of the Crawford party, which in 1824 had won a strong majority in Virginia and had come in second to Jackson in North Carolina. Because Crawford's defeat and incapacity (he had suffered a stroke) made it impossible for his party to hold together, his followers started looking for a new home. Like Troup, other southern Crawford men tended not to support Adams. When offered a position in the Adams administration, Bartlett Yancey, speaker of the senate in North Carolina, turned it down. Other Crawford men, however, especially in the North, responded favorably to Adams's nonpartisanship. Before the year 1825 was over, the Crawford party had split—half for and half against Adams.[5]

The movement of some Crawford men toward Adams had an immediate effect on journalism in Washington. Early in the 1820s the *National Intelligencer* had deserted the Monroe administration in favor of Crawford. In retaliation, Monroe's secretary of state, John Quincy Adams, cut off all executive patronage to the *Intelligencer*. But Adams's willingness to appoint Crawford men so impressed the publishers of the newspaper that they began to support the new president. This change of heart gave Adams a significant political advantage. While Congress was in session, almost all the important political news came out of the capital. Since most out-of-town newspapers could not afford to keep reporters in the city, they had to rely on the Washington editors for news. Adams, who already had the support of the *National Journal*, now had the backing of the two strongest newspapers in the city.

In addition, Adams had won the favor of Hezekiah Niles, the publisher of *Niles' Weekly Register* in nearby Baltimore. Whereas many newspapers considered Adams's election in the House of Representatives undemocratic, Niles called it a useful process, free from partisanship. Niles filled his pages with valuable economic data and was an unabashed supporter of manufacturing, tariff protection, and federal internal improvements. In the fall of 1825 he ran detailed stories about three canal projects—the Erie, the Hudson and Delaware, and the Chesapeake and Delaware.

While the Crawford men were making up their minds about the administration, the Jacksonians remained loyal to the Old Hero. Convinced that Adams had stolen the election, some of the rank and file rioted, burned Clay and Adams in effigy, and staged mock funerals. Although less violent, party leaders picked up their pens when they learned that Jackson planned to run again. Only days after Adams took office, Jackson's New Jersey friend Samuel Swartwout published a letter he had received from the Old Hero stating provocatively that "Mr. Clay never yet has risked himself for his country."[6] In June Charles Tutt of Virginia promised the Clinton people that if they supported Old Hickory, Clinton could succeed him as president. Since Jackson was already intimating that he was too old and too sick to last more than one term, Clinton was interested.[7]

Jackson's morbid hints about his health were not just political ploys. After fifty-eight years of violent frontier life, he was a sick man. He carried one bullet in his chest between his heart and lungs and another in his upper left arm. Over the years he had contracted malaria and dysentery, developed a persistent cough, and suffered from frequent stomach disorders. Preoccupied with his many ailments and suffering constant pain, he complained regularly about his health. His letters often read like a doctor's report.

Ill health was one of several reasons why Jackson was uneasy about returning to the U.S. Senate in December. In addition, he had never been comfortable in either house, and he was wary of committing himself on Senate roll calls while running for president. After mulling over the question during the spring and summer, he decided to resign. He carried out his decision in a carefully orchestrated series of events that began in the first week of October when the Tennessee legislature nominated him for president. On October 12, 1825, Jackson drew up a letter of resignation and the next day rode some forty miles to Murfreesboro, where the legislature was sitting, and delivered it in person.

The letter was a skillful campaign document. He was resigning, he said, because of the "inconsiderable fatigue" from traveling to and from Washington and the possibility of being accused of casting "selfish" votes designed to help his campaign. He endorsed two constitutional amendments—one restricting the election of presidential electors to the vote of the people in all the states, the other preventing members of Congress from holding a federal office during their congressional terms and for two years after. The first amendment was an obvious appeal to the democratic spirit of the times; the second was designed, he said, to protect the separation of powers, but it was also an attack aimed at Henry Clay. He couched the letter in old-fashioned republican terminology, using words such as "sacred," "morals," "wisdom," "experience," and "virtue" to oppose "encroachments of power," "corruption," "intrigue," and "evil." Jackson's letter, which was published in many newspapers, and Adams's inaugural address set a republican tone for the campaign.[8]

The next day Jackson delivered a speech to the members of both houses, thanking them for what he called their "very marked and respectful attentions."[9] When Clay learned about the proceedings, his response was far less respectful. In a letter to Charles Hammond he called the "scene" at Murfreesboro "ridiculous," an "imitation" of George Washington's resignation from the army and the congressional reception for

Lafayette. He laughed at Jackson's "briny tears" and his feeble attempts to play the "affected part" of Cincinnatus retiring to the plough.[10] Jackson had run for the Senate in 1823, Clay sneered, to bolster his first presidential campaign and was now resigning from the Senate to strengthen his second. The general, he added, would not have lectured about corruption if he had won. Cynical and harsh as they were, Clay's words were not far off the mark.

When December 1825 finally arrived, the Nineteenth Congress, consisting of 48 senators and 213 congressmen, convened in Washington. Almost all the members moved into the sixty or so boardinghouses that had sprung up around the Capitol and along Pennsylvania Avenue. A typical member boarded with half a dozen men from the same party and same region of the country as he. One notable boardinghouse was Williamson's, in which six of the eight boarders were opposed to the administration and five—Martin Van Buren, Louis McLane, Churchill C. Cambreleng of New York, John Forsyth of Georgia, and Edward Livingston of Louisiana—became future Jackson stalwarts.[11]

On paper the House of Representatives was tilted slightly in favor of the administration, and the Senate was about even, but factional alignments were so fluid that it was impossible to make political predictions. In the House John W. Taylor of New York, still linked to his Federalist, antislavery background and ably supported by Clay and Webster, was elected Speaker by a narrow margin over Crawford men Andrew Stevenson of Virginia and Louis McLane. Vice President Calhoun was president of the Senate.

When Adams ran a draft of his first annual message by the members of his cabinet, they all urged him to be cautious. One of the two Virginians, James Barbour, suggested that he say something conciliatory that would ease southern fears about the future of slavery. The other Virginian, William Wirt, warned him not to enflame states' rights sentiment by saying too much about national internal improvements. And when Adams mentioned that he planned to propose a national university, even the strongest nationalist, Henry Clay, objected. Wirt, who understood the Old Republican fear of central authority, was afraid that expensive national programs would justify southern charges that Adams was "grasping for power."[12]

But Adams ignored the advice. From the vantage point of twenty-first-century liberalism, his message was the most enlightened presidential message of the early republic. Observing that "the spirit of improvement

[was] abroad upon the earth," Adams called on Congress to advance the "moral, political, intellectual," as well as economic condition of mankind. The message was high drama. All that was lacking was an in-person presentation, as Adams followed the precedent of Thomas Jefferson and sent the message to Congress in writing.

Unfortunately for Adams, the message was sent not in the twenty-first century but two centuries earlier, and to many, it must have seemed an outrageous violation of states' rights. Starting with foreign affairs, Adams proposed reciprocal trade agreements with the new republics of Latin America and announced that he planned to send delegates to a Pan-American conference at Panama. This early version of Franklin D. Roosevelt's good-neighbor policy was a logical follow-up to the Monroe Doctrine, which Adams had helped write only two years before.[13]

Turning to domestic matters, Adams offered a dazzling series of national initiatives—a national bankruptcy bill, a militia bill, national standards for weights and measures, a Department of the Interior, and a revised patents law. To this he added an expanded program of federal internal improvements, highlighted by a canal between the Chesapeake Bay and the Ohio River and a national road from Washington to New Orleans. To cap it all he asked for a national university, a naval academy, and a national observatory.

Making it worse, Adams used themes and arguments certain to antagonize the many Americans who believed that a powerful central government would threaten individual liberty, as well as those who hated the British and liked the idea of being cut off from Europe. Turning republicanism on its head, he announced that "liberty [was] power" and said that Americans, who had been given so much liberty, had the responsibility of supporting a powerful government. As the model for standardized weights and measures he described the British system. And he called an observatory a necessity because there were 130 of them in Europe.

At times his words were ill chosen. Trying to goad the members of Congress into action, he seemed to be saying that democracy could not be trusted. The members must not, he said, "slumber in indolence or fold up [their] arms and proclaim to the world that [they were] palsied by the will of [their] constituents." Most dangerous of all for a politician, Adams left himself open to ridicule by calling observatories "lighthouses of the skies." The words would be used against him throughout the campaign. Even Adams himself admitted that his message was "a perilous experiment." As Stephen Skowronek has pointed out, Adams had "assembled . . . the ingredients of a great political reconstruction" without the "political rationale" or the political backing to carry it out. He had a program but not a party.[14]

The response, particularly from southern Old Republicans, was not favorable. With nothing in the message to reassure them, the congressional delegation from South Carolina concluded that Adams believed in abolishing slavery. Word sifted in from Virginia, where a substantial minority had backed Adams, that the state was now united against him. The Old Republican *Richmond Enquirer* published a savage attack on the message. It was, said editor Thomas Ritchie, "the wildest construction of the express, enumerated powers given by the Constitution" he had ever seen.[15] One congressman from the South, Edward Livingston, did react favorably, but he was a transplanted nationalist who had moved from New York to Louisiana and was thus a special case. It was not surprising that nationalist Hezekiah Niles applauded the message; what was surprising was his choice of words. The message, he said, was "plain, republican, practical."[16] Since a majority of the members of Congress disagreed, Adams's proposals made little headway.

The administration's shaky control of Congress was quickly revealed when Speaker Taylor and President of the Senate Calhoun appointed committees. Even though Taylor gave the administration a majority in seven of the nine most important House committees, the ratio in four was only four to three, and in two the committee selected a member of the opposition as chair. In the Senate the situation was much worse. Calhoun gave the opposition control of seven of the ten most powerful committees, and in three the ratio was five antiadministration senators to none or four to one.

The importance of the makeup of committees became apparent when, on December 26, Adams nominated two delegates, Richard C. Anderson of Kentucky and John Sergeant of Pennsylvania, to the Panama Congress. The matter was referred to the Senate Committee on Foreign Relations, which consisted of four antiadministration southerners, including Nathaniel Macon of North Carolina and Littleton Tazewell of Virginia, and only one Adams man. Still, prospects for the Panama mission looked good, for it was one of the few items in the annual message that had received popular support. The idea of a Pan-American congress had originated with Simon Bolivar, the charismatic soldier who had overturned Spanish rule in much of South America. Adams and Clay saw the invitation as an opportunity to build up trade in Latin America and gather support for the Monroe Doctrine. They were particularly interested in having inter-American backing in case Spain sent a fleet to the Caribbean to put down a popular uprising in Cuba. How could the republic that had freed itself from the tyranny of the British monarchy refuse to join the new republics to the south?

But Van Buren and Calhoun did not see the issue that way. The two men had spent the spring, summer, and fall reshaping their political careers—Van Buren trying to regain power, and Calhoun rethinking his constitutional views. Van Buren had made some progress; in the fall election his Bucktails had recaptured the New York legislature. But De Witt Clinton was governor, and the Little Magician, still on the defensive, did not dare commit his state party openly to Jackson. Calhoun, making the transition from nationalist to states' righter, had begun to separate himself from the administration. His first direct move came in September, when he advised his close friend Congressman Samuel D. Ingham of Pennsylvania that he approved of plans to bring Duff Green in from Missouri to start an anti-Adams newspaper in Washington.[17]

Sensing the chance to use the Panama issue to build a pro-Jackson, anti-Adams party, Van Buren made a bold move by calling on Calhoun. Although he did not know the vice president well, he had joined him in opposing John W. Taylor for Speaker in 1821, and he knew that Calhoun was on good terms with the Jackson men.[18] He found Calhoun very receptive, and the two agreed to oppose the Panama mission. Within two weeks they were joined by the southerners on the Foreign Relations Committee, who prepared a blistering report attacking the mission. Written by Tazewell and delivered by Macon, the report defined the proposed congress as a confederacy that only the states or the people of the United States had the authority to join. Adams had no right, said the report, to accept the invitation without consulting the Senate. Van Buren expanded on the theme with a resolution calling on the Senate to refuse to confirm the nominations. The report and the resolution were states' rights pronouncements designed to upstage Adams's appeal to nationalism.

In the long debates that followed, southern senators introduced the theme of race. Calhoun's friend Robert Y. Hayne of South Carolina and others pointed out that if the American delegates attended the congress, they would have to sit down with black delegates from Haiti and vote on the troublesome subject of the slave trade. Hugh L. White of Tennessee suggested that the Latin American delegates were planning to foment a rebellion in Cuba. The arguments were similar to those put forth by Troup in the Georgia Indian affair. In the end they were not enough. On March 14, 1826, the Senate voted 25 to 18 to confirm the two delegates, and on March 25 the House voted the necessary appropriations.

But politically the opposition had been successful. The debate over states' rights and slavery had brought together Jackson men, Calhoun men, and Crawford men in the North-South alliance that Van Buren had long been seeking. Voting against the confirmation were five senators who would later serve in Andrew Jackson's cabinet: Van Buren, Levi Woodbury of New Hampshire, Jackson's biographer and 1824 campaign manager John H. Eaton of Tennessee, John Branch of North Carolina, and John M. Berrien of Georgia. Although they lost the Panama vote, Van Buren, Calhoun, and their allies were able to block almost all of Adams's other proposals.

One of the southerners voting nay on the Panama mission was slave owner John Randolph of Virginia. With the death of John Taylor of Caroline County, Virginia, in 1824, only Nathaniel Macon equaled Randolph in his devotion to Old Republicanism. He was one of several southerners who had warned that a national government that could build roads and canals could also abolish slavery. Randolph had served in the House of Representatives for many years, dating back to 1799, and was a member of the House when the Nineteenth Congress convened. His unexpected election to the Senate in December (to replace new secretary of war James Barbour) demonstrated the strong support for Old Republicanism in Virginia at the time.

To say that Randolph was strange would be an understatement. An early illness had left him with a high-pitched voice and unable to grow a beard. Perhaps to compensate for his apparent lack of masculinity (he never married), he developed a sharp, hateful, yet brilliant and erudite speaking style that could not be matched. During the Panama debate and other controversies he would sweep into the Senate dressed for the hunt, sometimes followed by his dogs and his retainers, who would supply him with port during his long diatribes. His most notorious speech came on March 30, 1826, when, infuriated by his defeat in the Panama affair, he used two characters from Henry Fielding's *Tom Jones* to lash out at Adams and Clay. He had been beaten, he complained, by "the coalition of Blifil (Adams) and Black George (Clay)—by the combination, unheard of until then, of the Puritan with the blackleg."[19] When Clay challenged him to a duel, they met on the field of honor, but neither was hit in the wild exchange of bullets that followed.

The disputes over Federalism, the Georgia Indians, and the Panama mission were the opening guns in the 1828 election and an early indication of the role that race and states' rights would play in the campaign. In each case states' rights advocates opened their attack by accusing the national government of overstepping its powers, but as the debates intensified, racial fears and assumptions crept in. To twenty-first-century Americans the racial arguments—that Federalists were bent on ending slavery, that it was dangerous for American diplomats to sit down with foreign black officials, or that Adams's efforts to enforce Indian treaties proved that he was an abolitionist—are not convincing. But at the time many Americans took them seriously.

The controversy over race also reflected the differences among the groups opposing the administration. In attacking Adams's policy, Old Republican Crawford men seized on the racial issue, Calhoun and other southerners felt that Troup and his followers had gone too far, Jackson men were undecided, and Van Buren and the northern radicals did not stress the issue.

Ever since the convening of the Congress, Calhoun's behavior as president of the Senate had increasingly put him at odds with the administration. He had appointed antiadministration committees, he had sympathized with the opponents of the Panama mission, and when the debate over Panama grew heated, he refused to use his power as presiding officer to preserve order and rein in overly harsh critics of the administration. The Adams men were understandably outraged when Calhoun sat passively and allowed Randolph to vent his spleen for hours.[20]

Calhoun was in a difficult situation. His immediate predecessors as president of the Senate had not exercised much authority. The last one, Daniel D. Tompkins of New York, a notoriously heavy drinker, had rarely bothered to take the chair. In 1823, when the Senate took the unusual step of giving the presiding officer the power to appoint committees, Tompkins did not choose to exercise it, and the appointments were made by the president pro tem.

Although Calhoun did not wish to use the power of his new office indiscriminately, he did intend to use it. He decided to appoint committees, but since he was not a senator himself, he refused to use the power of the presiding officer to control senators in debate. When Randolph and others let loose their tirades, Calhoun insisted that it was the duty of the other senators to take the initiative in calling the offender to order. Since both these policies hurt the administration, Adams and his friends were angry.

By the end of the winter of 1826 Clay was convinced that Calhoun was "up to the hub" with the opposition, and the *National Journal* had begun to attack the vice president for his partisanship.[21] On April 15 the Senate passed an amendment to the rules, stripping Calhoun of his power to name committees. Then on May 1 "Patrick Henry" published a long article in the *Journal* denouncing Calhoun for not preserving order. Three weeks later "Onslow" (after a famous Speaker of the House of Commons) replied, defending the vice president. Everyone knew that "Onslow" was Calhoun himself, but no one was sure whether "Patrick Henry" was Adams or simply someone who wrote under Adams's direction. The writer most often suggested is Philip R. Fendall, an Adams man and clerk in the State Department, but Clyde Wilson, editor of the Calhoun Papers, argues on internal evidence that the author must have been a New Englander, and Fendall was from Virginia. The exchange of letters went on for almost half a year, with a total of five letters from "Patrick Henry" and six from "Onslow."

At the beginning the authors stuck to narrow questions concerning the powers of the vice president, but they soon moved on to a revealing debate over the meaning of republicanism in the new democracy. Both agreed that power in government came from the people, but Adams, who had equated power with liberty in his annual message, thought of it as a positive tool for the government to maintain social order, while Calhoun interpreted it as something to be diffused for the safety of the people. For Adams, power came from the office; for Calhoun, it came from a popular consensus. Adams would use power to advance society; Calhoun would control power to protect the people. The half-year debate had implications for Calhoun both intellectually and politically. Intellectually it played a major role in his shift from National Republicanism to Old Republicanism, and politically it brought his split with the administration out in the open.[22]

And long before the debate was over, Calhoun had committed himself to the Jackson movement. On June 4, after Congress had adjourned, Calhoun sent Jackson an important letter. The two men had corresponded frequently while Calhoun was secretary of war but had not written to each other for more than a year. Calhoun wrote the letter two weeks after he published his first reply to Adams and directly after a long talk with John H. Eaton, Jackson's closest contact in Washington. To keep the letter secret, Calhoun had given it to Eaton to carry back to Tennessee, instead of using the post office.

"The liberties of our country," Calhoun began, "are in danger." The issue had been drawn "between *power* and *liberty.*" In the campaign ahead the nation would determine "whether the real governing principle in our political system be the power and patronage of the Executive, or the voice of the people." The Adams government believed that it "can mould the publick voice at pleasure by an artful management of the patronage of office." If so, "our government may indeed retain the forms of freedom, but its sperit [*sic*] will be gone. Nor will it be long before the form will follow the spirit," and "we shall soon consider the form of electing by the people a mere farce." The people will then accept "the transmission of the Executive power by hereditary principle, in some imperial family." But Calhoun "hope[d] for better things." He had faith, he said, "in the intelligence and virtue of the people, which have safely carried us through so many difficulties." He was confident that Jackson was and always had been "on the side of liberty and [his] country." Jackson would be "the instrument, under Providence, of confounding political machinations" and "perpetuating our freedom." As for himself, he concluded, with a bit of self-pity, "much of the storm will fall on me. . . . I deem it my glory to be selected as the object of attack in [this] cause."[23]

This polished expression of the essence of Old Republicanism, liberty over power, together with the arguments in his "Onslow" letters, marked the completion of Calhoun's transition from nationalism to states' rights. In the letter he captured the providential, republican, yet also democratic spirit of the American people. The letter expressed all their anxious suspicion of government, corruption, and party patronage. The confidence in Jackson echoed the same spirit Eaton had presented in his "Letters of Wyoming" to Philadelphia's *Columbian Observer* in the 1824 campaign. In these letters Eaton had portrayed Jackson as a virtuous, republican hero out of the Revolutionary past who, like Washington, would defend the American people against power and corruption. It is interesting to note that these overtures to Jackson made no mention of slavery or the tariff issue.

In his reply Jackson was more aggressive and political than republican heroes were supposed to be. Adams, he wrote, had "followed the footsteps of his father" and had "revive[d] the asperity which marked the struggle of 98 and 1800." He had "steere[d] his political course, with a hypocritical veneration for the great principles of republicanism in the one hand, and an artful management of patronage in the other." Like "the enemies of freedom in all ages," he counted on the "*credulity* and *apathy* of the people" as the "foundation of [his] power." Jackson was not "surprised . . . to see the ministerial journals wantonly assailing" Calhoun. But, he promised, "the people are awake, and are virtuous." Jackson "trust[ed]" that his "name [would] always be found on the side of the people" and that he and Calhoun would "march hand in hand in their cause."[24]

Calhoun's and Jackson's letters committed the two men to a politically effective combination of Old Republicanism and democracy. They also brought many of Calhoun's supporters over to the Jackson side, including Senator Robert Y. Hayne of South Carolina and Congressmen Ingham of Pennsylvania and George McDuffie of South Carolina. Calhoun and his friends were already trying to win over other southerners. In writing to Littleton Tazewell of Virginia, Calhoun said there could be "no reaction in favour of liberty" that did not "come from the slave holding States, headed by Virginia and sustained by Pennsylvania." It was up to Virginia, he said, to decide whether Jackson would be the sole candidate to oppose the administration in 1828. After rubbing elbows with southern politicians at Ballston Springs, New York, Hayne's brother Arthur reported that Crawford men were swinging toward Jackson in Virginia and that North Carolina was safe for Jackson.[25]

The most loyal Calhoun man supporting Jackson was Duff Green. The plan to bring Green to Washington was carried out in February 1826 when he was installed as assistant editor of a small Washington newspaper renamed the *United States Telegraph*. Within three months Eaton had arranged a loan of $3,000, enabling Green to buy the paper. The names of the congressmen endorsing the loan give further evidence of the range of men flocking to Jackson. They included three original Jackson men, James K. Polk of Tennessee, George Kremer of Pennsylvania, and James Hamilton Jr. of South Carolina; Calhoun's friend Ingham; and a Crawford man, John S. Barbour of Virginia.

The rough-and-ready Green brought vigor, nastiness, and political as well as editorial skills to the job. He joined the assault on the Panama mission, saying that Clay had thought up the idea to distract attention from his corrupt bargain with Adams. Loyal to Calhoun, he doggedly defended the vice president against the attacks in the *Journal*. He also revealed his strong attachment to slavery with a series of articles defending the institution.[26] But like Calhoun and Jackson in their exchange of letters, Green's primary theme was the corruption of the Adams administration. Determined to link Adams and Clay to republican charges of corruption, he kept repeating his motto: "Power is always stealing from the many to the few."[27]

Green's editorials blended nicely with a report of a select committee of the Senate accusing Adams of wasting money and using the appointment power to bolster his own personal political party. The committee was made up entirely of members of the opposition, including Macon, Van Buren, White, Robert Y. Hayne, and Richard M. Johnson of Kentucky, but the strongest voice was that of Colonel Thomas Hart Benton, who had fought in the War of 1812 and was one of the first two senators elected from the new state of Missouri. Benton had once engaged in a bloody brawl with Andrew Jackson but was now one of his most ardent supporters. In a sarcastic speech in the Senate Benton accused Adams of trading jobs for votes: "The President wants My vote, and I want his patronage; I will VOTE as he wishes, and he will GIVE me the office I wish for."[28] Benton proposed six restrictions on the executive's power of appointment, and even though all were tabled, the colonel had made his point. It is ironic that the founders of the Democratic party, which would soon bring a large-scale spoils system into the government, should be accusing John Quincy Adams, who was stoutly resisting party patronage, of misusing the power to appoint.

While Calhoun and Green were openly opposing the administration, Van Buren remained noncommittal. Although he privately favored Jackson and had used the Panama mission to start a new party, his position in New York was still not strong enough to allow him or his party to come out publicly for the Old Hero. After his faction had gained control of the New York legislature in the fall of 1825, Van Buren had begun to bargain with Clinton. The governor offered to let the Little Magician succeed him if Van Buren did nothing to keep Clinton from becoming president. Van Buren had no interest in running for governor, but he did want to be reelected senator. At the same time Clinton needed to be reelected governor to keep his presidential hopes alive. So in the spring of 1826 Van Buren and Clinton were playing a strange game—political observer Jabez Hammond called it "back stairs intercourse."[29] It was rumored that when the gubernatorial and senatorial elections came up in the fall and winter of 1826–1827, the Bucktails would put up only token resistance against Clinton, and the Clintonians would reciprocate for

Van Buren. For the next half year Van Buren and the Bucktails would remain uncommitted on the presidential election.

This "coquetry" with Clinton left Van Buren in a weak position when the question of establishing another Jackson newspaper in Washington came up.[30] When Congress adjourned in May 1826 Van Buren suggested to Calhoun that the Jacksonians bring in editor Thomas Ritchie to set up a second and presumably official Jackson newspaper. Van Buren wanted Ritchie because they had both been Crawford men and because he needed Ritchie and his Richmond Junto to achieve his North-South alliance.

But Calhoun, who did not get along with Ritchie and preferred Green as party editor, demurred. After Ritchie decided that he did not want to move to Washington, Van Buren recommended New York congressman Churchill C. Cambreleng as an alternative, but Calhoun, unhampered by state politics, still stood in the way. "A paper is already in existence," he wrote smoothly in July, "and it does seem to me, that two on the same side must distract and excite jealousy."[31] There would be no second newspaper. Van Buren would have to clean up his affairs in New York before he could openly assert himself in the Jackson movement.

Meanwhile, in his self-imposed exile in Tennessee, Andrew Jackson was doing his best to keep in touch with his supporters. The Hermitage was isolated. It was more than an hour by carriage to Nashville and ten days by steamboat and carriage to Washington. Mail moved a little faster, but not much; the express mail of the 1830s was still a decade away. The only close political friends that Jackson saw on a regular basis were the members of the Nashville Junto, which had brought him into national politics. These included his secretary Andrew Jackson Donelson, whose plantation bordered on the Hermitage; his adviser and amanuensis William Berkeley Lewis, who lived a few miles down the road; and in Nashville, his old business partner and political colleague John Overton. John H. Eaton owned property just south of Nashville, but his duties as senator and unofficial campaign manager kept him out of the state much of the time.

But Jackson liked to write letters, and despite the myths about his inability to communicate, he wrote reasonably clear prose, spelled about as well as anyone in the early republic, and was fully capable of expressing complex ideas. A man with deep emotions, he was able to inject feeling into his letters—a valuable trait in the new democratic politics. As soon as Jackson settled down at the Hermitage he began to exchange letters with more than forty different friends, most frequently with planters John Coffee in Alabama and Richard Keith Call in Florida, both of whom had served under him against the Creeks and the British. A familiar sight for mail drivers in Tennessee was the gaunt figure of the Old Hero standing at the end of his driveway, waiting for his mail. Some of the letters, especially those to and from Coffee, concerned cotton growing, horse trading, slave management, and other concerns of southern planters, but most were about politics. With the campaign just getting started, Jackson used his correspondence to define himself, express his views, and keep himself and his friends informed. Later, when his party became better organized, his letters would influence the campaign.

Jackson's first and overriding goal was to write and behave in the way his republican audience expected. His letters, such as his reply to Calhoun, were filled with republican words and concepts. On receiving an accolade from the citizens of Jackson, Tennessee, he replied that he had always acted "for the benefit and advancement of our common country, the last spot on the globe where liberty has found a resting place." To make certain that "our government go down unimpaired to posterity," the citizens must beware of the "silent inroads which intrigue, ambition, and cunning" may bring. In selecting a person to act as their agent they should make certain that "virtue and purity" have "taken up their abode" with him.[32]

When asked to accept speaking engagements outside of Tennessee, Jackson invariably declined, frequently with the republican argument that the people would consider such behavior as "manoeuvering [sic] for my own aggrandizement." Several times, however, he used the more pragmatic argument that public speaking would drag him into the snares of "local politics." A third reason may have been that Jackson was no orator. "I must be excused," he once replied, because "having lost many of my teeth . . . I can articulate" only "with great difficulty."[33]

The controversies over the Georgia Indians and the Panama Congress gave Jackson an early opportunity to express his opinions. In each case his efforts had a military ring. He would move the Indians out of the Southwest, he wrote, because "a white population, instead of the Indian," would strengthen "the defense of the lower country."[34] He opposed the Panama Congress because it might drag the United States into wars with European nations.

Jackson's correspondence brought him detailed political reports from all parts of the nation except New England. In addition to the letter from

Arthur P. Hayne at the New York spa, he had letters from Samuel Swart-wout about politics in New York and New Jersey and from Eaton describing the situation in Congress as it adjourned in May. Jackson used the information in these and other letters when he wrote his own letters to his many friends.

Some of these friends had been Federalists. Although Jackson stressed his republican sentiments and once said that he would have hanged all the Federalists at the Hartford convention if he had had the chance, he kept the door open for Federalist supporters. In October 1816, when he first began to think about politics, he wrote to presidential candidate James Monroe recommending Federalist colonel William Drayton of South Carolina as secretary of war. He went on to advise Monroe to "consult *no party*" in any of his appointments.[35] Several other letters followed between the two men. When the Crawford party forced Eaton to release the letters during the 1824 presidential campaign, Jackson's opponents used them to portray him as an amalgamator and to cast doubt on his republican credentials. Now in another campaign, Jackson defended his republicanism and insisted that he would accept only "good" Federalists (those who had backed the War of 1812). The controversy did much to encourage Federalists to come out for Old Hickory.

While Jackson was writing letters, the administration continued to fumble with political patronage. One reason, of course, was the president's stubborn refusal to use patronage as a weapon. Another was the behavior of Postmaster General John McLean, a holdover from the Monroe administration who controlled more patronage than anyone else. McLean ran the Post Office well and had a large following in Ohio, but unfortunately for the administration, he was more loyal to Calhoun, Jackson, and himself than he was to Adams and Clay.

Doubts about McLean's loyalty arose early in the Adams administration when, on the advice of Calhoun, he appointed Henry Lee, son of Revolutionary War hero "Light Horse" Harry Lee, to a minor post. It was a bad appointment. Besides Lee's reputation as a Calhoun man, it was common knowledge that he had committed adultery with his wife's sister. The doubts about McLean grew stronger when Lee was accused of writing antiadministration material for a Washington newspaper. After being forced to resign in 1826 Lee moved on to Tennessee, where he joined the Jackson campaign and started a biography of the Old Hero. Other examples of McLean's disloyalty continued to plague Clay throughout the campaign.[36]

One vital Post Office appointment, however, pleased Clay and others in the administration. When Nashville postmaster Robert B. Curry resigned in 1826, the Tennessee congressional delegation, all Jackson men, recommended Curry's nephew for the post. Since the Nashville post office was one of the largest in the system, the president, not the postmaster general, had the authority to make the appointment. Behaving more like a party man than usual, Adams ignored the Jacksonian recommendation and appointed John P. Erwin, editor of the pro-administration *Nashville Whig*. The delegation appealed to a sympathetic McLean, who took the case back to Adams, but the president stuck with Erwin.

Clay was delighted. The new postmaster was the brother of Clay's son-in-law, and even more important, Clay knew that Erwin's appointment would infuriate Jackson. The Old Hero hated Erwin because he was the son of Andrew Erwin, leader of the political clique that had long opposed Jackson's state organization. Young Erwin was also the brother-in-law of John Williams, the senator that Jackson had unseated in 1823 after a bitter campaign. Feelings were so high in Nashville that Jackson's close friend Congressman Sam Houston got into a duel with William White, who was associated with the new postmaster. In Washington Duff Green accused the administration of appointing Erwin to "spy" on Jackson's correspondence.[37]

Few administration appointments were as clearly partisan as Erwin's. Politicians who should have been rallying behind Adams were continuing to complain that he was not appointing his friends. Many of the complainers were good Republicans, but others were Federalists who claimed that Adams had not followed through on his promises to appoint them. Prominent Federalists Henry R. Warfield in Maryland and Richard Peters in Pennsylvania angrily told Clay that the president should be appointing more Federalists. Even Republicans, such as Speaker John W. Taylor, warned that Federalists who had been ignored were turning toward Jackson.[38]

By the fall of 1826, halfway between the election of 1824 and the election of 1828, the political landscape was changing. Adams and Clay men were backing the administration; Jackson and Calhoun men were forming the nucleus of an opposition. Crawford men were divided. Former Federalists were trying to find their place in politics. But no real political parties had appeared. Much depended on New York, where Van Buren and Clinton were playing a waiting game. Van Buren was opposed to

Adams but not openly committed to Jackson; Clinton was taking offers from both sides. Although there had been much skirmishing on issues, neither side had established a program around which men could gather. Old party labels still existed, even though there was no longer a Republican party or a Federalist party. During the late summer and fall a referendum of sorts had taken place when thirteen states held congressional elections. The results were not conclusive: eight states chose delegations with an administration majority; five chose opposition delegations. If the election of 1828 was to make a real difference, political parties would have to emerge at both the national and state level.

3 ORGANIZING AT THE TOP, 1827

The convening of Congress in December 1826 for its short session brought leaders of both parties to Washington, giving them another and perhaps last opportunity to agree on party policies and build party organizations before the presidential election. The setting was not ideal, for second sessions of Congress were always short, often lame duck, and rarely productive.

Adams's second annual message gave no indication that this session would be any different. Whereas his first annual message had been a long, demanding, path-breaking declaration of policy filled with high morals, great expectations, and vivid language, the second was short, perfunctory, and rather dull. More significant, it offered neither the spirit nor the theme nor the program to unite a party. Anxious to conciliate the South, Adams said nothing about the tariff. He wanted to push hard for the Chesapeake and Ohio Canal but left it out of the message when even Henry Clay, the great supporter of internal improvements, counseled against its inclusion. Adams asked for nothing new, nothing exciting. Even the references to the deaths of his father and Thomas Jefferson lacked any special vigor. One committed young Jackson man, first-term congressman James K. Polk, sniffed that the tone was less than "towering," while his hero, Andrew Jackson, dismissed the message as "modest." Adams, he concluded, had held back because he had "felt the lash" after his first bold effort.[1]

The message set the tone for the session. Even though Adams men controlled most committees, they were no more able to carry out the demands of Adams's first message than they had been the year before. The United States was never represented at the Panama Congress. Richard Anderson died of fever in 1826 en route to the first session, and John Sergeant remained at home to avoid a similar fate. A second session, scheduled to meet in Mexico in 1827, was never convened. The request for a national university and an observatory never reached the floor of the House. When Webster brought in a bankruptcy bill, it failed to pass. Congress rejected a naval academy, calling it a dangerous source of executive patronage. The government carried on with the National Road, but the dream of a road from the District of Columbia to New Orleans remained a dream. Even in diplomacy, at which Adams and Clay excelled, the efforts of the administration fell short. When the president retaliated against British port closures in the West Indies by closing American ports to ships from the Indies, the policy backfired. U.S. exports to the British West Indies fell from $2,079,000 in 1826 to $26,000 in 1828. The sharp decline in West Indies trade, which the Jacksonians blamed on Adams's inept diplomacy, became an important issue in the 1828 election and was damaging to the administration.[2]

Two other issues that would have a political impact dominated the session. The tariff question found the administration uncertain, divided, and, in the end, unsuccessful. Coming from a state that had recently changed its position on the tariff, Adams would not join Clay and Richard Rush in calling for tariff protection, but Daniel Webster, Adams's strongest supporter in New England, was more committed. Responding to pressure from his Massachusetts textile friends, he joined the protectionists and strongly endorsed a House bill raising tariffs prohibitively on woolen manufactures and more moderately on raw wool.

The bill irritated many because of the deceptive way in which it raised rates. It made no change in the old ad valorem tariff rate of 33 percent for woolen manufactures but added a schedule of minimum valuations, whereby woolens in a given value range would be charged based on the highest amount in that range. All woolens valued between $0.40 and $2.50 a yard, for example, would be treated as though they were worth $2.50. Thus a common category of cheap woolens worth $1 a yard would be charged a tariff of $0.83 ($2.50 × .33) instead of $0.33 ($1 × .33). The bill brought Jacksonians together, especially those from New York, Ohio, Kentucky, and Missouri, states that produced wool, iron, hemp, flax, and other raw materials. The Jackson men tried to broaden the scope of the bill by increasing the protection of these products, but the bill passed without substantive change. When it went to the Senate it met similar resistance from southern and western Jacksonians and was tabled in March 1827 just before Congress adjourned.[3]

The way it was tabled revealed the growing desire for unity among men at the top of the Jackson party. Intent on building a North-South alliance, Van Buren was so torn between the protectionism of his northern friends and the antitariff views of those in the South that he thought it best not to vote. So he conveniently wandered off to visit the Congressional Cemetery (that was his story), missed the roll call, and set up a tie vote. His ally, Vice President John C. Calhoun, anxious to show southerners that he was no longer a nationalist, cast the deciding vote that tabled the protectionist bill. In 1828 the Adams men and the Jackson men would have one last chance to shape a tariff bill that could pass Congress and help their party in the election.[4]

The Jacksonians had more success in exploiting the issue of political patronage. During the first session they had attacked the administration rather vaguely for its supposedly corrupt use of the power of appointment. This time they could be more specific because Clay was in the process of shifting printing contracts from dozens of anti-Adams newspapers to those supporting the administration. On February 1, 1827, opposition senator Romulus Saunders of North Carolina offered a resolution requiring Clay to report on the removals. The resolution and Clay's response occupied much of the Senate's time for the rest of the session, and even though no legislation came out of the debate, the Jackson men were able to invigorate their already powerful antipatronage position. By hammering away on this theme they laid the foundation for a strong party message in 1828.

The session, however, was not a lost cause for the administration. During the winter Adams and his top administrators were able to work face-to-face with their congressional friends in building a party organization. Although Adams hated "electioneering," he was the titular head of the party and did not always shy away from politics. When the subject of a New York appointment came up during the session, he announced firmly that he would not appoint Federalist chancellor James Kent. He had obviously learned from the appointment of Rufus King the pitfalls of bringing Federalists, especially famous ones, into his administration.

Adams demonstrated his political awareness in other situations. He kept himself informed when the Senate investigated charges against one of his opponents, John C. Calhoun, and poured cold water on a proposal to send another, Martin Van Buren, to Great Britain. He shared New Hampshire senator Samuel Bell's worries about politics in the Granite State and Speaker John W. Taylor's pessimism about the makeup of the New York congressional delegation. His concern over the health of Senator Elijah H. Mills of Massachusetts showed not only his humanitarianism but also his political instincts. Mills's potential resignation raised the tricky question of whether Webster, a stalwart in the House, should be the one to replace the senator. If Webster moved up to the Senate, Adams wondered who would fill his leadership role in the House. Adams was a shrewd judge of politicians. When Senator Richard M. Johnson of Kentucky, a Clay man who had gone over to Jackson, denied being against the administration, Adams wrote dryly in his diary that Johnson liked to "keep upon good terms with all parties."[5]

But the president was never comfortable dealing with politics, and he never solved the problem of the Federalists. When told that the port collector of Philadelphia had resigned, Adams groaned, "Now comes the usual struggle of competition for the appointment as his successor." The end of Congress in March 1827 brought little relief. The day after adjournment Adams complained that he could not "conceive a more harassing, wearying, teasing condition of existence." What made it worse was the knowledge that even with Congress gone, the pressure would remain. "The weight," he moaned, "grows heavier from day to day."[6]

To help carry the load Adams turned to his cabinet. In the early republic cabinet members had great power, and the posts were highly prized, especially that of secretary of state, which had regularly served as a pathway to the presidency. Monroe's cabinet had been crowded with prominent men—Adams, Crawford, Calhoun—each with presidential aspirations. So Adams respected his cabinet and called frequent meetings—at least eleven during the first three months of 1827.[7]

Within the cabinet the president depended most heavily on Henry Clay. "Mr. Clay," he wrote with grudging admiration, "says that these times of trouble are the times which try the spirits of men."[8] Adams's reliance on Clay is surprising, because the two men had been rivals and were completely different. Adams was cold, aloof, pessimistic, puritanical, and judgmental; Clay was warm, accessible, optimistic, pleasure loving, and tolerant. When they served together at the Peace Conference at Ghent, Adams noted in his diary that on arising early one morning he had encountered Clay returning from an all-night game of brag. But Adams needed Clay's hard work and his skill in dealing with people. The president was clearly shocked early in the session when Clay reported that a number of their friends wanted him to leave the cabinet and run for vice president. Adams hastily told him that he would prefer that Clay stay in the cabinet.[9]

Clay was indispensable because he loved and understood politics, and it soon became clear that he, not Adams, was the real head of the Adams party. Clay, Adams, and four cabinet members—James Barbour, Samuel Southard, and, to a much lesser extent, Richard Rush and William Wirt—served as an informal central committee. Calhoun and McLean were left out because of their Jackson connections. During the session of Congress this committee strengthened its ties with influential legislators such as House Speaker Taylor and Senator David Barton of Missouri. Clay would keep in touch with these men and other members of Congress after they returned to their homes.

With this modest start Clay turned to the task of party building. Although Martin Van Buren, Amos Kendall, Isaac Hill, and other Jacksonians have received more credit for party organizing than their Adams–National Republican opponents, Clay and his allies deserve more than a cursory glance. Clay's reputation as the Great Compromiser and the model Speaker of the House and his long career as congressman, senator, secretary of state, and three-time candidate for president have forced historians to give him his due; yet his efforts to create a second political party to match the Jacksonians deserve far more attention than they have received. These efforts began during the 1828 campaign, at a crucial moment when the public was beginning to accept the concepts of national political parties and a two-party political system.

Clay's first significant contribution to forming a party was his aggressive policy of shifting federal printing contracts. Before the Adams presidency had reached the halfway mark, Clay had taken contracts away from thirty-three of the more than eighty newspapers printing the federal laws. His purge struck all but six states. In New Hampshire, the only New England state that showed any signs of deserting Adams, Jacob B. Moore's *New Hampshire Journal* replaced Isaac Hill's *New-Hampshire Patriot*. In Pennsylvania, the strongest Jackson state north of the Mason-Dixon Line, John Binns's *Democratic Press* replaced John Norvell's *Franklin Gazette*. To strengthen Adams in Jackson's home state, Clay rewarded the *Nashville Whig* at the expense of the *Nashville Republican*. And to build up support in his own state, he transferred the printing in Frankfort from Amos Kendall's *Argus of Western America* to the

Commentator. He also tried to shore up support in Ohio by giving the printing to Charles Hammond's *Liberty Hall and Cincinnati Gazette.*

Two of the other moves were surprising. Even though the *National Intelligencer* had come back to the administration, Clay gave the patronage in Washington to the more politically aggressive *National Journal,* published by Peter Force. And in Albany, New York, either because the political lineups in New York were too complicated to challenge or because there was no good alternative, he left the printing with Van Buren's *Albany Argus.* Clay's purge drew sharp battle lines between outspoken critics of the administration such as Hill, Kendall, and Norvell and staunch Adams men such as Binns, Hammond, and Force.[10]

More important to Clay than these editors was a small group of close personal friends with whom he corresponded on a regular basis. The group included Webster and Hammond as well as Francis T. Brooke of Virginia, Peter B. Porter of New York, John Sergeant of Pennsylvania, John J. Crittenden of Kentucky, Josiah S. Johnston of Louisiana, and Edward Everett of Massachusetts. The emerging Adams party drew much of its character from these men and others like them.

Brooke, who at sixty-three was older than the rest, had joined the Revolutionary army at age sixteen and fought alongside Lafayette and General Nathanael Greene. When the war was over, he started a law career in Richmond. That was where he met Clay, who was studying law with Brooke's brother Robert, the former governor of Virginia. After serving in the state legislature, Francis Brooke held a seat on the Virginia Supreme Court of Appeals for forty years.

Politically more powerful than Brooke was Peter B. Porter of Buffalo, New York. Born in Connecticut just before the Revolution, Porter graduated from Yale and established himself as a wealthy lawyer in western New York. Elected to Congress in 1808, he joined Clay and other War Hawks in calling for war with Great Britain. After fighting in the war, he was elected secretary of state in New York and later ran unsuccessfully for governor against De Witt Clinton. In 1824 he managed Clay's campaign for president, and in 1828 Adams would bring him in to replace Barbour as secretary of war.

In Philadelphia Clay's connection was John Sergeant, whose father Jonathan D. Sergeant had been a member of the Continental Congress. After graduating from the University of New Jersey (now Princeton University), young John rose to become a prominent Federalist lawyer serving the establishment of Philadelphia. Like John Quincy Adams he

Edward Everett. One of the most precocious figures in American history, he was minister of the Brattle St. Church in Boston at the age of twenty and served as a member of Congress during the 1828 presidential campaign.

Senator John H. Eaton, who lived near the Hermitage in Tennessee, introduced General Jackson to American politics with a biography and his "Letters of Wyoming" in 1824.

The militiamen handbills. Published in late 1827 by Adams editor John Binns of Philadelphia, the handbills attacked Jackson for unfairly executing six militiamen under his command.

Francis Preston Blair, Amos Kendall's assistant editor, did much to help Jackson carry Kentucky in 1828.

shifted over to Republicanism and held a seat in Congress from 1815 to 1823. Early in 1827 Sergeant was on his way to the Panama Congress, but when it was called off he returned to Philadelphia to run again for Congress. In 1832 he would run for vice president on the Clay ticket.

John J. Crittenden grew up in Woodford County, Kentucky, not far from Clay's plantation in Lexington. After studying at William and Mary College he served as attorney general of the Territory of Illinois, speaker of the Kentucky House of Representatives, and U.S. senator before settling in as a court attorney in Frankfort, Kentucky. His clients included Clay, whom he supported in the election of 1824. In 1827 Adams would appoint Crittenden a U.S. district attorney.

Clay also had a loyal backer in Senator Josiah S. Johnston of Louisiana, the one southern state where, because of the port of New Orleans, commercial interests outweighed the agricultural and support for Clay's "American System" of internal improvements was strong. Johnston, a transplanted Yankee, graduated from Transylvania College in Lexington, Kentucky, and then set up shop as a lawyer in the Red River frontier of Louisiana. Elected to the U.S. Senate in 1823, Johnston served as one of Clay's campaign managers in the election of 1824. The two men were such close friends that Johnston acted as Clay's second in his duel with John Randolph.

The last of Clay's correspondents was Edward Everett. The precocious and brilliant Everett was the most gifted of the Unitarian intellectuals who found their way into the Adams–National Republican (later Whig) party of Massachusetts. He graduated from Harvard at age seventeen and took the pulpit of the prestigious Brattle Street Church in Boston when he was twenty. After four years of study and travel in Europe, Everett became professor of Greek literature at Harvard and editor of the influential *North American Review* by the time he was twenty-five. He was already famous for his oratory, which was often compared to Webster's. Like others of his generation he abandoned the pulpit and academe for politics, and in 1827 he became a junior congressman from the Bay State. On the eve of the Civil War he would run for vice president on the Constitutional Union ticket.

These men had several things in common. All save Hammond had attended college, and all but Everett were lawyers. All but one (Johnston) came from one of the large, key political states of Massachusetts, New York, Pennsylvania, Ohio, Kentucky, and Virginia. All held high office. They were all knowledgeable, well-placed, upper-class leaders—members of the elite, or the "aristocracy," as the Jackson men would call them. Strategically located throughout the nation, they were ardent Clay men. They joined the Adams-Clay party at the top.

Some idea of the extent of Clay's politicking can be seen in the two hundred letters he exchanged with politicians and others during the first four months of 1827, which have been made available in the recent edition of his papers. The letters were sent to or from nineteen of the twenty-four states, and almost 30 percent were exchanged with the close friends previously described, ranging from fifteen with Sergeant down to three with Hammond. The distribution of the letters coincided roughly with the political importance of the states, with thirty-five letters exchanged with New Yorkers, thirty with Kentuckians, and twenty-nine with Pennsylvanians.[11]

Clay had apparently made arrangements to correspond with many members of Congress, because soon after the session ended he began to receive reports from a number of them about their trips home. On March 11 Congressman Philip S. Markley wrote from Philadelphia that his contacts in the city strongly approved of the administration's policies on the tariff and the Georgia Indians. A day later Congressman Francis Johnson of Kentucky reported from the steamboat *William Tell* that Maryland was safe and western Pennsylvania was excited about the woolens bill. On March 13 Congressman Elisha Whittlesey warned from Ohio that the Jackson men were buying up newspaper presses. A persistent lot, Clay's informants let nothing—not even ill health—stand in their way. Detained in Philadelphia because of sickness, Massachusetts congressman Benjamin W. Crowninshield reassured Clay that the Quakers of Pennsylvania were for Adams. Clay inquired solicitously about his friend's health and pointed out that Crowninshield's observation was similar to others emanating from the Keystone State.[12]

The most important letters were those between Clay and Daniel Webster. During the War of 1812 no two men could have been farther apart than these two. The tall, slender Harry of the West, with his flashy, sharp, often sarcastic speaking style, leader of the nationalist, Republican War Hawks, seemed the exact opposite of the powerful, stocky, dark and brooding, godlike Daniel, the states' rights Federalist opponent of the war. After the war the differences gradually faded as Clay fought for his American System of internal improvements, a national bank, and the protective tariff, which Webster now endorsed.

The Clay-Webster alliance was formed in 1827, first in person while

Congress was in session and then in writing as the two men exchanged some two dozen letters during the year. It began to take shape in March when Webster stopped on his way home from Congress to send Clay a blunt letter assessing the condition of the Adams party in Baltimore and Philadelphia. Webster was dismayed by the lack of party spirit in either city and the refusal of the newspaper editors "*to take a side.*" His recipe for success was party patronage, starting with the *Baltimore Patriot.* "All protection, all proof of regard, all patronage, which can justly be afforded by the Executive Government," he told Clay, "must be given to friends; or otherwise it is impossible to give any general or cordial support to the Administration before the people."[13]

He was writing to a kindred soul, for Clay answered: "The principle ought to be steadily adhered to of appointing only friends of the Administration in public offices. Such I believe is the general opinion in the Cabinet. . . . We should, on all occasions, inculcate the . . . truth that *now* there are but two parties in the Union, the friends and the enemies of the administration, and that all references to obsolete denominations is for the purpose of fraud and deception. In this way, the efforts in particular places to revive old names may be counteracted."[14]

When Webster reached Boston in mid-April he wrote to Clay again, this time extending his survey to New York and New England. He predicted that New Yorkers would soon abandon Jackson in favor of Clinton. He also suggested having state legislatures in New England pass resolutions supporting the Adams administration. Clay replied promptly that he had already written to Senator Samuel Bell about the resolutions. Having state legislatures pass resolutions of support became standard Adams policy and was later copied by the Jackson administration. In these four letters Clay and Webster got the Adams campaign going in at least seven states.[15]

By early May it had become clear that Senator Mills would not be returning to the Senate and that Webster was the most likely replacement. Webster sent Clay a letter outlining the political ramifications of the situation and was rewarded by a detailed reply. The secretary of state was now acting like a party chairman, trying to decide whether Webster would be more valuable in the House or the Senate. The answer hinged on who could replace Webster as party leader in the House. Former Federalist Thomas Jefferson Oakley of New York, who had recently been elected to the House, was one possibility; John Sergeant was another. Unfortunately, Oakley was flirting with the Jacksonians, and Sergeant had not yet been elected. In the regular congressional election in 1826 Sergeant had tied with his opponent and now faced a special election. On June 7 the Massachusetts legislature settled the matter by electing Webster to the Senate.

The concern about Oakley called attention to the persistent problem of what to do about the Federalists. On this issue Webster and Clay disagreed: Webster represented those who would welcome Federalists into the party, Clay those who would keep them out. There was hardly a state in which the Adams party did not face this problem. It was particularly acute in Pennsylvania, where Federalists held the balance of power, and in New Hampshire, where Webster had difficulty convincing Senator Bell that Federalists should be invited to party conventions. Webster was also conscious of the political importance of the enclaves of New Englanders, many of them Federalists, who had moved west to key states such as New York, Pennsylvania, and Ohio.

Just as Clay and Webster were coming together, they were shaken by a newspaper article that appeared on March 27, 1827, in Fayetteville's *Carolina Observer*. Virginia planter Carter Beverley wrote that he had just returned from Andrew Jackson's plantation, where Old Hickory had told a revised version of the bargain charge. According to Jackson, just before Adams's election in the House, Henry Clay and his friends had offered to make the Old Hero president if he would agree not to retain Adams as secretary of state. Old Hickory, who told the story to a large number of guests with great relish, said that, of course, he had rejected the offer. Here was a twist on the original bargain charge, with Clay once again making a corrupt offer, but this time trying to deal with Jackson, not Adams. Hoping that Beverley's story would reinforce the charge, Duff Green ran it in the *Telegraph,* but the story was false. The Clay people had wanted to prevent Adams from staying on as secretary of state, but they had never made a specific offer. Clay, who knew the story was false, thought it would backfire on the Jacksonians. He decided to deny the charge and wait for Jackson to get in over his head. His patience was rewarded in early June when Jackson published a long letter endorsing and elaborating on Beverley's story. In the letter the general stated that he had been informed of Clay's offer by "a member of Congress of high respectability."[16]

Jackson's letter appeared just as Clay was embarking on an important political trip to western Pennsylvania and down the Ohio River to Kentucky. Aware that both the farmers and the manufacturers in the states through which he would pass—Pennsylvania, Ohio, and Kentucky— were in favor of internal improvements and protective tariffs, Clay was planning to use the trip to establish his American System as the central theme of the Adams campaign. The trip had started auspiciously in late June with large dinners at Uniontown, Pittsburgh, and Washington in western Pennsylvania and at Steubenville, Ohio. To the seven hundred who listened to his Pittsburgh address, he predicted that with the help of the protective tariff, "the value of our exported manufactures [would] exceed [the value] of all the exports of raw produce from our country."[17]

But all this changed on the night of June 23 when Clay's steamboat docked at Wheeling, Virginia, and he got his first glimpse of Jackson's letter. On reaching Lexington he issued another denial and demanded that Jackson reveal the identity of the congressman with "high respectability." On June 29 Clay reviewed the entire bargain charge story in a long speech before a thousand listeners in Lexington. From that point on he abandoned the subject of the tariff.[18]

Word soon leaked out that the man of "high respectability" was Jackson congressman James Buchanan of Pennsylvania. Although Buchanan did not admit his responsibility until August 8, Clay knew it a month earlier. Buchanan had apparently made up the story to bring Clay and Jackson together and, in the process, advance his own career. This confession was a major victory for Clay, and if he and the Jackson men had let the bargain charge drop there, it might have helped turn the election in Adams's favor, but that was not to be. Clay kept the original story alive by publishing evidence to refute almost every Jacksonian charge. His most widely circulated document was a well-publicized major address late in December. On the Jackson side, Amos Kendall started a series of public letters to Clay in which he revealed that just before Adams's election Clay had written a letter to Francis Preston Blair of Kentucky, announcing that he would vote for Adams and urging Blair and his friends to put pressure on the other Kentucky congressmen to do the same. For the rest of the campaign Kendall, Green, Hill, and other Jackson editors would not let the story die.[19]

Clay and Webster had another opportunity to exploit the tariff issue on July 30, 1827, when a national tariff convention was held at Harrisburg, Pennsylvania. Ever since the rise of the textile industry, manufacturers, newspaper editors such as Hezekiah Niles, and northern intellectuals such as political economist Matthew Carey had joined politicians in calling for tariff protection. The failure of Congress to pass the woolens bill in March 1827 had made the tariff the central economic issue of the day. As with the issues of the central bank and internal improvements, interest in the tariff was strongest in Pennsylvania and the other Middle Atlantic states and among Adams men rather than Jacksonians. Taking advantage of the growing interest, the Pennsylvania Society for the Protection of Manufacturers organized the convention.

Webster and Clay did all they could to make the convention a success. Webster used his considerable powers of persuasion to convince his brother Ezekiel, who detested traveling, to make the difficult trip from New Hampshire to Harrisburg. "It might be well perhaps to go," Daniel gently suggested. "You will have good company, & a good opportunity to see the middle States." He was more businesslike in dealing with New Yorkers, sending duplicate letters to John W. Taylor and several other prominent political figures. If Taylor could not arrange a large meeting to choose delegates, wrote Webster, why not try a number of local meetings?[20]

Thus it was not surprising that Adams men dominated the conventions called to nominate delegates. About one hundred delegates were elected from thirteen states—nearly all of them Adams men. It was so one-sided at one Philadelphia meeting that Peter P. F. Degrand, publisher of the financial periodical *Degrand's Weekly Report,* humorously apologized to Clay, saying that the one Jacksonian who had managed to slip in had been able to do so because the organizers did not realize he was a Jackson man. The Harrisburg convention was so completely an Adams affair that several Jacksonians in favor of tariff protection, including Henry Baldwin of Pennsylvania and Louis McLane of Delaware, chose not to attend.[21]

During the three-day session the delegates drew up protective tariff schedules to be presented to Congress. They proposed raising the ad valorem rate for woolen goods from 33 percent to 40 percent and keeping the system of minimum rates proposed in the 1827 woolens bill. That combination would raise rates much higher than ever before. The convention gave the Adams men a great political opportunity, because tariff protection was already popular in many northern states, but they failed to take advantage of it. Jacksonian protests about the political bias of the convention put the Adams men on the defensive, and they stopped short of using the convention to support Adams candidates. In the concluding ceremonies not a word was said about John Quincy Adams.[22]

Even so, the convention gave a much-needed lift to the Adams campaign in the northern states. It put the Adams men on the popular side of a powerful issue, and the process of holding a major convention had given them experience in political organizing. The Harrisburg convention made it even more imperative for the Jackson party to deal with the tariff in the next Congress.

As Clay and Webster became increasingly involved in organizing the Adams party, they were forced to spend more and more time dealing with party newspapers and campaign expenses. Since Webster was in close contact with the leading money men of Boston, New York, and Philadelphia, he became the de facto treasurer of the party. To help spread party doctrine in the crucial state of Ohio, he first offered to raise money to send copies of the *Massachusetts Journal* to a number of Ohio printers but then agreed to a less costly plan of exchanging copies of the *Journal* for copies of several Ohio newspapers.[23]

As the election drew closer Clay became more aware of the role played by the party press and the needs of the individual newspapers. In his view the "most efficient and discreet" newspaper on the Adams side was Hammond's *Liberty Hall and Cincinnati Gazette*. Since Hammond was "poor [and] proud," Clay told Webster, something must be done to keep such a talented editor in business. When Clay asked Webster to provide Hammond with "a new set of types," the godlike Daniel replied that he would be glad to do it. Estimating that new types would cost between $500 and $600, he said he knew "a few Gentlemen here who would be willing to bear a part."[24]

At this point Clay came up with an imaginative plan: they would set up a fund to help needy, useful newspaper men, and in return, the editors would be expected to circulate a number of copies free of charge. By November 18 Clay and Webster had established a fund to be administered by Josiah S. Johnston and Edward Everett and had extended help not only to Hammond but also to John H. Pleasants, editor of the *Richmond Constitutional Whig*. Everett had already raised more than $700 from wealthy Boston merchants and manufacturers, including Peter Chardon Brooks, Nathan Appleton, Abbott and Amos Lawrence, and Colonel Thomas Handasyd Perkins. These men were in the same social class as the members of Clay's inner circle.[25]

The Jackson party was also organizing. In New York, Martin Van Buren's "back stairs intercourse" with De Witt Clinton seemed to be paying off.[26] After his Regency, as agreed, put up a weak gubernatorial candidate in the fall of 1826, Clinton won reelection and was presumably ready to let the Little Magician return to the Senate when the New York legislature voted in February. But Van Buren, a chronic worrier, was still not sure. New York City editor Mordecai Noah, who spoke for Tammany Hall, had announced for Jackson and was attacking the Little Magician for holding back. Van Buren also learned in December that the administration was trying to convince John W. Taylor to run against him in February and that one of the strongest Jackson men, Samuel D. Ingham of Pennsylvania, had recently been defeated for the Senate. So Van Buren still did not dare to come out publicly for Jackson.

Van Buren also had a more immediate reason to be anxious. He was about to have another of his political conferences with Calhoun, one that promised to be just as difficult as the others because it concerned Thomas Ritchie, who distrusted Calhoun. In the past Ritchie and his Richmond Junto had opposed Calhoun because of his nationalist views and his close ties with the northern state of Pennsylvania. Snubbing Calhoun, they had supported Crawford in the election of 1824. But Ritchie now seemed ready to join Calhoun and Van Buren in opposing the administration. Badly frightened by Adams's nationalism in the first annual message, Ritchie was fearful that the nation, including the Old Dominion, would succumb to the wiles of the administration. More immediately, he was afraid that John Tyler, a friend of Adams, would defeat the strongest antinationalist in the Senate, John Randolph, in the coming senatorial election in the Virginia legislature.

When Congress paused for Christmas 1826, Van Buren and Calhoun left for Fairfax County, Virginia, to spend the holidays at Ravensworth, the estate of wealthy planter William Henry Fitzhugh. Despite the sensitive issues, the conversations between the two men went far better than either might have expected. Before long, Van Buren recalled, they had "united heart and hand to promote the election" of Andrew Jackson.[27] They agreed that Van Buren would write a letter to Ritchie urging him to bring the Richmond Junto and the state of Virginia into the Jackson movement. To make sure that Calhoun's northern allies would approve, Van Buren agreed to show the letter to Congressman Ingham before sending it.

The letter, a classic in American political history, strongly endorsed the new positive concept of political parties. "We will always have parties," Van Buren wrote, "and the old ones are the best." He called for a return to the old party system of Federalists and Republicans, which, he asserted, had reduced the dangers of sectionalism by uniting North and

South. By substituting *"party principle* for *personal preference,"* they would "unite the planters of the South and the plain Republicans of the North," thus preventing conflicts between the two. He pointed out that after the first party system broke down, "the clamour agt Southern Influence and African slavery" arose in the North. Would Ritchie join him and Calhoun in restoring the old Republican party "by combining Genl. Jackson's personal popularity with the portion of old party feeling yet remaining?"[28]

Some scholars have read overarching themes into this letter. They have portrayed Van Buren as a modernist calling for an entirely new concept of national parties. They have called him a doughface selling out to slavery in the South or an ideologue eager to lead the nation back toward classical republicanism. To accept any of these concepts is to misunderstand Martin Van Buren. The Little Magician was not an ideologue; he was first and foremost a very capable, pragmatic politician. The letter is far more political than it is ideological. By returning to the old system, he predicted, they would steal New Hampshire away from Adams in the election. Although still advocating the caucus system to nominate candidates, Van Buren wrote that he was willing to call a national convention to nominate Jackson, not because it would be more republican or more democratic than the present system but because it would help the revived Republican party win the election. Holding a Republican convention would help the party outmaneuver Adams and Clinton and counter the impression engendered by Jackson's letter to James Monroe that Old Hickory was an amalgamator or, even worse, a Federalist lover. In the end, however, neither a caucus nor a convention was held. Van Buren ended this pragmatic letter by warning that if Ritchie did not follow his plan, the nomination could go to Clinton rather than Jackson.

Those who use this letter to attack Van Buren for defending slavery are applying the moral attitudes of twenty-first-century Americans to a situation that took place nearly two hundred years ago. They fail to ask two crucial questions: What did Americans then know about the problem of race? And what were Van Buren's alternatives? The answer to the first is that compared to today they knew very little. Many Americans, to be sure, were against slavery, but many of those were less than enthusiastic about having free blacks living next to them. The answer to the second is that Americans like Van Buren were more concerned that abolitionism would destroy the Union than they were about the immoral treatment of African Americans. The terrible irony, of course, is that slavery came very close to destroying the Union and took the lives of vast numbers of Americans. To expect Van Buren to have anticipated all this is unreasonable.[29]

Once Van Buren, Calhoun, and Ingham had agreed on the letter, the pieces began to fall into place for the Jackson party. Ritchie promptly joined. Just a few days before the letter (which was dated January 13, 1827) arrived, he learned that Randolph had lost his Senate seat to Tyler. Now more determined than ever to stop Adams's nationalism, Ritchie had no choice but to fall in line. On February 6, 1827, the New York legislature, with Clinton's blessing, reelected Van Buren for a second term, and he was soon able to come out openly for Jackson. The election of Van Buren and three other Jackson senators—Thomas Hart Benton of Missouri, Louis McLane of Delaware, and Powhatan Ellis of Mississippi—provided a great boost for the Jackson party. Van Buren was now free to make overtures to Jackson and his Nashville Junto. He was already friendly with one member, Alfred Balch, and he had been working in the Senate with another, John H. Eaton. Now he began to correspond with William B. Lewis and in a few months would be writing directly to Jackson.[30]

Van Buren was also free to formalize the antiadministration party that had been gathering around him and Calhoun in Congress. Using the congressional caucus system that had nominated Crawford in 1824 as a model, he started calling meetings of Jackson senators and representatives. Among those attending were Calhoun; senators Eaton, Benton, and Johnson; and congressmen Sam Houston of Tennessee, Ingham, Buchanan, and Thomas P. Moore of Kentucky. *Niles' Weekly Register* called the meetings the work of "a new cabalistic party," and the *National Intelligencer* denounced Van Buren as the "Master Spirit" of an organization bent on taking over the functions of the government.[31]

Since Congress would adjourn in March, and since there would be only one more session in the almost two years before the election, Van Buren and his group established a year-round central committee of Washingtonians that would keep in touch with state organizations and answer charges coming from the administration. The chair of the committee was president of the Bank of the Metropolis John P. Van Ness, a member of the aristocratic Van Ness family of New York. Van Ness had served in Congress for two years before moving to Washington, where he became a man-about-town, holding positions such as councilor, alderman, mayor, and general of the militia. His brother Cornelius P. Van Ness had recently retired as governor of Vermont. Other members of the committee included such prominent local citizens as Dr. William Jones, who was later postmaster; his brother-in-law Thomas Corcoran Jr.; former Federalist congressman Philip Stuart of Maryland; register of wills Henry C. Neale; and land and pension agent Joseph Watson.[32]

The most important member of the committee was editor Duff Green, who was making the *United States Telegraph* the most powerful voice in the Jackson party. A tireless, bold, fierce debater willing to stretch the truth, Green stood ready to rebut attacks on Jackson or to justify his often contradictory positions on economic issues. And when Green went on the attack, as Whig editor Nathan Sargent later recalled, the "charges . . . were made in so bold, positive, and confident a manner, and in such thundering tones, and . . . so oft repeated, that the people of the United States, . . . not knowing . . . that there was not a grain of truth . . . in them, . . . were astounded and some even convinced."[33] What Green said counted because the circulation of the *Telegraph* rose to 20,000, greater than any other newspaper at the time, and because his articles were promptly copied and republished in the growing network of Jackson newspapers.

Early in 1827 Green was paying more attention to the tariff, internal improvements, and slavery than anything else. The debates in Congress had shown that large numbers of Americans representing diverse interests from many parts of the country were in favor of tariff protection and national roads and canals. Southern slave owners, however, opposed these policies because they considered them unconstitutional, against their economic interests, and a first step toward the abolition of slavery.

Green and the Jackson party generally avoided constitutional arguments, resorting instead to vague statements or specific arguments tailored to local concerns. Green would point out that Jackson had voted for roads and tariffs when he was in the Senate, or he would quote Jackson as saying that he favored a *"judicious"* tariff, especially tariffs that would strengthen the nation against foreign attacks.[34] Green would also argue that subjects such as the tariff and internal improvements obscured the real republican issues—democracy, corruption, and the character of the candidates. He hammered away on the theme that the Adams party had failed on all three counts.

In defending slavery, Green used arguments that later became the hallmark of Jacksonian democracy. Adams men, he said, often Federalists in disguise, agitated for the abolition of slavery simply to win votes in the North. Their agitation endangered the Union. Slavery, he conceded, was undemocratic but could be abolished only over a long period of time.

Green also used the *Telegraph* to promote Calhoun's vice presidential hopes. In the absence of a congressional caucus or a national nominating convention, presidential and vice presidential candidates had to be nominated by state legislative caucuses or conventions, most of which had not yet taken place. Since Calhoun had come out openly for Jackson, and since he was already vice president, many assumed that he would become the Old Hero's running mate. Although they said nothing publicly, the many conferences between Van Buren and Calhoun suggested that they had agreed on the South Carolinian for vice president.

But there was strong opposition to Calhoun, led by supporters of De Witt Clinton, whose reputation as the builder of the Erie Canal made him a well-known, popular figure. In the South many Old Republicans preferred Nathaniel Macon or some other constitutional traditionalist. Green vigorously opposed Clinton, saying that his nomination would cost Jackson votes by alienating Van Buren supporters in New York. He also pointed out that Clinton had opposed the War of 1812 and had won the support of many Federalists when he ran against Madison for president. Clinton, he warned, would have the Hartford convention "thick about his ears."[35]

Green also had to defend Calhoun against charges that, as secretary of war, he had misused funds for military construction at the Rip Raps shoal in Chesapeake Bay. Calhoun had insisted on a Senate investigation and had stepped down as president of the Senate while it was going on. On February 13, 1827, he was vindicated when the Senate cleared him of any misdoing.[36]

But despite the vindication, southern suspicion of Calhoun remained. Even though Ritchie and Virginia had been won over, there were still questions about the lower South. To strengthen his position in North Carolina, Calhoun personally sought the support of two of the most important Old Republicans in the state. He made a conscious effort to court former congressman Willie Mangum, and later, on his way home from the Senate, he attended a dinner in honor of retiring congressman Romulus Saunders, whose patronage resolution had sparked such controversy.

Van Buren was also traveling through North Carolina. After Congress adjourned in March 1827 he and a party of friends headed for Charleston, South Carolina. Accompanying him were congressmen James

Hamilton Jr. and William Drayton, of Charleston, and Churchill C. Cambreleng, a native North Carolinian but now a New Yorker. Their goals were to win Old Republican support for Calhoun as vice president and to bring Crawford supporters in the Carolinas and Georgia into the Jackson ranks. It would be a difficult task, for only one of the three congressional delegations—the South Carolinians—had voted for Jackson in 1825; the delegations of both North Carolina and Georgia had voted for Crawford. The trip was no secret. Hamilton told Jackson enthusiastically that Van Buren was *"zealously cordially* and *entirely"* with them and intended to spend "his Spring in Carolina and Georgia."[37] On the administration side the *Intelligencer* reported dourly that "intrigues [were] on foot."[38]

Traveling by carriage, the party made its way through Virginia and North Carolina, stopping to greet political friends and make new ones along the way. After arriving in Charleston late in March, they stayed for almost a week to attend a dinner honoring Senator Robert Y. Hayne. Here Van Buren offered a toast calling for "a speedy extinguishment of Sectional and State jealousies—the best and most appropriate sacrifice that can be made on the altar of State Rights," words pleasing to Old Republican ears.[39]

After a short trip to Savannah by sea, they went inland to Crawford's plantation at Woodlawn in the Broad River Valley of up-country Georgia. Although Woodlawn was almost close enough to Calhoun's plantation at Pendleton, South Carolina, to make the two men neighbors, and even though they had served together in James Monroe's cabinet, they were not close personally and had crossed swords on many occasions. Crawford had recovered some of the eyesight lost because of his stroke, but he was now more an Old Republican symbol than an active politician. When Van Buren asked him to support a Jackson-Calhoun ticket, the stricken old man gasped, for he hated Jackson almost as much as he did Calhoun. After some hesitation, however, he finally gave in and agreed to back the Old Hero. For vice president, however, he held out for Nathaniel Macon instead of Calhoun, to which the ever diplomatic yet firm Van Buren gently replied that Calhoun was indispensable to the movement. They parted united for Jackson but not for Calhoun.

On the way home Van Buren and Cambreleng passed through Columbia, South Carolina, and Raleigh, North Carolina, before reaching Richmond in early May. Here they were joined by Calhoun's strongest spokesman, the passionately "churlish" George McDuffie, who helped the two New Yorkers make the case for a Jackson-Calhoun ticket. When he reached Washington on May 12 Van Buren paid a courtesy call on President Adams. Although the two men merely exchanged pleasantries, Adams understood exactly what was happening. A few hours after the conversation he wrote in his diary that Van Buren had become "the great electioneering manager for General Jackson."[40]

Adams was eventually proved correct, but at the time, Jackson was relying more on Senator John H. Eaton than on anyone else. Eaton had lived at the same boardinghouse as Jackson when they were both senators, and he had written Jackson's biography. As his campaign manager in 1824 he had published the "Letters of Wyoming" in the *Columbian Observer*, portraying Old Hickory as a republican hero. After Jackson lost the election, Eaton positioned him for 1828 by drafting the letter in which George Kremer accused Adams and Clay of a corrupt bargain. In the winter of 1826–1827 Eaton had been reporting back to Jackson from the Senate.

The contents of three of those reports give a good indication of how the Jackson party viewed the election. The letters reeked with paranoia. In two of them Eaton warned Jackson to beware of his friends and pointed to James Monroe, who, he said, was as much a part of the administration "gentry" as Clay, Southard, or Barbour. Monroe, who had been secretary of war at the time of the Battle of New Orleans, had claimed that he should receive as much credit for the victory as Jackson. Eaton began to suspect that Monroe was the source of talk that Jackson had disobeyed his orders in the Seminole War and that Jackson had urged Monroe to appoint Federalists in 1816. Eaton's suspicions went well beyond Monroe. Jackson must be alert, he said, to make sure that "no enemy" could find his way into the general's "camp" in "the garb & character of a friend." According to Eaton, obvious enemy Charles Hammond had written him "a very insiduous [sic] and friendly letter." Eaton's greatest fear concerned the Post Office. Convinced that no letter was safe, he compared the administration's espionage with that practiced by the radicals in the French Revolution.[41]

In a third letter Eaton turned his attention to administration efforts to get Jackson to commit himself on economic issues. He passed along advice from the other Tennessee senator, Hugh Lawson White, who said that Jackson should offer no opinions at all, even though his views were perfectly sound. By remaining silent he would keep his enemies from taking advantage of anything he might say and would leave himself "entirely free to shape his course [according] to the best interest of the Country." These letters reflect the intense suspicions of the Jacksonians and their basic republican assumption that they were virtuous and their opponents corrupt.[42]

The Jacksonians were jittery because the Adams men had launched a series of personal attacks on Jackson. In the fall of 1826 Charles Hammond announced in the *Liberty Hall and Cincinnati Gazette* that he intended to explore rumors about Jackson's marriage. When Andrew Jackson and Rachel Donelson married in 1791, they believed erroneously that Rachel's first husband, Lewis Robards, had obtained a divorce. After learning that they had been mistaken, they waited until they received official word of the divorce and then married again in 1794. In their own eyes they had done nothing wrong, but their enemies were whispering that they had committed adultery. On learning of Hammond's threats, an outraged Jackson concluded that Clay was responsible and asked Eaton to investigate. He was less than satisfied when Eaton reported back that Clay denied any involvement.

On February 12, 1827, Thomas Dickens Arnold, an Adams party candidate for Congress from eastern Tennessee, brought the marriage question into the open by publishing an article stating that Jackson, "a lump of naked deformity," had "tor[n] from a husband the wife of his bosom," that he had "driven [Robards] off like a dog, and had taken his wife."[43] Hammond published a similar attack on March 23 and continued his charges throughout the rest of the campaign. Jackson, who had once killed a man in a duel for taunting him about his marriage, was furious.

Meanwhile, Jackson had to deal with another serious charge when on March 19 two Adams congressmen from Kentucky, Richard Buckner and Francis Johnson, separately accused Jackson of having cruelly and illegally executed six Tennessee militiamen for mutiny. The incident occurred near Mobile in the Mississippi Territory in the late summer of 1814, while Jackson was in command of the entire Southwest. At the court-martial, which was held on December 5, 1814, the six men maintained that they were innocent because their terms of duty had expired, but the court ruled otherwise. Jackson was not present at the court-martial, but on January 22, 1815, shortly after the Battle of New Orleans, he approved the court's findings, and on February 21 the men were executed. The charges against Jackson were serious. For a man being compared with Cincinnatus and Washington as a person of great virtue and the savior of his nation, the accusations of stealing a wife and murdering soldiers were career threatening.

At first the Jacksonians responded individually and locally. The *Nashville Republican* called the criticism of the marriage nothing but "innuendoes and insinuations," and Amos Kendall ran a similar article in his *Argus of Western America*. But when the charges kept coming, Jackson and his Nashville friends decided to set up an organization that could respond to attacks on the Old Hero.[44] Called officially the Nashville Central Committee, it was made up of about twenty people, including John Overton and William B. Lewis, who directed operations; Alfred Balch; justices of the state supreme court John Catron and Robert Whyte; federal district judge John McNairy; speaker of the state senate Robert C. Foster; and former U.S. secretary of the treasury George W. Campbell. Many of these men were members of the Nashville Junto, which had launched Jackson on his career. Aware that republican dogma disapproved of candidates participating in elections, Jackson at first tried to separate himself from the committee, but it soon became clear that he was often calling the shots.[45]

After gathering data for several weeks the new committee published formal responses to both charges. In defense of the marriage they reproduced official records and testimony allegedly demonstrating the young couple's innocence. They published documents showing that the executed men had stolen food and supplies and that their terms of enlistment had not expired. They also pointed out that the mutiny and court-martial had taken place while the United States was under attack and that the men had been executed before word of the peace treaty arrived in New Orleans.

The committee made sure that word got around. Committee members sent copies of their statements to Duff Green to be published in the *Telegraph* and to other Jackson newspapers. Late in May Anthony Butler wrote to Jackson from Mississippi asking for copies of the committee's response to the marriage charges. And the administration followed the situation closely. Late in April Clay received a letter from Francis Johnson reporting that "last nights mail brought a package of hand Bills—from the Nashville Jackson committee—signed by 'John Overton' in which Mr Buckner and myself are noticed."[46] A month later Francis T. Brooke told Clay that news of the Nashville committee had reached Virginia. Clay himself wrote to Edward Everett and sarcastically noted the "vindication from the Nashville Comee" of the militia "affair."[47]

Duff Green's response to the marriage charges offers a good example of the ruthless, holier-than-thou way he used accusations, hints, insinuations, and threats to fight off attacks. "It now appears," he wrote, that Jackson's "enemies, not content with slandering his public character, have determined to assail his life" and that "his wife is to come in for her share of slanderous abuse." But, he continued, the Jackson party would not resort to "just recrimination . . . materials for which are abundant, and at hand." Green insisted slyly that he had "no desire to trace the *love* adventures of the Chief Magistrate, nor to disclose the manner, *nor the time,* at which he . . . led [his] *blushing bride* to the hymenial altar."[48] But, he suggested, he would not hesitate to do so if the *Journal* renewed its libel.

While fending off these charges, Jackson was also forced to deal with an issue that had worried Eaton—that Monroe deserved much of the credit for defeating the British at New Orleans. In the summer of 1826 an old enemy of Jackson's, Jonathan Roberts, published an article in Philadelphia's *Democratic Press* stating that Monroe had planned the defense of New Orleans and then had to order Jackson to move out of Florida to defend the city.

Earlier in the summer the same subject had come up at a dinner party at the home of Dr. John S. Wellford in Fredericksburg, Virginia. As the members of the party drank wine after dinner, Dr. John H. Wallace, an ardent Jackson man, argued that the Old Hero's skill in defending New Orleans proved that he was well qualified to be president. Secretary of the Navy Samuel Southard, who was present that evening, conceded that Jackson deserved praise for the victory but insisted that Monroe should be given a share of the credit. Anticipating the charges that Roberts would make a few weeks later, he pointed out that Monroe had made plans for the defense of the city and had alerted Jackson to the approach of the British.

Southard had not meant to make an attack on Jackson, but the emotional Wallace considered his words an insult. He reported his version of the conversation to Congressman Sam Houston, who passed it on to Jackson in October. Jackson, who was outraged, prepared a harsh letter to Southard, which he asked Houston to deliver on his return to Washington in December. The affair then escalated from a misunderstanding between Jackson and Southard into a full-blown controversy involving the leadership of both parties. Instead of delivering the letter, Houston showed it to Jackson supporters in Washington, who suggested that Old Hickory compose a softer letter or, better still, do nothing. Meanwhile, Southard, who had gotten wind of the contents of the letter, took the matter to Adams and Clay. Adams, who was both amused and scornful, commented that Southard's remarks had had the same effect on Jackson as "a scarlet blanket upon a tiger."[49]

On February 3 Southard received a short letter from Jackson in which the general accused him of saying that Monroe deserved all the credit for the victory at New Orleans and that Jackson had left his army before the battle and had to be ordered back by Monroe. Jackson also surmised that Southard was speaking for the "executive branch of our government."[50] When Southard brought this inflammatory, hyperbolic letter to Adams, the president told him to deny that he had said anything about Jackson leaving his post but to ignore the worrisome charge that he was speaking for the government. Southard followed this advice.

But Jackson was not satisfied. On March 6, 1827, he wrote Southard an embarrassing, viciously sarcastic letter saying that he had expected "a frank answer" from Southard, not an "argumentative one." He went on to lecture the secretary about the "historical facts," which Southard had apparently forgotten in his "*unofficial* zeal" and his "*wine drinking.*" Suggesting that a duel might ensue, Jackson ended by saying that he "close[d] this correspondence."[51] When the letter arrived on April 2, the administration was dumbfounded. Southard sat down and composed a thirty-one-page memorandum to himself, summarizing the affair. Adams dismissed Jackson's letter as one written in a "coarse and insulting style, . . . with passion partly suppressed," and he ordered Southard to avoid getting drawn any further into the affair.[52]

By this time the Southard-Jackson controversy was public knowledge. The *National Journal* cited the correspondence as good evidence of Jackson's "violence and intemperance"; Green's *Telegraph* defended the heroic general.[53] The squabble attracted public attention because it was a direct conflict between the upper echelons of the two parties, but it soon faded from view in many of the states because of other events involving state parties. With the election now less than a year and a half away, and with the two parties increasingly organized at the top, the outcome would depend on how well they could organize at the bottom.

ORGANIZING AT THE BOTTOM

By the time the Southard-Jackson controversy reached the newspapers, politicians at the state, county, and town levels were beginning to make plans for the coming presidential election. Ideally, a thorough study of the election would entail an analysis of all twenty-four states, but since space limitations make that impossible, I chose six representative states. Four—New York, Pennsylvania, Virginia, and Ohio—were the largest states and would have the greatest impact on the outcome. The other two—New Hampshire and Kentucky—add geographic balance by including one state from New England and one from the Old Southwest.

No six states can perfectly represent the Union in 1828, but these come reasonably close. They offered samples of almost all the economies of the young republic—fishing, hillside farming, cotton and tobacco planting, wool growing, and textile manufacturing—as well as free and slave cultures. They included the two largest, most metropolitan states, New York and Pennsylvania; two rapidly growing western states, Ohio and Kentucky; and two slowly growing eastern states, New Hampshire and Virginia. They were home to almost half of both the American people and the electoral college. They included three of the four states with the closest presidential elections in 1828. Eight of the twelve men to be reckoned with in the election were identified with one of these states. And ten of the first fifteen presidents of the United States came from them.

All six states had already left their mark on American

politics. In New Hampshire Isaac Hill had gained a national reputation because he so perfectly represented the new-style editor–politician– regency head who openly embraced the new attitude toward political parties. For years New York had been the scene of fierce battles between the master of old-style politics, De Witt Clinton, and the manipulator of new-style techniques, Martin Van Buren, head of the Albany Regency. Though still without its own regency, Pennsylvania had consistently led the way toward democracy and political parties. No state could claim more ruthlessly political newspapermen than Ohio, and politicians were already looking at Kentucky politics for hints about the next national presidential election. Virginia, of course, had been the birthplace of presidents.

These six almost contiguous states cut a broad swath across the land, stretching southwestward from the Atlantic coast to the junction of the Ohio and Mississippi rivers. All but New Hampshire were created and held together by the great pathways between East and West—the Erie Canal, the National Road, the Ohio River, and the trail down the Valley of Virginia and through the Cumberland Gap. National patterns of migration had left their mark on five of the six. New York City and Philadelphia were already the great entryways for Irishmen, Englishmen, Germans, and other Europeans migrating to the United States. New York was so much the product of migration that in 1825 half the members of the state legislature had been born outside of the state, most of them in New England. These Yankees had settled in the Mohawk Valley and counties to the west——the route of the Erie Canal. In Ohio farmers from Connecticut had moved into the Western Reserve on the shores of Lake Erie. Daniel Webster referred to these transplanted New Englanders affectionately as the "universal Yankee Nation," which, he claimed, would "give a good account of [itself] from the bottom of Lake Erie to [the] Penobscot River" in Maine.[1] He meant, of course, that they would vote for Adams.

Two other migrations were shaping Ohio and Kentucky. One, down the Ohio River, brought settlers, some of German stock, from Pennsylvania to central and southern Ohio and northern Kentucky. The second, from Virginia, was made up of planters, small farmers, and slaves from Virginia who migrated through the Cumberland Gap to Bluegrass Kentucky and across the Ohio River to the southern part of the Old Northwest. Henry Clay, who moved from Virginia to Lexington, Kentucky;

Duff Green, whose father acquired land in Woodford County, Kentucky; and Abraham Lincoln, whose family settled in Hardin County, Kentucky, were products of this migration.

This chapter and the next one look at the election of 1828 from the vantage point of these six representative states.

NEW HAMPSHIRE

The first statewide party contest in New Hampshire arose in 1796 when minority Republicans ran a slate of candidates against the well-established Federalists. The Republican efforts failed miserably—John Adams and the Federalists swept the state—but the Republicans kept up the battle and in 1805 won their first victory. From then on they lost only four of the annual state elections, their final defeat coming in 1815, after which the Federalists gradually disappeared as an organized party.

Voting patterns had developed that carried over into the 1820s. Federalism was strongest in the so-called Old Colony along the seacoast—the first settled, most highly developed, commercial and political center of New Hampshire—and in the towns along the east side of the Connecticut River, which divided New Hampshire from Vermont. The mountainous north country and the hilly, farming interior of the state between the Old Colony and the Connecticut Valley were more likely to vote Republican.[2]

During these years New Hampshire had become increasingly democratic. Governors served terms of only one year. The early state constitution granted almost universal adult male suffrage, including blacks. The Toleration Act of 1819 allowed all Christian denominations (not just the Congregational Church) the right to receive local tax support. And after 1800 New Hampshire had a relatively advanced system of political parties. Each party was directed by a caucus that met during the state legislative session in June and chose candidates for Congress and state offices. A central committee set policy and sent out circulars to county committees, which nominated state officials and got out the vote. They did their work well. Sixty-two percent of eligible voters voted for president in 1808, 75 percent in 1812, and 81 percent for governor in 1814.

After the collapse of the Federalists the Republicans united behind governors William Plumer and Samuel Bell and ran the state harmoniously for several years. But in 1822 the party began to split into factions. The dominant Republican faction was led by party secretary Isaac Hill, who, though only thirty-four, had accumulated great political power. In addition to being party secretary and editor of Concord's *New-Hampshire Patriot,* he was state printer and state senator and would soon become federal printer and a federal mail contractor. Firmly settled in Concord in the hills of central New Hampshire, Hill and his Concord Regency were fast becoming the spokesmen for the Republican farmers of the state.

Resentful that all the governors had come from the Old Colony, Hill first tried (unsuccessfully) to elect a western candidate and then made an alliance with a rising young lawyer who had moved from the interior to the Old Colony port of Portsmouth. The handsome, cautious Levi Woodbury was everything the crippled, ruthless Hill was not. Woodbury had been educated at Dartmouth and had married into wealth; Hill was uneducated and had earned his way as a low-class printer. To make sure that no one forgot it, he always wore a black suit and worked standing up at a high desk. With Hill's help Woodbury was elected U.S. senator and took his seat in December 1825 in time to join the opposition to President Adams.

Until 1824 Hill stayed out of presidential politics, but that year he, like Van Buren, supported William H. Crawford against John Quincy Adams, the only candidates on the New Hampshire ballots. As a result he suffered a temporary setback when Adams carried New Hampshire by the overwhelming margin of 9,389 to 634. Shaken by the defeat, Hill moved into the Jackson party. An anonymous writer in the *Patriot,* perhaps Hill himself, ran a series of attacks on Adams; Hill supporters in Dover set up an anti-Adams newspaper; and Hill began to communicate with Jackson supporters in Tennessee, Ohio, and New York. When the legislature met in June 1826 Hill strengthened his party by reviving the party caucus and then left for Albany to visit Van Buren and tour Revolutionary War battlefields. In committing to Jackson, Hill was ahead of Kendall, who made the move in the fall of 1826, and Van Buren, who did not come out openly for Jackson until the fall of 1827. In all three cases the goal was personal and party political advancement more than ideology.

Hill also continued his search for a gubernatorial candidate from western New Hampshire. He found his man in Benjamin Pierce, a rough, coarse tavern keeper who had fought in the Battle of Bunker Hill. Well known in the state as a Republican, Pierce had marched with other heroes from the Revolution when Lafayette visited Concord in 1825.

After losing the election of 1826, Pierce was elected governor a year later.

By this time Hill seemed almost unbeatable. He was, said one Adams man, "traversing the State, like a flying dragon, attending all caucuses, & organizing his regulars." Now the largest mail contractor in the state, he was "disseminating his base slanders" without paying postage fees. It was often impossible, said another critic, for Hill's enemies to get their mail delivered. Federalist Jeremiah Mason told his friend Daniel Webster that Levi Woodbury was working with Hill, trying to elect "true blue Jacobins" in Portsmouth.[3] Another Federalist, Daniel Webster's brother Ezekiel, said that there was hardly a town in which Hill did not have representatives. He used pamphlets, speeches, and newspapers "to address the passions-feelings, & prejudices of the voters." Hill's chain of newspapers, Ezekiel reported, had a far greater circulation than the Adams papers, and the *Patriot* alone had more readers than all the administration newspapers combined.[4]

The Adams leadership in Washington was especially concerned because they knew that Hill's influence extended into Vermont and Maine. Copies of the *Patriot* were already circulating widely in Maine, and Hill was on good terms with Governor Cornelius P. Van Ness of Vermont. The spread of the Anti-Masonic movement into Vermont and the rise of a Jackson faction in Maine contributed to political instability in both states. The Adams men were worried because the combined number of presidential electors held by New Hampshire, Maine, and Vermont totaled twenty-four—fourth highest among all the states.[5]

Trying to build an Adams party, Clay admitted he had "not a single regular correspondent in New Hampshire." Fortunately he was able to fall back on Adams's friend Senator Samuel Bell and New Hampshire native son Daniel Webster. Rallying behind Bell, the administration started to fight back. Bell came home from Washington in the spring of 1826 and set up two new administration newspapers—the *Butterfly* in Dover and the *New Hampshire Journal* in Concord, the latter edited by Hill's former partner and now bitter enemy Jacob Bailey Moore. In the fall of 1827 Clay removed Hill as printer of the federal laws and gave the contract to Moore. Bell also forged an alliance with Concord postmaster Joseph Low, who publicly sided with Bell by rejecting Hill's suggestion that he speak out against President Adams.[6]

The administration realized that it could never defeat Hill without help from the Federalists. The voters of New Hampshire were divided into three groups: the Hill Democratic-Republicans, who were growing rapidly; the remainder of the Republicans, now led by Bell; and the former Federalists, who made up about one-third of the state vote. A sizable number of Federalists were joining the Jackson party, while a majority of the remaining Federalists and Republicans, including all the congressmen save one, preferred Adams.

But Bell and many of the Republicans so detested the Federalists that they refused to work with them or invite them to meetings. In the spring of 1827 both Webster and Clay urged Bell to start including Federalists in party affairs. The first opportunity came in June 1827 when Webster asked Bell to present resolutions to the legislature endorsing the Adams administration. Bell agreed, but when he called a meeting to draw up the resolutions, he invited only Republicans. And those at the meeting were not content to praise Adams's policies; they gratuitously pointed out that Adams was not a Federalist. The resolutions were defeated by a vote of 137 to 70. Federalist Ezekiel Webster, who spoke for the resolutions, was outraged. "Let the cause of the Administration be supported," he said, "on just and liberal principles: not proscribing men by classes, not for past political opinions . . . or let it not be supported at all."[7]

Fortunately for the Adams men, Bell was flexible enough to step back from disaster. During the fall of 1827 he wrote to leading Republicans in the state, asking their advice. A solid majority told him to reorganize the Adams supporters and invite the Federalists to join them. Bell agreed, and during the rest of the fall he implemented an organizational plan similar to those that Van Buren, Hill, and Kendall were using in their states and that the Adams party was putting into effect in Kentucky and Pennsylvania.

At the top was a central committee in Concord, chaired by editor of the *New Hampshire Journal*, Jacob Moore. Three-man committees from each district of the Governor's Council were empowered to authorize town committees to call conventions to select candidates for county offices. Bowing to the Federalists, the plan announced that "*all the friends of the Administration*" would be invited to all meetings and would be eligible for all offices. To prepare for the March election, Bell considered calling a convention but decided against it because of the hard feelings that still existed between Republicans and Federalists. Instead he allowed the county committees to choose the gubernatorial candidate and decided to start with the Hillsborough committee because its members agreed with the central committee that there should be a new candidate. Tough-minded politicians seemed to be taking over.[8]

Things went so smoothly that Bell finally got up enough nerve to call a state convention. In November, before he departed for Washington, he announced a convention for friends of the Adams administration, Republicans and Federalists alike, to be held in Portsmouth, where Hill was not very popular. The convention would have much to say about the political future of northern New England.

NEW YORK

With its thirty-six electoral votes, New York would be the largest plum in 1828. The electoral votes would be split, however, because New Yorkers had chosen to vote in electoral districts instead of adopting the general winner-take-all system. Democracy was increasing in the Empire State. In 1825 the legislature had taken one democratic step by shifting the power to select presidential electors from the legislature to the people. In 1826 a constitutional amendment was passed removing a taxpaying requirement, the last significant restriction on adult white male voting in the state. A few blacks—those with a $250 freehold—could vote.

Politics in New York had almost never been a clear-cut battle between Federalists and Republicans. After 1801 Republicans held the upper hand, but in most cases the party in power was a factional alliance of a Republican family group (usually Clinton or Livingston) with minority Federalist support. In 1827 both the Van Buren Bucktails and the Clintonians called themselves Republicans, but most of the Bucktails had fallen in line behind Jackson, while the Clinton men favored Adams (even though Clinton himself was a Jackson man).

In the early months of 1827 the presidential election appeared to be a toss-up. The recently elected New York congressional delegation, which would take office in December, was evenly split between Adams and Jackson men. The Jackson party was strongest in New York City and the rural central part of the state, while the Adams party had steady support in the western counties settled by New Englanders and the old Federalist strongholds on the Hudson River. The Adams party had two advantages: many New Yorkers preferred voting for a northerner over a southerner, and New Yorkers in general endorsed much of Adams's national republicanism. The Jackson party, however, was clearly better organized. Despite their setbacks in 1824 and 1825, the Bucktails were once again the predominant party in the state. Van Buren ran the central committee—the Albany Regency—from his law office at 111 State Street in Albany, supported ably by his number-two man, state comptroller William L. Marcy. Behind them were rising young men such as Van Buren's law partner and Albany County attorney general Benjamin F. Butler, state senator Silas Wright, and editor Edwin Croswell of the Regency newspaper, the *Albany Argus*.

These and the other Regency men were the "plain republicans of the north" to whom Van Buren had referred in his letter to Thomas Ritchie.[9] None came close to being aristocrats or commanding figures like De Witt Clinton. Nor were they drawn from the ranks of the poor. Van Buren, Butler, and Croswell were sons of tavern keepers; others grew up on small farms. They were common, ordinary, bourgeois Americans, more plebeian than patrician, adept at taking advantage of the opportunities offered by the new openness of American society. Like many Americans they moved about as they moved up. Marcy and Wright had migrated west from New England but had not joined the Adams "Yankee Nation." Committed to political parties, they were not ashamed of "electioneering." Wright considered himself nothing more nor less than a "political party man," and Marcy saw "nothing wrong in the rule, that to the victor belong the spoils of the enemy."[10]

The Regency's party discipline was never tighter than early in 1827. Van Buren's political machine had representatives in every county, and he did not hesitate to call on them. Duff Green marveled at the Magician's control of party caucuses, county committees, and a newspaper chain of at least fifty presses. With the Regency, he exclaimed, "*party* is everything."[11] But the Little Magician, who had been burned by mixing state and national politics several years before, had not yet announced that his party was backing Andrew Jackson.

The Magician was acting wisely, for the Regency was faced with serious problems that would have to be addressed if it hoped to carry the state for Jackson. First and most obvious was dealing with De Witt Clinton. Since Clinton and Jackson thought highly of each other, Regency men were afraid that Jackson and his inner circle would insist on nominating Clinton for vice president. This would win votes for Jackson in New York, but it would also threaten the position of the Regency. If a Jackson-Clinton ticket prevailed in the election, then Clinton, not Van Buren, would represent the new president in New York, and patronage would go to Clintonians rather than to Bucktails. This is one of the reasons Van Buren insisted on keeping Calhoun as vice president.

Another, less plausible worry was that Jackson, who was old and sick, might drop out of the race at the last minute and be replaced by Clinton. Van Buren had mentioned the possibility in his letter to Ritchie, and rumors about it surfaced later in the campaign. There were also fears that Clinton would run as a third-party candidate and force another vote in the House of Representatives. This was not a wild stretch of the imagination, for the House had elected two of the first six American presidents.[12]

A third concern was southern dominance, which was always an issue in New York because of the Virginia dynasty. Even in the tightly controlled Regency, Van Buren's choice of a southern slaveholder like Jackson did not meet uniform approval. Rudolph Bunner, a New York City Federalist who had joined the Bucktails, was afraid that Jackson would become "a monster of a President," dominated by Calhoun as well as by Clinton.[13] Wright was willing to ally with the South, but only if the North played the leading role. Another Regency man, Azariah Flagg, was alarmed at the prospect of having an all-southern slate of national leaders—president, vice president, and perhaps Speaker of the House. One Adams man whom Van Buren much respected told him that he could not understand why powerful northern states like New York and Pennsylvania had to accept another southern, slave-owning president.

The most pressing problem was that New York had become a high tariff state, with both iron and woolen manufacturers and upstate wool growers demanding increased protection. Only in New York City, where merchants supported an auction system that allowed the British to dump goods in the city, was there any substantial support for free trade. On arriving home in May 1827 Van Buren found that the demand for protection had grown dramatically. During that spring alone New Yorkers had sent nine memorials to Congress favoring protection. According to Marcy, "manufacturing excitement [was] rageing [sic] all over the State."[14]

In Van Buren's own Albany, the Farmers, Wool Growers, and Friends of the American System had called a conference for July, where protectionists threatened to attack Van Buren and Congressman Cambreleng, a confirmed free trader, for not voting for high tariffs. At the meeting Van Buren succeeded in placating his critics by calling, rather vaguely, for increased protection on raw wool but not on woolen manufacturing.

When asked later about his performance at the convention, he admitted that "directness on all points had not been [the] most prominent feature" of his remarks.[15] To keep both farmers and manufacturers on Van Buren's side, the *Albany Argus* came out in support of Clay's American System and published a letter from Jackson and L. H. Coleman of Virginia in support of a "judicious examination and [upward] revision" of the tariff.[16]

The statement in the *Argus* was a direct response to the approaching tariff convention at Harrisburg, Pennsylvania. So many New York Adams men had been chosen for the convention that the Jacksonians were forced to scramble to make certain they were represented. They managed to send enough delegates to keep the meeting from becoming entirely an Adams affair.

Meanwhile, Van Buren had to deal with another more local and more immediate crisis—the Anti-Masonic movement, now almost a year old. On September 10, 1826, in the village of Batavia in western New York, William Morgan, a Freemason, was arrested for a petty crime. Two nights later he was abducted and never seen alive again. Since Morgan had recently threatened to publish an article revealing secrets of the order, suspicion arose that the Masons had murdered him. New Yorkers had long resented and feared the Masonic Order because of its political and economic power and its supposedly evil secret rituals—feelings that had been exacerbated by the panic of 1819. The Morgan abduction triggered deep Anti-Masonic sentiment, which soon spread throughout the western counties.[17]

Intensified by a wave of evangelical revivals in the same region, Anti-Masonry grew into a powerful political-social movement. Unlike most political organizations, which sought (or claimed to seek) political equality for Americans, the Anti-Masons also called for social and economic equality. They played an important role in the rise of democracy because, lacking political and religious institutions such as caucuses and church meetings, they quickly turned to democratic conventions to organize their members and spread their ideas.

After holding a large convention in western New York in January 1827, the Anti-Masons began forming local parties and nominating candidates. Calling Masonry the world of Satan and swearing never to vote for a Mason, they won spring elections all over Genesee and Monroe counties. When the Masons fought back and succeeded in ousting the popular old treasurer of Rochester, Anti-Masons became so angry that the city became the center of the movement. The Anti-Masons met so often to prepare for the November state election that the summer of 1827 became known as the "convention summer."

The sudden emergence of a new political party in western New York, long a center of Adams power, upset the political balance of the state. If the Anti-Masons ran as a third party, they were likely to take votes away from Adams candidates, but if they united with the Adams men, the combination would pose a dangerous threat to the Jackson party. Van Buren was concerned because members of the Regency had outraged the Anti-Masons by blocking a thorough investigation of Morgan's death. Anxious to find out about Anti-Masonry for himself, he made a tour of the West late in the summer and concluded that the Jackson party must take the movement very seriously. When prominent Jackson editor Mordecai Noah, who was a Mason, told the Anti-Masons to stay out of New York City, Van Buren was appalled. He promptly ordered Cambreleng to "beseech [Noah] to let the Morgan affair alone."[18]

Van Buren was worried about politics in New York City because he would need the support of Tammany Hall in the state and presidential elections the following year. Tammany Hall was the Republican political organization in New York City, formed in 1817 as an offshoot of the earlier Society of St. Tammany. After splintering into a number of factions in the early 1820s, Tammany Hall briefly came under the control of the Clintonian People's party in 1824. In 1826 it divided again into a Regency faction, which cooperated with Clinton and delayed supporting Jackson, and a Mordecai Noah faction, which came out immediately for the Old Hero. Because of Adams's strength in upstate New York and the uncertainty engendered by Anti-Masonry, Van Buren had to have a united pro-Jackson Tammany Hall in New York City to secure a strong Jackson majority in the state.[19]

The Adams men faced even greater difficulties than the Jacksonians. Two years had passed since Adams's election, yet they still had no organization dedicated to reelecting him. Just setting up an Adams party was difficult because there was no tradition of presidential parties in the state. Starting one with Clinton men was even more difficult because Clinton preferred Jackson. Furthermore, New York State was so large and sprawling that just holding a meeting or exchanging letters took great effort. This was especially true for the Adams men because they had to unite two widely separated blocs of supporters, one along the Hudson River and the other in western New York. It took almost a week to travel from New York City up the Hudson River to Albany and along the Erie Canal to the western counties.

The administration, however, was fortunate in having a number of strong, highly respected leaders along this route. Its most prominent spokesman in New York City was speaker of the state assembly and former congressman Peter B. Sharpe, who had made a comfortable living manufacturing horse whips. Two-thirds of the way up the river, in the thriving port town of Hudson, lived former Federalist orator and lawyer Elisha Williams. Farther up the river, south of Albany, was another old Federalist, Congressman Stephen Van Rensselaer, the eighth and last patroon and heir to the great Van Rensselaer landed fortune. Van Rensselaer had led New York militiamen somewhat ingloriously in the War of 1812 and had recently founded Rensselaer Polytechnic Institute. He was the New York congressman who had succumbed to Webster's blandishments and cast the decisive vote for Adams in the House election of 1825.

In Albany and to the north lived two of the most influential Adams men. Practicing law and writing history in Albany was Jabez Hammond. Perhaps the best scholar-politician in New York history, Hammond later published a three-volume history of political parties in the state that is still a valuable source. Saratoga County was the home of Speaker of the House John W. Taylor, the congressman who had antagonized slave owners by opposing slavery in Missouri.

In Anti-Masonic country west of the bridge at the foot of Lake Cayuga, Adams's fortunes lay in the hands of one old politician, Henry Clay's trusted friend Peter B. Porter of Buffalo, and two young men, editor Thurlow Weed of the *Rochester Telegraph* and state representative Francis Granger of Canandaigua.

Respected and talented as these men were, they were having great trouble forming a party, for the distances separating them were daunting. Porter told Clay that he felt at a great disadvantage because he lived so far out on "the extreme borders of the State."[20] Other impediments were pessimism, friction, and disinterest, which stood in the way of cooperation. When the state legislature convened in January, Porter reported to Clay, without citing much evidence, that "a considerable majority of the members [were] opposed to the administration."[21] At the same time Jabez Hammond complained that he had been unable to get Porter and others to agree on Van Rensselaer as the candidate to oppose Van Buren for the U.S. Senate. With no organized opposition, the legislature had elected Van Buren almost unanimously. Angry and frustrated, Hammond pleaded with Clay to "urge" Porter and his friends to cooperate.[22] Clay was sympathetic, but he was disgusted with the lack of interest. In a sharp letter to Van Rensselaer he protested that he found the degree of "apathy among our friends . . . discouraging."[23]

Hammond, however, was far from apathetic. Perhaps hoping that Clay would quote him to the others, he issued a challenge. "*NOW* is the time," he said, "to form a strong administration Party in this state—if the present moment is neglected the opportunity may not again occur."[24] Apparently he was successful, for two months later he told Clay optimistically that majorities in the senate and assembly were "friendly to the Administration."[25]

One subject on which the Adams leaders agreed was the lack of patronage from the administration. Both Hammond and Van Rensselaer called on Clay to provide more federal jobs. Patronage, said Hammond, was indispensable because "no portion of the Union [was] so much influenced by the distribution of Patronage" as New York.[26] New Yorkers, he protested, held only six of the three hundred federal civil offices in Washington. The highest office held by a New Yorker was chief clerk in the Treasury Department.[27]

The question of appointments had bothered Adams's supporters in New York since 1825, when Thurlow Weed had made his fruitless trip to Washington to get positions for himself and James Tallmadge. Adams continued to appoint men of all persuasions, including Federalists, and the Federalist issue continued to cut both ways. Appointing Federalists angered loyal Adams men because they wanted the jobs for themselves and their friends. But not appointing them was just as troublesome, for when Adams failed to reach out sufficiently, they began to move toward Old Hickory.

The political history of Thomas Jackson Oakley of Poughkeepsie was a case in point. One of the leading Federalists and lawyers of his day, the "majestic" Oakley represented New York in Congress during the War of 1812 and later served as Federalist leader of the state assembly.[28] He was so highly respected that when he was elected to Congress for the term beginning in December 1827, Henry Clay counted on him to assume leadership of the Adams party in the House, which Daniel Webster, who was moving to the Senate, would be giving up.

But there was one important caveat. No one knew whether Oakley, who had run as a Clintonian, would commit to Adams or Jackson. As a result, Oakley's political decision was a source of great anxiety among Adams men. "What [do] you hear from or about Oakley?" Clay asked Webster in April, and ten days later Webster admitted that he was "very anxious" about Oakley.[29] In June Supreme Court justice Joseph Story asked Webster, "Have you seen Oakley?"[30]

Early in June Webster caught up with Oakley in New York City, and after a long conversation he came away somewhat reassured. Oakley, he reported, would vote to reelect John W. Taylor as Speaker of the House, would support a woolens bill, and would never become the "tool . . . of the Southern members of the opposition."[31] But Webster was still not sure about the man. Oakley opposed national internal improvements, was "an attached friend of Mr Clinton," and could not be counted on to remain in Congress.[32] He did not sound like a good party man.

So the problem of what to do about the Federalists remained. The Adams party in New York prided itself on its republican orthodoxy and refused to consider Jacksonians true Republicans. They criticized the Jackson men for accepting Federalists, and they used Jackson's 1816 correspondence with Monroe to show that the Old Hero was far from a pure Republican. But the Adams men needed the Federalists' votes, and as the election drew closer they would be forced to reach out to the Federalists and accept the taunts of becoming amalgamators.

Behind much of the administration's uncertainty in New York was the lack of a newspaper strong enough to cope with the Jacksonians' *Albany Argus* and *New York Enquirer*. The *Daily Advertiser* in Albany and the *American* in New York City were anti-Jackson, but their allegiance was to Clinton rather than to Adams. Well aware of this weakness, Hammond, Porter, Van Rensselaer, and administration men in New York City started raising money to finance presses in both cities. It was slow work, but in the summer they finally took over Noah's old paper, the *National Advocate* in New York City, and turned it into an administration organ. No Adams paper appeared in Albany until 1828.

One of the criteria for a new Adams newspaper was that its "polar star" must be "the encouragement of domestic manufactures & support of the tariff."[33] The tariff question, which had become a headache for the Jacksonians, was a boon for the Adams party. Porter told Clay how popular the tariff issue was in New York, and Peter Sharpe and Elisha Williams played prominent roles in the Albany tariff convention. When Webster wrote to Taylor advising him how to get delegates for the Harrisburg convention, he pointed out "the great importance of having New

York represented at the meeting."[34] Taylor did his job. Twenty-one delegates from New York—more than from any other state—attended the meeting. They were predominantly supporters of the administration.

The greatest opportunity for the Adams men lay in the rise of the Anti-Masonic movement, but they were slow to react. Thurlow Weed, for one, was too preoccupied with his *Telegraph* to take a position, and he did not join the movement until August 1827—almost a year after Morgan was abducted. Shortly after he joined, a dramatic event took place that sealed his commitment. On October 7 a decomposed body that bore some resemblance to Morgan washed up on the shore of Lake Ontario near the mouth of the Niagara River, setting off a series of wild charges and countercharges and stimulating intense interest in the fall election. Now convinced that the Masons had murdered Morgan, and sensing a political opportunity, Weed threw himself recklessly into the movement. When critics suggested that the body might not be Morgan, he cynically replied that the corpse was "a good enough Morgan until after the [fall] election."[35] However, he still had made no effort to merge the Adams and Anti-Masonic parties.

Interest in politics was also high in New York City. The bitter conflict to determine which party would gain control of Tammany Hall came to a head a few weeks after the body was found. On September 26 the General Republican Committee of New York City met at Tammany Hall and passed a series of resolutions that reflected the growing unity of the Jackson party. Brushing aside all internal conflicts, the committee resolved to support the election of Andrew Jackson, "the man whom the American people delight to honor," and recommended that in the state election their "republican fellow citizens" vote only for candidates "favorable" to the Old Hero.[36] At precisely the same time Van Buren, the Albany Regency, and fifty New York newspapers came out for Jackson. Years later, in his history of New York politics, Jabez Hammond admitted that "the effect was prodigious. All the machinery [of Van Buren] was suddenly put in motion, and it performed to admiration."[37]

Caught by surprise, the Adams men on the committee could make only a feeble gesture. As Hammond recalled, Peter Sharpe and eleven other "respectable members of the general committee, protested the resolutions as 'unauthorized, violent, and unprecedented,' and published their protest."[38] The use of the word "violent" by Sharpe and his friends revealed their underlying admiration and fear of the Jacksonians. Porter had also called them "violent" and at other times had described the

Jackson movement as "clamorous" and "confident." Both Porter and Webster referred to the Jackson "fever."[39] Meanwhile, Daniel Mallory apologetically described his Adams compatriots as "mostly quiet moral people—men of wea[l]th and influence."[40]

There it was: emotion and spirit on one side, morality and wealth on the other. And emotion and spirit seemed to be winning. The last few weeks between the Tammany resolutions and the state election were filled with this dichotomy. According to twentieth-century historian De Alva Alexander, it proved to be "a canvass of unusual vehemence, filling the air with caricatures and lampoons. . . . From the moment Jackson became the standard-bearer, the crowds were with him. . . . When everything in favour of Adams was carefully summed up and admitted . . . the people, fascinated by the distinguished traits of character [of Jackson] and the splendour of the victory at New Orleans, threw their hats into the air for Andrew Jackson."[41]

Outside of New York two concerned observers expressed their fear about what was happening. In Philadelphia John Sergeant described the "alarm" of many in the administration that the Jackson forces would gain control of the New York legislature and take back the power to choose presidential electors—thus guaranteeing Jackson all thirty-six votes. "If they succeed," he said, "we shall have everything to fear. 'Shadows, clouds, and darkness' you know rest upon all political prospects in that State."[42] Leaving for Massachusetts after a short visit to New York City, Daniel Webster expressed contempt as well as concern. "There is no part of the Country," he told Henry Clay, "in which our cause has been so badly managed as here. . . . The prevailing error has been *timidity*."[43]

The election on November 5–7 confirmed the worst of these fears. The Jacksonians won ninety-eight (two-thirds) of the seats in the assembly, the Anti-Masons fifteen, the Adams party only twelve. Almost all of the thirty senate seats went to the Jackson party. It was a victory for party organization, "violence," "clamor," and the personal popularity of the candidate. In Alexander's words, "The eloquence of [Elisha] Williams could carry Columbia County; [Peter B.] Porter, ever popular and interesting, could sweep the Niagara frontier . . . but from the Hudson to Lake Oneida the Jackson party may be said to have carried everything by storm."[44]

On the long trip from New York City back to Buffalo after the election, and in the weeks that followed, Porter tried to summarize for Clay what had happened. The "extraordinary result of our late elections," he concluded, had been "produced . . . by stratagem & party discipline on the part of the Jacksonians, and by apathy [and] want of concert among the friends of the administration." Trying to put the best face on the outcome, he said that perhaps it was "desirable, as it would rouse our friends to some energy."[45]

PENNSYLVANIA

Pennsylvania politicians had also been building from the bottom and looking ahead to a fall election. In writing the history of early America, historians have paid too little attention to the story of Pennsylvania—perhaps because it lacked a popular, simple central theme. There was no Puritan tradition like the one in Massachusetts, no presidential dynasty as in Virginia, and no new-style party organization like the Albany Regency in New York. Presidential politics at the time showed the same neglect. In the first half century of the new nation (1789–1841), a Virginian served as president or vice president for thirty-six years, a New Yorker twenty-seven years, a man from Massachusetts seventeen years, and a South Carolinian and a man from Tennessee eight years each. No one from Pennsylvania held either office. The neglect is strange, because Pennsylvania had already earned its nickname, the Keystone State. With its large size and strategic location linking New England and New York with Virginia and tying the East to the West, Pennsylvania was the natural place for the Continental Congresses, the crucial military campaigns during the darkest days of the Revolution, and, for a short time, the national capital and the site of the constitutional convention.

Pennsylvania was also in the forefront of the rise of American democracy and capitalism. With its powerful single-house legislature and its weak twelve-man executive, Pennsylvania had the most democratic constitution of all the new states. Although the revised Pennsylvania Constitution of 1790 established a much stronger executive and a more cumbersome bicameral legislature, the new government retained many democratic features. All adult males, white or black, could vote, and the small voting districts in the counties made it easy for voters to get to the polls. State elections were held annually in October.

Throughout these years Pennsylvania had the most advanced industrial economy in North America. On the eve of the Revolution more tonnage moved in and out of Philadelphia than at any other port in the British colonies, and Philadelphia shipyards rivaled those in New England. By the 1820s Pennsylvania, with eight rolling mills, had become the center of the American iron industry, and ten years later Pennsylvania had more weaving looms than any other state save Massachusetts. Most of the early manufacturing (and half the population) of Pennsylvania was concentrated in Philadelphia and a few nearby counties. But far across the state, Pittsburgh was well on its way to becoming a model industrial city and was already known as the Gateway to the West. During the War of 1812 Pittsburgh equipped most of the American fleet on Lake Erie, and in the decade that followed it became a center for coke ovens, rolling mills, foundries, and glass houses.[46]

Because of its advanced economy, Pennsylvania's government officials, businessmen, and even farmers supported protective tariffs and encouraged state banks and corporations. It was not by chance that Philadelphia became the home of the Bank of the United States. But despite their economic strength, Pennsylvanians were jealous of the advantages that the Erie Canal and the National Road were bringing to New York and Maryland, respectively. In 1826 the Pennsylvanians initiated an economic program, called the State Works, to build a network of canals running west through the Allegheny Mountains. The State Works eventually connected Philadelphia with Pittsburgh, but it never matched the Erie Canal because the mountains were too high, and the system had to depend on an awkward railroad portage between the Juniata River and Johnstown.

This meld of democracy and capitalism fostered the rise of party politics, which, like banking and manufacturing, was centered in the southeastern corner of the state. As in New York, the Jeffersonian Republican party overwhelmed the Federalists in the presidential election of 1800, and from then on, elections were contests waged between Republican factions. There still remained, however, tens of thousands of Federalists (or former Federalists) who had the power to swing elections. The Republican organizations were usually led by county politicians and newspaper editors, who called themselves Democrats or Democratic-Republicans. They were among the first to use party patronage as a political weapon, but unlike the politicians in New York, they had been unable to build a statewide party.

After the War of 1812 politicians in Pennsylvania divided into New School Democratic-Republicans, who supported banks, tariffs, and corporations, and Old School men who leaned toward the Old Republicanism of the South. But parties in Pennsylvania resisted ideological labels.

By 1824 a party of New School Republicans and former Federalists (hence called the Amalgamators) had emerged. Led by iron manufacturer Henry Baldwin of Pittsburgh and former Federalist congressman James Buchanan of Lancaster County in the southeastern part of the state, the Amalgamators were among the first to support Andrew Jackson. Opposing them was an alliance of politicians from Philadelphia (George M. Dallas) and Pittsburgh (William Wilkins) that became known as the Family party because it was held together by an intricate network of marriage ties. One of the strongest members of this party was prominent congressman Samuel D. Ingham of Bucks County (near Philadelphia). The Family party had favored John C. Calhoun in the 1824 election, but when support for Jackson rose dramatically in the winter of 1823–1824, the party fell in behind Old Hickory, thus earning the nickname of Eleventh-Hour Men. On March 4, 1824, Jackson was nominated at a state convention at Harrisburg with only one dissenting vote. With the strong support of both factions, he carried the state in the fall of 1824, winning 36,000 of the 47,000 votes cast. Adams won only 5,000 votes.[47]

Jackson seemed well positioned to carry the state again in 1828. He still had the support of the two Democratic-Republican factions; Ingham of the Family party and Buchanan of the Amalgamators were already vying to determine which faction would win the party patronage if the Old Hero took office. In March 1826 the Jackson men held a successful convention in Harrisburg at which they endorsed Jackson's nomination and formed vigilance committees in Philadelphia and other cities and towns. As the October 1826 congressional and state elections drew near, Buchanan told Old Hickory not to worry. "Outside of Philadelphia," he said, there was not "sufficient division in public sentiment to disturb our repose." In the "large wealthy & populous" Lancaster County, Adams would not win 500 votes.[48] Buchanan was correct, for the Jackson candidates won handily, carrying twenty of the state's twenty-six seats in Congress and maintaining control of the state government. When he heard the good news, Jackson wrote complacently that "all things are going on well" in Pennsylvania.[49] Confident of victory, the Jackson legislative caucus announced in April 1827 plans for a state convention to meet on January 8, 1828, the anniversary of the Battle of New Orleans.

Just as in New York, the Jackson bandwagon was moving so fast and so violently that one visitor described the Adams men as "paralised" by fear. Convinced that they would be "overwhelmed," Adams legislators were not willing to "take the field" against the Jacksonians. "If Pena.

was polled [today]," one Adams man wrote in April 1827, "Genl Jackson would have two thirds of all the votes."[50]

Despite the long odds, Clay, Webster, and other Adams party leaders were determined to make a strong effort in Pennsylvania. For the next year and a half Clay devoted a substantial proportion of his letter writing to politics in the Keystone State. Webster visited the state on several occasions and reminded one of his friends of "the great importance of Pennsylvania."[51] John C. Calhoun, who knew more about Pennsylvania politics than any other southerner, was impressed by the intensity of the administration's effort. "The enemy," he told Littleton W. Tazewell, "is resolved to detach, if possible, Pennsylvania from the good cause."[52]

Clay and his allies were determined because they knew that Adams's chances were much better than they seemed on the surface. A major reason was the press. Within a year after Adams took office, the strongest Jackson newspaper in the state, Stephen Simpson's *Columbian Observer* of Philadelphia, had gone bankrupt and been forced to close. At the same time, more than fifty newspapers had come out for the administration, many more than those declaring for Jackson. The most prominent Adams newspaper in the state was John Binns's Republican *Democratic Press*.[53]

There was also Robert Walsh's Federalist *National Gazette and Literary Messenger.* The son of a wealthy Baltimore merchant, Walsh graduated from Georgetown College and studied law before traveling in Europe, meeting famous men such as George Canning along the way. After returning to America he moved to Philadelphia and began a successful career as a Federalist scholar and journalist. In 1827 he was editing the *American Quarterly Review* as well as the *National Gazette*.[54] Walsh and jurists Joseph Hopkinson and Richard Peters Jr. were leaders of an elite group that maintained the tradition of Philadelphia as a Federalist stronghold.

If the Democratic-Republican press could join hands with the Federalist press, the Adams party would have a good chance of winning. There were 150,000 eligible voters in Pennsylvania, three times the number that had voted in 1824. Of this number, 100,000 were said to be Democratic-Republicans; the majority were for Jackson, but a strong minority supported Adams. There were also some 50,000 Federalists. As in New Hampshire, Adams needed to unite his Democratic-Republican base with a majority of the Federalists. Webster pleaded with the administration to do all it could to get Walsh's full support, pointing out that

"Mr. Walsh's opinions [had] great weight" with the Federalists.[55] Ideologically this union made sense because the Adams administration and the Federalists both supported the Bank of the United States, protective tariffs, and internal improvements. But it would not be easy, for Binns and Walsh treated each other as rivals, and although Walsh was, as Adams remarked, "friendly to the Administration *in his way*," the editor was "not always happy in his manner of shewing it."[56] The Adams party was depending on two talented prima donnas.

The administration was also counting on Governor John A. Shulze. The well-educated son of a prominent Lutheran clergyman, Shulze had enjoyed successful careers in the church and in business before turning to politics. He was elected governor with a majority of 25,000 in 1823 and three years later was reelected almost unanimously. As the driving force behind the State Works program, he was Pennsylvania's De Witt Clinton.[57] Although Shulze had been reelected in 1826 as a Jackson–Family party man, he was showing signs of moving toward Adams. In his message to the legislature in December he had gone out of his way to praise the manner in which the presidential election of 1824–1825 had been handled. In May 1827 former congressman Philip S. Markley reassured Clay that the governor was "decidedly friendly to the re-election of Mr. Adams."[58] Other Adams men, however, wanted Shulze to speak up more openly for the administration.

Shulze was especially important because he was a second-generation German. Aside from the English and Scotch-Irish, the most powerful ethnic group in Pennsylvania was the large enclave of Germans who had settled in more than a dozen counties west of Philadelphia between the Delaware and Susquehanna rivers. When properly mobilized, the Germans voted as a bloc and swung elections. Since 1808 every Pennsylvania governor save one had been of German stock. The German vote was so important that the state legislature published its journal in German as well as in English.

But the Germans seemed disaffected with the Adams administration. In April 1827 a realistic John Binns reported grimly to Clay, "Our German population, and they move pretty much altogether, are generally opposed to us."[59] So wooing the Germans became a central theme in the Adams campaign. Binns urged Governor Shulze to speak out for Adams and bring the Germans along with him. He and other administration printers prepared more than 10,000 campaign documents in German. When Edward Everett produced a pamphlet supporting internal improvements, the party circulated a German translation. Samuel Mifflin, president of the Union Canal Company, was so set on getting the Germans to vote for Adams that he promised to spend most of his time for the next year and a half talking with them and pointing out the dangers the Jacksonians posed to the Germans. The Adams party was determined to win the support of the German newspapers. After visiting several of them on his way to the state capital, Philip Markley promised Clay that the *Harrisburger Morgenrothe Zeitung* would soon come out in "a decisive tone" and would "be followed by other German papers."[60] Thus in 1827, with the election only a year and a half away, the hopes of the Adams party rested on the press, the Federalists, the governor, and the Germans.

There is no doubt that Binns was the strongest Adams editor in the state and that his press was the center of party activity. In a report on politics in Pennsylvania, Clay's friend Benjamin W. Crowninshield of Massachusetts called Binns "the mainmast of [party] power in the interior."[61] Binns was certainly busy. During two weeks in April 1827 he received forty-four letters about the upcoming election, wrote at least as many, and distributed innumerable printed circulars.[62] Webster called the *Democratic Press* the most committed administration paper in Philadelphia.

But Binns was not a happy man. He was miffed at the administration for not giving him any patronage beyond the tiny sum he got for printing federal laws. He was particularly angry at the postmaster of Philadelphia, Richard Bache, who refused to give him the contract for post office printing. In the spring of 1826 Binns went over Bache's head, first taking his case to then-congressman Philip Markley, later to Postmaster General John McLean, and finally to Henry Clay. McLean, who was opposed to the spoils system and had little interest in the future of the Adams administration, replied bluntly that he never intervened in such matters. Even though he understood the value of patronage, Clay did nothing.

A month later Binns protested to Clay again. Half a year ago, he said, when the *Columbian Observer* had been forced to shut down, the Jackson men had offered him patronage and the newspaper's subscription list if he would support the Old Hero. He had refused the offer and continued to work for Adams, and thanks to his efforts, the tide began to turn in Adams's favor. He "flattered" himself, he continued, that he would be rewarded with the printing for the post office and the customhouse as well. But it was "quite otherwise." His treatment was "all wrong—unless in Politics we practice, what we preach in Religion, and render Evil for Good and Good for Evil."[63] Clay still did nothing.

In the spring of 1827 Crowninshield took up the cause. He told Clay that Binns was so important to the party in Pennsylvania that he should be given all the printing contracts that were available. Clay wrote back rather defensively that he could not interfere with the Post Office and suggested that Crowninshield write directly to the president. Whether Crowninshield passed Clay's letter on to Binns is unknown, but a month later Binns wrote to Adams, complaining bitterly that the administration did not "support its friends, and intimat[ing] that sacrifices in time and of money must be made." The friction between himself and Bache had grown to the point, he said, that the postmaster had attacked him physically. When Adams received the letter, he clearly was not moved. He had "observed," he said, "the tendency of our electioneering to venality, and shall not encourage it." He would not put money "in the channels of the press."[64]

Binns's rival, Robert Walsh, was also having difficulty getting party patronage. When Markley, a favorite of Clay, was defeated in the fall 1826 election, the administration named him naval officer in Philadelphia, a post that Federalist Joseph Hopkinson had been eyeing. Webster was disappointed and Walsh was outraged that the administration had refused to do something for a prominent Federalist. In March 1827 Walsh traveled to Washington to make his case. Preceding him were letters from Webster to Adams and Clay, urging them to listen carefully and sympathetically to what Walsh had to say. But whatever he said, it was not enough. After Walsh's return, Hopkinson sent the bad news on to Webster. Walsh had come back, he said, with the impression that if allowed to follow his own views, Adams would welcome the Federalists, but Clay, Republican to the core, stood in the way. Clay, said Hopkinson, was "full of subtle explanations, and polite reasons" rooted in "his inveterate dislike to all Federalists."[65] Walsh had joined a swelling group (Weed and Binns) who had gone to Washington and come home empty-handed.

During the hot Philadelphia summer of 1827 harmony vanished from the ranks of the Adams party. Sensing that their prospects had improved during the spring, the Adams men decided to make a "show of our strength" on the Fourth of July. They hoped to receive support from Walsh, but according to one Adams man, the angry Federalist "employed all his energies to decry our proceedings."[66] On the Fourth of July hostility increased when all but one of the men holding federal patronage jobs—the postmaster, the district attorney, the naval officer, the coadjutor, and the customs collector—refused to attend the celebration. The only one at the dinner was printer of the laws Binns, and he left before the oration. A month later, when President Adams stopped overnight in Philadelphia on his way home to Massachusetts, he tried to make amends by spending time with Walsh but succeeded only in antagonizing the Democratic-Republicans, who felt slighted.

The Adams movement in Philadelphia faced a dilemma. The national administration was refusing to reward the leading Democratic-Republican and Federalist editors in the city. The editors in turn were ridiculing and boycotting party celebrations, and the federal officeholders were refusing to attend. For a party that counted on a vigorous press and on cooperation between Democratic-Republicans and Federalists, the situation was perilous. Responsibility for the dilemma was divided: Adams can be blamed for not using party patronage, Clay for not accepting Federalists, Binns and Walsh for acting like prima donnas, McLean and Bache for disloyalty to Adams.

The difficulty of uniting Federalists with Democratic-Republicans can be seen in John Sergeant's two-year campaign to win one of the Philadelphia seats in the Twentieth Congress, which would convene in December 1827. A Democratic-Republican with close ties to Federalists, Sergeant was a strong candidate. He was a friend of Clay, he had already served four terms in Congress, and Adams had appointed him a delegate to the Panama Congress. But Sergeant was at a disadvantage because he was an Adams man and his opponent Henry Horn was a Jacksonian.

Before the Democratic-Republicans met to nominate candidates in October 1826, the Federalists tried to nominate Sergeant, but he refused the offer. When the Democratic-Republicans could not decide whether to nominate Sergeant or Horn, a fight ensued, and the meeting broke into an Adams faction, which nominated Sergeant, and a Jackson faction, which nominated Horn. Since the Federalists nominated no one, the election provided a good test of whether the Adams men could attract enough Federalist votes to overcome their minority in the Democratic-Republican party. They almost succeeded, for the election on October 10, 1826, ended in a tie, and the vote was postponed for another year. Sergeant then left for the Panama Congress (which, as noted earlier, never met) and did not return until the following summer.

Winning the German vote was as difficult as getting the Federalist vote. The impact of the Germans and of German governor John Shulze on the Adams campaign was not as great as party leaders had hoped. A chance to win German votes came in June 1827 when a new canal opened in one of the German counties. Members of the party wrote to Adams and invited him to the ceremony, where he could "show [himself] among the German farmers and speak to them in their own language." It was a choice political opportunity. Adams, who spoke German well, could help win over a vital constituency. Unfortunately, the president replied curtly that although he was "highly obliged to [his] friends for their good purposes," he felt strongly that "this mode of electioneering suited neither [his] taste nor [his] principles."[67]

During the first half of 1827 Governor Shulze seemed ready to take the lead in the Adams campaign. One observer claimed that all of Shulze's appointees were Adams men, and others believed that Adams would carry the state if he put Shulze on his ticket as the vice presidential candidate. But Shulze would not come out and campaign openly. The influence of another prominent German, assembly speaker Joseph Ritner, was even less positive. In mid-September Ritner disappointed the Adams party by announcing that he had voted for Jackson in 1824 and intended to do the same in 1828. The announcement was especially disappointing because Ritner had great influence in western Pennsylvania, where Adams needed high-profile leadership.

As the state election and Sergeant's second chance to gain a congressional seat approached, the Adams organization began to take shape. The party had always been strong in Philadelphia County, but now the organization had spread out to Lancaster and other neighboring counties in the southeastern part of the state. After visiting Philadelphia in September 1827, Adams senator Josiah S. Johnston of Louisiana reported back to Clay that party spirit was far stronger than before, not only in the southeast but throughout the state. He cited an increase in the number of Adams newspapers, several of them German, and predicted that the German bloc would back the administration. Before departing Johnston left plans for a statewide organization, with a committee of a hundred in each county responsible for superintending the elections and bringing voters to the polls.

But Johnston also noted that Pennsylvania was still a Jackson state and that the Jacksonians were "ready for anything . . . in popular excitement." They "marshall in their ranks a class of Men, not easily Contrould [sic]." Society in Pennsylvania, he observed, was "Cut horizontally, leaving only a few political Leaders."[68] Sergeant, too, commented that he was impressed by the "ferocious course" of the Jacksonians and noted that the Adams party would have "everything to fear" if the Jacksonians won in New York.[69] These observations, like the references to Jacksonian "violence" in New York, show a common pattern of swashbuckling, free-wheeling Jackson men intimidating their decent, moralistic opponents.

A good example of this pattern was the way the two parties dealt with the possibility that Henry Clay might visit Philadelphia. On August 13 and again on the sixteenth the Adams men met and debated whether to invite Clay, who at the time was under heavy attack for his "corrupt bargain" with Adams. After much debate they decided that it was too risky and agreed simply to make plans to welcome him in case he happened to visit on his own. A hundred-man committee was appointed to make arrangements.[70] Even this modest plan was enough to stir up the Jackson men. On August 17 they held their own meeting—a boisterous event—and appointed a committee of 113 (outnumbering the Adams committee) "with full power . . . to take such measures as may afford the people an opportunity . . . to *counteract* the designed effect" of a Clay visit. On any "information of the arrival of HENRY CLAY IN, OR NEAR, THIS CITY," the Jackson men would "*immediately*" assemble.[71] They would act like minutemen. The Adams response was much less aggressive. They deplored the Jacksonian plans as "conducive to violence," expressed their right to approve "the principles and conduct of public men" and to show "decorous hospitality towards eminent citizens," and raised the number on the committee to two hundred or more.[72] That same day Sergeant wrote to Clay and suggested that he not come. Clay never came.

Another problem facing the Adams party was the voters' reluctance to give up the old party structure. This was good news for Van Buren, who had plotted for years to restore the old party conflict between Federalists and Republicans. Following this theme, Jackson men in New York, Pennsylvania, and many other states were calling themselves Democratic-Republicans and their opponents Federalists. "The old names are kept up," Sergeant complained to Clay, "the old machinery is employed, and elections turn entirely upon this distinction, so that there is no effective mode of operating in mass."[73] Clay himself had warned of this problem back in April when he told Webster that they must "inculcate the incontestible [sic] truth that *now* there are but two parties in the Union, the friends and the enemies of the administration."[74] The Adams men in Pennsylvania knew they could not win without the Federalists.

The most important tests of their chance of winning were the state election and Sergeant's second effort to regain his seat in Congress, both set to take place on October 9, 1827. Sergeant's election had great symbolic value—nationally as well as in Pennsylvania—because he was so prominent. There was talk that if he won and the Adams party retained control of Congress, he would become Speaker. Sergeant's fears were eased somewhat when the Federalists again chose not to nominate anyone, but they were raised when the Jacksonians nominated Joseph Hemphill, an incumbent who was popular with the Federalists. The campaign was spirited—Sergeant called his supporters "zealous" and the Jacksonians "abusive."[75] This time, backed by a stronger organization, Sergeant won the election.

As election results began to filter in from other parts of the state, the Adams party had every reason to be encouraged. It had carried Philadelphia County by a wide margin over the "martial" party.[76] Returns from other counties in the southeastern corner were "encouraging." Enough of the German counties went for Adams to renew hope for a large Adams swing in 1828. In the northeastern corner of the state, where many New Englanders had settled, the returns were good. Even more important, the turnout was enormous—up 50 percent in Sergeant's election and between 20,000 and 30,000 throughout the state. Sergeant called it a "decisive" victory.[77] Making the election even more dramatic, President Adams and Secretary of the Navy Southard were both in Philadelphia as the returns came in. Never one to exude excitement or confidence himself, Adams wrote in his diary: "The excitement and confidence of my friends in Philadelphia is at this moment in the flood."[78]

But the party still had a long way to go. Sergeant had won only 51 percent of the vote. The returns from many counties, including James Buchanan's Lancaster, were misleading because of a confusing variety of party names. One newspaper in Harrisburg announced that it would support Adams at the national level but Jackson at the state level. The results, especially in the western part of the state, were far from complete. The governor remained loyal to Adams, but no one could say with any assurance that Adams men or Jackson men controlled the legislature. And the German vote was still uncertain. Perhaps Sergeant put it best. "I am persuaded," he told Clay, "we have a majority in the State, if we can only bring it out."[79] He was referring, of course, to the Federalist and German votes.

5

ORGANIZING AT THE BOTTOM
THE WEST AND THE SOUTH

OHIO

In the fall of 1827 politicians in Ohio were also sorting out the returns from a state election. As in New York and Pennsylvania, the population of Ohio was heavily concentrated in certain well-defined regions. The most densely populated was Hamilton County, including Cincinnati, in the southwestern part of the state, which had attracted farmers and merchants from Pennsylvania and Kentucky. With a population of 20,000, Cincinnati had grown into a commercial center known as the Queen City of the West. Other concentrations were in the Scioto River Valley, running from Columbus in the middle of the state to Portsmouth on the Ohio River, and in the "backbone" counties along the eastern border, settled by Scotch-Irish and Germans from Pennsylvania. Somewhat less developed were New England settlements in the Western Reserve on Lake Erie and in Marietta and other townships on the upper Ohio. Because of these demographic patterns, economic and political power in Ohio radiated out from Cincinnati in the southwest rather than from the east, as was the case in the states along the Atlantic.

Four powerful themes shaped politics in Ohio: explosive growth in population, faith in democracy, opposition to slavery, and enthusiasm for internal improvements. Expanding at a rate of 60 percent a decade, Ohio was the fastest growing large state in the Union. The steady influx of so many new voters made it difficult to predict the outcome of elections. And since electoral votes were allotted according to the census figures determined at the start of each decade, Ohio was sure to be underrepresented by 1828. The state's electoral vote had jumped from eight in 1820 to sixteen in 1824 and 1828 and would rise again to twenty-one in 1832.[1]

Ohio had been quick to establish the rights of white male voters. Almost all adult white males could vote, and there were no property requirements for holding office. Former Federalists sometimes held the balance of power in state elections, but Federalism was far less significant than in Pennsylvania or New Hampshire. Although the turnout in presidential elections was as low in Ohio as in other states, there was no lack of interest in the federal government. The turnout for congressional elections was high, often greater than for state elections. As revealed by the overthrow of the Presbyterian-Federalist standing order in Dayton in the early 1820s, the panic of 1819 had democratized and intensified Ohio politics.[2]

Ever since the days of the Northwest Ordinance banning slavery, Ohioans had hated the institution. Benjamin Lundy had started an antislavery society at St. Clairsville, Ohio, in 1815, five years before founding his *Genius of Universal Emancipation* in nearby Mount Pleasant.[3] One of the most unforgettable experiences in the life of Amos Kendall, who owned slaves in Kentucky, was a run-in with a pugnacious enemy of slavery while traveling through Ohio in 1827.

The overriding political and economic issue, however, was internal improvements. Voters, businessmen, and farmers alike highly approved of federal improvements, particularly the National Road, which had already reached Zanesville and was bringing in a steady stream of migrants from the East. Like voters in Pennsylvania, the citizens of Ohio envied New York's Erie Canal and sought to match it with a network of their own. In 1825, a year before Pennsylvania started its State Works program, the Ohio legislature passed the Canal Law, calling for waterways connecting Cincinnati, Portsmouth, and Marietta on the Ohio River with Toledo, Sandusky, and Cleveland on Lake Erie. The canals would be a great boon to the economy of Ohio and to the nation as well, for when completed, they would provide vital links for an inland waterway tying New York City to New Orleans.

As the presidential election of 1824 approached, two easterners drew early support. The friends of John Quincy Adams held meetings in Cincinnati and Columbus, while backers of De Witt Clinton reminded Ohioans of his role in building the Erie Canal. But Henry Clay, whose career as Speaker of the House and chief counsel for the Bank of the

United States in Kentucky and Ohio made him well known in the state, soon moved ahead. By July 1823 his supporters had formed committees, nominated "Harry of the West" for president, drawn up a slate of electors, and capped it all with a state convention.

Two Clay leaders had emerged: Charles Hammond, who was now practicing law and writing for the *Liberty Hall and Cincinnati Gazette,* and Congressman John C. Wright, a lawyer from Steubenville in the eastern part of the state. Born in Connecticut, Wright had worked as a printer and studied law at Litchfield before moving west. He and Hammond had become political and legal allies in 1820, when Hammond was still living in eastern Ohio. The hot-tempered Hammond soon found that he could count on the calm, composed Wright for political and emotional support. On one occasion when one of Hammond's sharply worded pamphlets got him into trouble, he quickly turned to Wright, admitting wryly that his "poor pamphlet [had been] quite out of season."[4] The demands of politics did not force the two friends to give up their law careers, although in one case they were forced to oppose the man they were backing for president. In 1823 they represented the state of Ohio before the U.S. Supreme Court in *Osborn v. Bank of the United States,* in which Clay was defending the bank. After hearing the case twice, John Marshall handed down a landmark decision granting the bank additional powers beyond those established in *McCulloch v. Maryland.*

Late in 1823 the Jackson movement began to spread into Ohio from Pennsylvania and Kentucky. It attracted the interest, but not the immediate support, of three unusually colorful Clintonian newspaper men, two in Cincinnati and one in the Scioto Valley. Moses Dawson, a short, stocky, heavily muscled man in his late fifties, was the frontier reincarnation of John Binns. An avid member of the United Irishmen, he had thrice been arrested for high treason by the British government, and only through luck had he escaped being hanged. In 1817 he came to America and started a school in Cincinnati. When the school was forced to close during the panic of 1819, Dawson turned to writing for the *Inquisitor and Cincinnati Advertiser* and was soon its editor. After supporting William Henry Harrison in a losing congressional campaign in 1822 and flirting briefly with the Clinton movement, he became one of the first Jackson men in Ohio.

Dawson quickly realized that he needed the help of Elijah Hayward, also of Cincinnati, whose Hamilton County political organization was the strongest in the state. Born in a small town in Massachusetts,

Hayward had failed in business before migrating to Cincinnati in 1819 and becoming editor of the *National Republican and Ohio Political Register*. In the spring of 1824 he was a committed Clintonian when word arrived that Clinton had been removed from the Canal Board in New York. Interpreting the news (incorrectly, as it turned out) to mean that Clinton's political career was over, Dawson and the Jackson men publicly challenged Hayward and the Clintonians to join them. Forced to make an immediate decision, Hayward dramatically changed sides and soon became the de facto leader of the Jackson movement in Ohio. Under his direction the Jackson party held a state convention in July, at which they set up a central committee and chose a slate of electors.

The third Jackson man was Caleb Atwater, the dark, massive, imposing scholar-editor of the *Friend of Freedom* in the Scioto River Valley town of Chillicothe. Although crippled for life when his hands were frozen while tending farm animals in Massachusetts, Atwater had gone on to graduate from Williams College in 1804. He then moved from one profession to another—schoolmaster, preacher, lawyer—before, like Hayward, losing all his money in a business venture. His failure drove him west to a town near Chillicothe, where he practiced law and started a lifelong scholarly career as an archaeologist, anthropologist, geologist, and historian. His interest in public matters, particularly education and the state canal system, drew him into Clintonian politics and newspaper publishing. In March 1824, a few weeks before Hayward changed sides, Atwater abandoned Clinton for Jackson. He attended the Jackson convention and was soon working alongside Hayward in the Jackson committee of correspondence.[5]

The Clay, Adams, and Jackson parties differed very little. They were strictly presidential parties, with no involvement in state and congressional elections. Personal ties outweighed ideological positions. All three called township and county meetings, held state conventions, published broadsides, and organized parades. There were, however, a few key differences. The Clay and Adams men were spread evenly across the state, while the Jacksonians were concentrated in the more heavily populated counties. And there was one difference that reappeared in the 1828 election: the Jackson newspapers were more national, exciting, and partisan than the others; the Adams press was more intellectual and moral.

The vigorous three-way presidential struggle that developed in the fall of 1824 drew a respectable 35 percent of Ohio voters to the polls, the highest to that point in Ohio history. It was second only to Maryland and far higher than the 20 percent that turned out in Pennsylvania, but it was much lower than the record-breaking 53 percent voting in the Ohio state election that fall. Clay carried the state by a small plurality with 19,225 votes, followed by Jackson with 18,457 and Adams with only 12,280. As expected, Jackson did best in the vicinity of Cincinnati, Adams in the New England settlements in the Western Reserve and southeastern Ohio. In the House of Representatives vote to select the president in 1825, the Ohio delegation was one of the three Clay delegations that voted for Adams.

After the election the three presidential organizations disappeared and were gradually replaced by early versions of the Adams and Jackson parties. The steady opposition to slavery and support for tariffs and internal improvements in Ohio gave the Adams men a decided advantage. Although Adams was not committed to the antislavery movement, he did not hide his hostility to slavery, and Clay's American System mirrored the strong nationalistic feelings in the state. The Jacksonians, in contrast, were badly divided on all three issues. During Adams's first year in office the Ohio public strongly favored sending delegates to the Panama Congress and opposed the pro-slavery arguments used by many Jackson senators in the debates. Harshly critical of John Randolph's tirades defending slavery, Charles Hammond could not understand why Virginia had sent such a man to the Senate.

But despite the hostile public opinion, Elijah Hayward held his Hamilton County machine together and continued to promote Andrew Jackson. In November 1825 he was lavish with his praise when Old Hickory, accepting the presidential nomination, called for an amendment giving the people the sole power to elect the presidential electors. "The corrupt bargains," he wrote, that had made Adams president "against the expressed voice of the People, should rouse the nation." When the next election was over, he concluded, "the political principles of *Andrew Jackson* . . . will . . . stand unshaken."[6] Like John Eaton's "Letters of Wyoming" a year earlier, Hayward's editorial presented the Old Hero as a combination of republican morality and military power, which appealed to the Ohio Jacksonians.

In 1826 the Adams and Jackson parties in Ohio expanded to support congressional candidates. Hoping to exploit the bargain charge and win a majority, the Jacksonians blacklisted the seven candidates who had voted for Adams in 1825 and made plans for a large Jackson meeting in Cincinnati. Encouraged by the small turnout at the meeting, Hammond told Clay that the administration party would carry all the congressional districts except the two surrounding Cincinnati. Elisha Whittlesey, a transplanted Yankee running for reelection in the Western Reserve, sent an equally optimistic letter to Daniel Webster. Cheered by the optimism, Webster wrote to Congressman John C. Wright, who was also a candidate for reelection, predicting that Wright's "constituents [would] send [him] back, notwithstanding all [his] sins."[7]

Hammond and Webster were correct. Both Whittlesey and Wright were reelected, and Adams men, including all seven who had voted for Adams in 1825, won twelve of the fourteen congressional seats. The only Jackson men elected were James Findlay and Irish immigrant William Russell, who represented the two districts in the southwest corner of the state. Even then, the Findlay victory was due more to family connections and personal popularity than it was to the strength of the Jackson party. Findlay, the former mayor of Cincinnati, had valuable business and family ties with the Family party in Pennsylvania and with Senator William Henry Harrison of Ohio, the hero of the Battle of Tippecanoe and an Adams man.

Administration men also won the governor's seat and the vast majority of other state offices. The new governor, Allen Trimble, who won 80 percent of the vote, was one of the best known figures in early Ohio. He had grown up in a log cabin fifty miles northeast of Cincinnati and during the War of 1812 had waged a successful campaign against the Indians in the upper Wabash River Valley. After the war he served as speaker of the Ohio senate and as one of the first commissioners for the Ohio Canal Fund. A staunch supporter of Clay's American System, Trimble was sympathetic with the administration but showed little interest in becoming a strong party man.

Elijah Hayward, however, had always been a party man. Directly after the 1826 election he set about rebuilding the Jacksonian party, which had fallen on hard times. In the early months of 1827 he could count on committees in only three of the state's sixty-five counties. Using his Hamilton County committee of vigilance and correspondence as a base of operations, he started building a new and stronger state party. By springtime he had arranged for Jackson meetings in ten counties and was corresponding with new committees in Wayne County in the north, Pickaway County in the Scioto Valley, and Jefferson County in the east. Hayward saw this as only a beginning, for his goal was to have a Jackson party in all sixty-five counties.

Newspapers played a major role in his plans. By the end of the year the number of Jackson newspapers had grown from six to twenty-four. The most important were Hayward's own newspaper, the *Cincinnati National Republican and Ohio Political Register*, Dawson's *Inquisitor and Cincinnati Advertiser*, and the *Ohio Monitor* in the state capital at Columbus. Most of the newspapers were small, struggling operations; the only two of any size were Hayward's *National Republican* and the *Muskingum Messenger* in Zanesville.

Large or small, the newspapers were indispensable. They brought to Ohio the same bold, passionate, often violent tone for which the Jackson press was notorious in New Hampshire, New York, and Pennsylvania— a tone the Adams party found improper and threatening. As in the three eastern states, the Jackson newspapers formed a tightly knit chain that tied the widely dispersed county committees to the state central committee and to Duff Green's central committee in Washington. Articles attacking the administration would appear first in the *Telegraph* and then be reprinted in local Ohio newspapers. The process could also be reversed, for Green often published articles from the state newspapers to demonstrate national support for Andrew Jackson.

According to Jacksonian rhetoric, Hayward's organization worked democratically from the bottom up. Local township meetings sent delegates to county conventions, which elected delegates for the state convention, which in turn selected presidential electors and candidates for state and federal office. For many years historians accepted this view. Writing in 1950, R. Carlyle Buley concluded that the Jacksonians, "the party of the 'common man,'" had "a distinct advantage over their opponents. They began at the bottom."[8] Fifty years later Donald J. Ratcliffe presented a different picture. The traditional view, he wrote, applied to Hamilton County and several others, but quite often the system was far less democratic, and in other cases the counties were barely organized at all. Here, in summary, is Ratcliffe's description of the way the system worked in Belmont County, which lay on either side of the National Road as it crossed into Ohio from Wheeling, Virginia:

A Jackson [county] meeting . . . appointed a general committee of correspondence of fifteen . . . which in turn appointed a five-man central committee. This small executive body then named . . . township committees, consisting of only two people each [which] were required to organize township meetings. . . . The real power still rested with the centrally appointed two-man committees, for they named, in August 1828, the party's ticket for local office in the fall election.[9]

Rather than working from the bottom up, the Jackson system in Ohio worked from the top down: from Washington down to the center of political power in Ohio—that is, Cincinnati and Hamilton County—and from there down to the counties and townships. The prominence of Cincinnati made it inevitable that Hayward and Dawson would run the show. Hayward held the reins, but the fiery Dawson commanded attention. When Dawson lampooned Hammond too aggressively, a tart note appeared in the pro-Adams Washington *National Journal* warning that if he did not "let Charley alone[,] depend on it there will be an 'improvement' made upon your press in short order." Dubbing it a "paltry threat," Dawson sent the note to Clay, saying it "must have emanated from some person who professes to be your friend."[10] Dawson also antagonized both Hammond and Wright by accusing Clay of buying their support by promising favors from his client, the Bank of the United States.

Outside of Ohio the third Jackson leader, Caleb Atwater, was better known than either Hayward or Dawson. The imposing, self-centered Atwater spent so much time writing to politicians and traveling that he left the impression, as one critic put it, that "he correspond[ed] with every great man in the nation."[11] During the campaign he was the only important Ohio Jacksonian to visit the Old Hero, write to him, or travel on his behalf. Just as dramatic and conspiracy minded as Old Hickory, Atwater warned Jackson in September 1827 that there was a "*spy—a double one—* for Clay and for McLean & Calhoun! . . . seated by *your side*."[12] He was referring to the black sheep of the Lee family, the immoral biographer Henry Lee, whom Atwater had seen at the Hermitage earlier in the year. There is no evidence that Lee was a spy. Atwater also made much of his contacts with De Witt Clinton. Later in 1827 he circulated a letter from Clinton promising to "take the field for Jackson."[13] Intrigued by Atwater's correspondence, historians once thought of him as the leading Jackson man in the state, but it is now clear that he played second fiddle. His base of power in the Scioto Valley could not match that enjoyed by Hayward and Dawson in Cincinnati.

Although it fell short of true democracy, the structure of the Jackson party in Ohio played a significant role in the spread of democracy in the state. Far better organized and much less deferential than the system that preceded it, the new system spread political ideas, involved more

citizens in the government, and increased the percentage of those voting. Even in local elections in Cincinnati, where the Jacksonians had
such numerical superiority that they did not have to work hard to get out
the vote, Hayward and Dawson consistently brought large numbers to
the polls. In the remaining months of the campaign the Jackson party
would become even more adept in the tactics of the new party system.[14]

Despite its early ideological advantage, the Adams party—like its
counterparts in New York and Pennsylvania—had a hard time deciding
how to compete with the Jacksonians. Even the most active Adams-Clay
man, Charles Hammond, was uneasy about accepting the new attitude
toward parties and adopting the new democratic, partisan tactics practiced by his opponents. In April 1827 Hammond laid out his democratic, antiparty sentiments in the *Liberty Hall and Cincinnati Gazette*.
He would, he said, "rather see the most ambitious and dangerous man
in the Union elevated to the presidential chair by the free voice of the
people, than the best and wisest elected by the efforts of a disciplined
party like the one Mr. Van Buren leads in the State of New York."[15]

Hammond feared that politics in Ohio would descend into the same
fierce partisanship already evident in Pennsylvania and New York. There
was "too little principle in the politics of the times," he told Clay. Men
were far more "devoted to personal interests and feelings" than to "the
Public good." Such "self-aggrandizement and self-interest" prevented
"that united feeling of attachment to men and measures, which is essential to hold politicians together."[16] He was especially alarmed by the
spirit of revenge that dominated the Jackson party and gave rise to an
organization that was designed "to perplex, degrade, and demolish."[17]
In this outburst, Hammond represented thousands of Americans who
were proud of democracy but afraid of it, envious of party but scornful
of it.

Other Adams men had fewer philosophic scruples. In Columbus the
editors of the powerful *Ohio State Journal* urged their party to copy the
Jacksonian ways, and after seeing firsthand how effective the Jacksonians were in Congress, Hammond's friend John C. Wright agreed. In a
letter to Daniel Webster he expressed his fear that Jackson men such as
George McDuffie and Samuel D. Ingham, "aided by the sarcasms of the
crazy Randolph" (recently reelected), would give the administration "a
hard trip" in the next session of the House of Representatives.[18]

Instead of railing against his opponents' lack of principle, Wright
decided to work doggedly to build a better party. At the state level he

organized a party meeting in Steubenville, publicized early attacks on Jackson's marriage, and arranged an exchange of newspapers between Adams editors in Ohio and Massachusetts. His interest in parties went well beyond the Buckeye State. In May 1827 he urged Webster to give in to pressure to move up from the House to the Senate because the party needed him in the upper house. In the same letter he gave his opinions on politics in New Hampshire, Massachusetts, New York, Kentucky, and western Pennsylvania as well as Ohio.[19] During the summer Wright returned to Washington, where he joined Webster, Josiah S. Johnston of Louisiana, and other administration men in making plans for the presidential election.[20]

Like Adams men in other states, Hammond and Wright ran afoul of Postmaster General John McLean in their efforts to build a state party. Even though McLean had grown up in Ohio and had been a popular Ohio congressman and chief justice of the Ohio Supreme Court, Hammond expected no favors from him. As early as January 1826 Hammond had protested to Clay that McLean was "devoted to Calhoun" and was "not to be trusted." "The Heroites," he believed, "derive a vast advantage from their controul of the Post office" in Cincinnati. When Hammond learned that the postmaster of Cincinnati, William Burke, was a defaulter, he pressed Clay to remove him. Hammond weakened his case, however, by pointing out that McLean would probably replace Burke with another Jackson man and recommended that Clay avoid "any stir or commotion."[21] Clay admitted that the situation was "to be regretted" and that he was no longer willing to defend McLean, but he did not "believe it practicable to prevail on the President to move in the affair." Adams, he added, had "great, if not inconquerable repugnance to turning any man out of office, merely for an opinion."[22] The Hammond-Clay connection was unable to deliver a significant amount of party patronage to the Ohio Adams men.

Yet the Adams men were confident that Clay's American System would make up for any deficiencies in patronage or party organization. They knew that Governor Trimble strongly supported the American System. They ridiculed and dismissed as counterproductive the attacks by southern Old Republicans on federal tariffs and internal improvements. When William B. Giles offered resolutions against the American System in the Virginia House of Delegates, Samuel Vinton of Gallipolis, Ohio, called his words "more precious to the Administration than Millions of *Gold and patronage* could be."[23] With this sort of backing, Clay was able to urge his Ohio friends to unite all supporters of manufactures and internal improvements, regardless of party identification.

On July 13, 1827, the Adams men responded by calling a bipartisan meeting in Cincinnati to choose delegates for the Harrisburg tariff convention, then only two weeks away. Apparently in command, they offered a strong slate of delegates and seemed to have the necessary votes to elect them. But suddenly the Jacksonians moved to adjourn the meeting—a maneuver designed to keep the Ohio delegates from getting to Harrisburg on time. When tempers flared, the managers had to adjourn the meeting, but three days later they showed their resilience by reconvening it and electing their slate of Adams delegates. Ohio was represented by Adams men at Harrisburg.[24]

As the fall elections of 1827 approached, the Adams men had reason to be optimistic. A majority of the voters agreed with them on the major issues. Their newspapers far outnumbered the Jackson press and enjoyed a larger circulation. In Columbus the Adams *Journal* had many more subscribers than the Jackson *Monitor*. Even with the rapid expansion of the Jackson press, there were five Adams newspapers for every two supporting Old Hickory. There were very few Jacksonians in the state legislature and only two in the U.S. House of Representatives.[25]

Thus the results of the state election in October 1827 came as a great surprise. The Jackson party increased its representation in the state legislature to forty-one, while the number of Adams men fell to sixty-six. Even more worrisome to Clay was the victory of a Jacksonian, William Stanbery, in a special election to replace a deceased Adams congressman. Stanbery's election increased the number of Jackson men in the House from two to three out of twelve, and it added one more name to the list of congressmen likely to vote against Clay's candidate for Speaker of the House.[26]

Hammond reassured Clay that these "advances" did not "indicate any Serious danger," but they did "impress upon us the necessity of activity." Realizing that they must take "measures to discipline and organize [their] friends for action," they had already published a circular announcing a state convention in December and were preparing a party address that would be adopted by the delegates.[27] Clay concurred. He was "glad to see that our friends in Ohio have resolved on organization and systematic exertion, in future. The other side is completely disciplined."[28]

This frank acknowledgment by Hammond and Clay that the Jackson party was much better organized than theirs echoed the sentiments coming out of New Hampshire, New York, and Pennsylvania. So did the undisguised fear and loathing of the opposition, as well as the admiration for it. "Some of the most persevering and artful men" in the state senate, said Hammond, "are against us. . . . There is no more chance to put down and Silence the lies of the Opposition . . . than there was of old to destroy the heads of the fabled dragon."[29] Jackson's moves were becoming so "extravagant," he continued, that they were making his followers more and more "violent." Hammond warned that "the Success of the opposition Seals the fate of the country."[30] Clay replied darkly that "the success of the opposition [is] pregnant with the fate of the Republic. . . . These are the darkest pages of our history." So, while the Adams men in Ohio were scrambling to match the organization of the opposition, they were, in Clay's words, "trembl[ing]" for the Republic.[31]

KENTUCKY

On his way down the Ohio River in 1831 Alexis de Tocqueville was struck by the dramatic difference between the free state of Ohio on the starboard side of his steamboat and the slave state of Kentucky on the port side. From the Ohio side came the "hum" of industry and agriculture; on the Kentucky side "man [was] idle." The difference, he concluded, was that Ohio was a free state, Kentucky a slave state.[32]

But Kentucky was not idle, and it was not monolithic. By the 1820s there were two Kentuckys. One was the relatively small Bluegrass region made up of the city of Lexington and surrounding counties in the northern hump of Kentucky, the earliest settled and most densely populated part of the state. The other was the rest of Kentucky. The rich soil and gentle climate of the Bluegrass had attracted planters from Virginia, and its location at the end of the Wilderness Road, not far from the Ohio River, had encouraged merchants and manufacturers to set up shop. Economically, socially, and culturally, the Bluegrass was much more highly developed than the other parts of the state. With its college, its newspapers, and its busy social life, Lexington had become known as the Athens of the West.

Kentucky was a democratic state, even more so than Pennsylvania and Ohio. Virtually all adult white males could vote, and 74 percent of them had turned out for the gubernatorial election of 1820. Jeffersonian from the start, Kentucky had no party competition to speak of until the panic of 1819 triggered the rise of the Relief movement. Alarmed by the spread of foreclosures, the Reliefers had succeeded in passing two radical bills in the state legislature—a replevin act, allowing debtors to postpone debts, and a banking act, setting up a state bank to lend money to debtors. Improved economic conditions, however, soon led to a backlash against the two measures, especially in the Bluegrass, and late in 1823 the state court of appeals declared the replevin act unconstitutional.

The decision of the court turned the state election of 1824 into a conflict between Reliefers and Anti-Reliefers. Since the Bluegrass had not suffered as much from the panic as the rest of the state had, the Relief movement was much stronger outside the Bluegrass than within it. As a result, leaders of the Relief party were most likely to come from outside the Bluegrass or from its outer fringes. There were other differences as well. Almost none of the Relief men but at least half of the Anti-Reliefers came from the wealthy elite. All the Reliefers were lifetime Republicans; half the opposition had once been Federalists. Even more striking, half the Reliefers had served in the War of 1812, but none of the Anti-Reliefers. In Kentucky politics, militaristic small farmers and businessmen of modest means from outside the Bluegrass were facing off against planters and men of commerce from inside.

The spokesmen for the Relief party were General Joseph Desha, who was running for governor, and Amos Kendall, editor of the *Argus of Western America*. Desha, who had fought in the War of 1812, lived north of the Bluegrass near the Ohio River. Kendall had given up his job tutoring the Clay children and had tried unsuccessfully to establish a law career in Lexington. Feeling out of place in upper-class Lexington society, he had moved to the capital city of Frankfort on the outer edges of the Bluegrass, where he took over the *Argus*.

During the campaign Kendall introduced a personal, slashing, sometimes humorous style of political writing that was far different from the traditionally analytical, stately, scholarly style of American editors. Instead of explaining the virtues of the replevin and banking acts in words that only men of learning could understand, he attacked the enemy by speaking directly in common words to the common people. He blamed Kentucky's economic woes on the Bank of Kentucky, the Bank of the United States, the state and federal courts, and a small group of "rich and well born" aristocrats, all of whom, he said, were stealing property from honest yeoman farmers.

To buttress his argument, Kendall introduced familiar republican themes—virtue (the Relief side) versus corruption (the opposition), outsiders (Relief) versus insiders (opposition), and liberty (Relief) versus power (opposition)—in a new, direct, democratic writing style that used personal names or nicknames, anecdotes (often fictional), and gross hyperbole. It was a colorful story, he told it well, and the public loved it. With this new style, Kendall soon emerged as one of the best of the new political editors—on a par with Jacksonians Duff Green, Isaac Hill, and Moses Dawson and with Adams men John Binns and Charles Hammond. He would later use this style in writing Jackson's bank veto. This new democratic writing style reached a higher level in the writing of Abraham Lincoln and Mark Twain.[33]

Kendall's aggressive style, Desha's vigorous campaigning, and the voters' widespread opposition to the court decision resulted in a decisive victory for the Relief party. Emboldened by their success, the Reliefers passed a Reorganization Act that replaced the original appeals court with a new one that favored the Relief side. This high-handed maneuver cost them dearly, however, because it transformed their loosely organized opponents into a political party almost as partisan as their own. When the old appeals court refused to disband, Kentucky found itself with two courts and two parties—the Relief party, now called the New Court party, and the Anti-Reliefers, now the Old Court party.

Unlike the evolution of politics in Ohio, where state parties followed presidential parties, in Kentucky the presidential system came second. In the presidential election of 1824 Henry Clay had an obvious advantage in Kentucky. The proprietor of a grand estate called Ashland on the outskirts of Lexington, he and his wife Lucretia had presided over Lexington society for years. Clay had already been elected to the U.S. Senate six times and to the House of Representatives seven. Eight of the twelve Kentucky congressmen elected in 1824 (including Clay himself) were Clay men. He was so popular in Kentucky that only Andrew Jackson dared oppose him there. During the campaign representatives of both candidates set up organizations and held county and presidential district meetings, but the parties were separate from the state parties.

Even though Clay was close to many of the Anti-Relief–Old Court men, he had steadfastly refused to take sides in the controversy. Within the New Court party Desha and others supported Jackson, while Kendall and his Frankfort friends, who had backed Clay for years, remained loyal to their fellow Kentuckian. In a lackluster election in which only 25 percent came out to vote, Clay won an overwhelming victory with 73 percent of the vote. The only strong Jackson support came from Louisville and from Campbell County across the river from Cincinnati, the center of Jackson power in Ohio.

But Clay's decision to support Adams in the House election and accept the position of secretary of state weakened his position in Kentucky. Many of his old friends, including large numbers in the New Court party, turned against him. Before long the New Court party had largely gone over to Jackson, and the Old Court party was backing John Quincy Adams. Historian Richard P. McCormick has argued that the new party system was simply a matter of personalities—Clay and Adams versus Jackson—but it seems more likely that it was an extension of the state party system. All nine leaders of the Relief party in 1824 had become New Court–Jackson men by 1827; nine out of ten Anti-Reliefers were in the Old Court–Adams party. Lexington, the heart of the Bluegrass and once the center of opposition to the Relief movement, was now the heart of the Adams-Clay party in Kentucky.

Amos Kendall tried hard not to commit himself. As a westerner he was anti-Adams, but he was far from enthusiastic about Jackson. During the 1824 campaign he had attacked Old Hickory for his "propensity to war."[34] More important, his longtime connection with the Clays kept him out of the Jackson camp. Even though most of his political allies had joined the Jackson movement, he could not bring himself to break his relationship with Clay. He was especially grateful to Lucretia Clay for nursing him back to health when he had almost died from bilious fever, and he looked to Henry Clay as a patron who could help him get a government job or a loan. A $1,500 loan from Clay in 1825 kept Kendall in this awkward position.

Meanwhile, Kendall's position in state politics had worsened. Public outrage against the Reorganization Act led to Old Court victories in the elections of 1825 and 1826 and gave the Old Court party control of the state legislature. Protected by his four-year term in office, Joseph Desha was still governor, but the prospects of the New Court party looked bleak. So did Kendall's future. Suffering from acute anxiety and a dangerous case of violent diarrhea, he was on the verge of getting out of politics.

But in the fall of 1826 Kendall recovered his health and swung back into action. Desha convinced him that they must shift public attention away from the court struggle by converting the faltering New Court party into a Jackson party. On October 4, 1826, Kendall announced that he had become a Jackson man because the Old Hero was more Jeffersonian and less "consolidating" than John Quincy Adams. Clay made the break complete in December by removing federal printing from the *Argus*. Kendall was sincere about his Jeffersonian beliefs, but he had made the move primarily to save his state party and his own career. He really had no other choice. If he had refused to shift, the Jacksonians would have set up their own newspaper in Frankfort, and the *Argus* would have been in deep trouble. His abrupt shift was like that of Elijah Hayward in 1824, when he had suddenly jumped from Clinton to Jackson, and like that of Isaac Hill in 1825, when he had abandoned Crawford for Jackson.[35]

Kendall joined a state Jackson party that already boasted well-known leaders and the beginnings of party organization. U.S. Senator Richard M. Johnson and *Argus* assistant editor Francis Preston Blair preceded him into the party's ranks. In Louisville and surrounding Jefferson County, which had gone for Jackson in 1824, editor Arthur Lee Campbell had set up a Jackson organization with a central committee in the city and sub-committees in the city wards and militia companies. Kendall's goal was to build similar organizations throughout the state. Again like Hayward and Hill, he went to work in the winter and spring of 1826–1827 to create a statewide organization. In the spring Adams congressman Francis Johnson warned Clay that a "Frankfort Junto," headed by Kendall had taken charge of Jackson politics in the state. Johnson was afraid that he would lose his seat to one of Kendall's minions who was tearing about his district quoting statements from "Amos" and the *United States Telegraph*.[36] One of the favorite "Amos" stories was a one-sided account of the way Clay had taken government printing away from Kendall.

As the August 1827 state election approached, it took on added significance as a possible harbinger of the presidential election of 1828. Kendall's belligerent campaigning made it appear that the Adams men were losing control of the state. Porter Clay reminded his brother Henry of the "excitability" of the Kentuckians. "Once [you] get them aroused," he warned, "you might as well attempt to control the currant [*sic*] of the Mississippi."[37] Looking for ways to boost the confidence of the Adams party, Clay urged John W. Taylor of New York to write an "encouraging" letter to Adams men in Kentucky.[38] And perhaps to buck up Taylor as well, Clay promised him that Kentucky would elect more administration congressmen in August than in the previous election, that is, more than eight out of twelve. It was a bold promise.

Aware that what had once been considered merely a state election had become a national event, Kendall broadened his message to include the two presidential candidates. As a result, his articles in the *Argus* give an excellent preview of the presidential campaign of 1828. He defended Jackson against the charges of adultery and of murdering the six militiamen and attacked Adams for installing a billiards table in the White House. The image of the president playing billiards blended well with Kendall's central theme—that the Jacksonians represented republican virtue, while the Adams men constantly violated it. Another morality tale, obviously untrue—that Adams had provided a woman for the pleasure of the czar of Russia—also appeared in the *Argus*.

In dealing with Kendall and the other Jackson editors, the Adams men had the same handicaps as their compatriots in the other key states. They were painfully slow in accepting partisanship. Clay's closest friend in Kentucky, John J. Crittenden, spoke for many Adams men when he condemned the opposition for the "malevolence of party spirit."[39] Aware that the persistent problem of patronage would not go away, Clay's brother Porter and editor William W. Worsley of Louisville took it on themselves to lecture Clay on the subject. Porter could not understand why Adams and Clay were so slow in appointing Crittenden, the obvious candidate, as U.S. attorney for Kentucky. Worsley reminded Clay that positions should be given to a party's "*decided* friends in place of its enemies or its lukewarm friends." "A contrary course," he gratuitously added, "has in no instance . . . conciliated an enemy, [but has often] made friends . . . a good deal cold to the cause."[40]

The Kentucky Adams men also faced the same post office problem that plagued their allies in New Hampshire, Pennsylvania, and Ohio. The day before Clay received the first election returns from Kentucky, an unpleasant letter arrived from a friend complaining that Lexington postmaster Joseph Ficklin would not allow his post riders to carry Adams handbills. Others suspected that he was opening and reading political letters. An entrenched and allegedly corrupt Jackson man, Ficklin had received his position through the help of prominent Jacksonians—Senator Richard M. Johnson and chief justice of the new court of appeals William T. Barry. His behavior was eerily similar to that of William Burke in Cincinnati and Richard Bache in Philadelphia, and just as in those cases, Postmaster General John McLean had no intention of removing him.

Most damaging of all was the attitude of the Adams men toward their opponents. Considering themselves morally, intellectually, and socially superior to the Jacksonians, they looked down on their rivals with great disdain, but these sentiments masked a deeper feeling of grudging respect and sometimes fear. Crittenden called the Jackson men "a clamorous band of political fanatics, mountebanks and pretended patriots."[41] John Harvie, chair of the state Adams party, came close to expressing the feelings of his colleagues when he told Clay that the administration and Clay himself were "too correct and unexceptionable" and thus too vulnerable to the "intrigues & machinations" of the Jacksonians.[42] As Crittenden looked ahead to the fateful state and presidential elections of 1828, he was filled not with enthusiasm but with fear. Quoting from *King Henry V* he told Clay that "the whole country resounds 'with fearful note of preperation [sic].'"[43] Unlike Henry V, he was prepared for defeat.

The Jackson men in Kentucky had none of these handicaps. After losing the state elections of 1825 and 1826, they were determined to return to power in 1827. With the panic of 1819 far in the past, they put old issues from the Relief war aside and ran on the Old Hero's record as a military commander. William T. Barry drew a crowd of 3,000 to hear him re-create Jackson's many exploits. Just before the three days of voting began in early August, thousands of Jacksonians marched through the streets of Lexington wearing hickory leaves on their heads. The new tactics paid off. These "clamorous" Jackson men won a victory in the legislature and made a false prophet out of Clay by reducing rather than increasing the number of Adams congressmen. Their number dropped from eight to five out of twelve.

Spurred by success, the Jacksonians wasted no time starting to plan for the two big elections of 1828: the state election in August, when a new governor would be selected, and the presidential election, which would be held in November. On August 20, 1827, the day that county sheriffs brought in the official election returns, a committee of twenty Jackson men, led by Kendall and Blair, began to draw up a revised party organization. Working from the bottom up, town and militia committees would elect delegates for county conventions, which would then choose delegates for a state convention, which would nominate candidates for office and publish a party address. Centralized control was placed in the hands of a central committee, which would appoint "trusty agents" to pass the word down to county and local committees.[44]

Just as significant as the party organization was the dramatic way Kendall and his associates implemented it. To build up party spirit they held a barbecue for seven hundred people on September 10 at Cedar Cove, outside of Frankfort. There were toasts, public addresses, bands playing, men marching, and hints, but nothing specific, about organization.

Then, two weeks later, on September 26 Kendall and Blair came out with an issue of the *Argus* in which they dramatically revealed that their Adams enemies were plotting to seize power. To prevent this from happening they called on all good Jackson men to form the local and county committees they had designed. They also announced a state Jackson convention to be held on January 8, 1828, the thirteenth anniversary of the Battle of New Orleans. All this was done in the "clamorous" Jackson style that the Adams men scorned and feared.[45]

There was one other piece of information, which Kendall chose not to announce: the name of the Jackson candidate for governor. Kendall was worried about an ugly split between the Frankfort wing of the party (Kendall, Blair, Desha, and Johnson) and the Louisville wing (Lieutenant Governor Robert McAfee, U.S. Senator John Rowan, and editor Shadrach Penn). McAfee wanted to run, but Kendall was afraid that this would lead to a fight between the two wings. To avoid this he hoped to convince William T. Barry of Lexington, who was committed to neither wing, to be the candidate. So on September 17, partway between the barbecue and the *Argus* announcement, he wrote to Barry asking him to run. Although Barry made no commitment at the time, he later agreed. Kendall's main argument to win Barry over was the promise that if he lost, he would be able to obtain a job from a grateful Andrew Jackson after he was elected president. In short, the Kentucky party would be part of a national party organization that had not yet been completed.[46]

To bring Kentucky into this national organization, Kendall decided to write directly to Jackson himself. This was a daring, even presumptuous decision, for the two had never spoken to each other or exchanged letters. Striking boldly on August 22, Kendall sent a letter giving Jackson advice on how to deal with James Buchanan's revelation concerning the bargain charge. A month later he issued the public letter revealing that he had seen a letter from Clay to Blair proving that Clay had planned to vote for Adams in 1825.[47]

Kendall also decided to go to Washington, where the Jackson party would control Congress when it convened in December. The trip would strengthen the national ambitions of his Kentucky party and give Kendall a chance to get a loan from the Jackson party treasury, which was controlled by Martin Van Buren and Duff Green. By the middle of October he was riding north on horseback through Ohio, heading for Cleveland, the Great Lakes, and the Erie Canal.

He left behind an Adams party desperately playing catch-up. Fearful that his home state might fall to Jackson in 1828, Clay on September 27 sent a letter with an enclosure to a half dozen of the leading Adams men in Kentucky. Blaming the defeat in the August election on Jacksonian *"organization,"* he called on his friends to build a party that could regain control of the state. Unlike the Jackson leadership, Clay was willing to tie the administration party to an ideological theme: "Let there be a public meeting called in every county of the State of the friends of the administration of the American System, and of H. Clay, if it is thought expedient to use his name." Each county was to have a committee of correspondence of ten or twelve people to correspond with similar county committees and distribute newspapers, political essays, and tracts that would "advance the success of the cause." There would also be county committees of vigilance made up of a hundred or more persons, sufficient to cover each town or neighborhood in the county. Clay put great stress on the committees of vigilance, which were to "watch over the interests of the cause; to vindicate it from error and aspersion; to disseminate information and documents . . . ; to animate their neighbors, and to stimulate and encourage them to attend the elections." Each of the two committees would have the power to call meetings of the people.[48]

The democratic idealism of Clay's document is palpable. He was certain that "every member of the two Committees would feel himself flattered by the appointment . . . to make the greatest exertions." As a result, "intelligence would be rapidly and certainly communicated throughout the whole community." And—on a practical note—the system would allow an "estimate" to be "correctly made of the strength of friends in every neighborhood." At the end Clay called for a "Central Committee of Correspondence" at Frankfort "to communicate with the other committees throughout the state." Buried in the middle of the document was the obvious general theme that "the principle on which our institutions are based, is the capacity of the people to govern themselves."[49] Clay's letter was so idealistic that it helps explain why the Adams men in New Hampshire, New York, Pennsylvania, Ohio, and Kentucky felt themselves morally superior to the Jacksonians.

Clay's friends responded well. Only a day or two after his letter arrived, Thomas Smith of Lexington reported that two meetings had already been held at his home and that plans were under way to carry out Clay's proposals. A meeting at Louisville had already taken place, the first Fayette County meeting—an important event—would be held within the next week, and meetings were scheduled for nearby Scott and

Bourbon counties. Even more significant, a date had been set for a state convention in Frankfort on December 17. And they were already arguing about who should be the candidate for governor.

There were, however, several worrisome notes. The Adams men kept repeating the mantra that they were morally superior to the Jacksonians. Crittenden promised Clay that the December state convention would be one of "the most respectable ever held in any state,"[50] and a Franklin County meeting praised Adams and Clay as "pure, patriotic, uncorrupted and incorruptible republican and accomplished statesmen."[51] Similar statements in the other states had not brought success. And in Kentucky the Jacksonians seemed to match or anticipate every move of the Adams party. When the Adams men got started in Frankfort and throughout Franklin County, they learned that the Jackson men there had already held a meeting and appointed a committee of correspondence. When Thomas Smith incorrectly informed Clay that Lieutenant Governor McAfee would be the Jackson candidate for governor, he was unaware that Kendall had already lined up Barry. Although perhaps morally and socially inferior to the Adams men, the Jackson men always seemed to be one maneuver ahead. Perhaps they were better politicians.

VIRGINIA

The republican tradition and the state constitution of 1776 hampered the growth of political parties in Virginia. Since voting and other political activities were carried out largely at the county level, where self-appointed justices of the peace controlled patronage, there was no pressing need for statewide parties. The tradition of filling elective offices with the best qualified men rather than party men was also discouraging. More often than not there was little competition for election to the lower house of the legislature. In addition, the governor's election by the legislature rather than by the people made parties seem superfluous. Perhaps the most important impediment was the constitutional provision restricting voting to those with a freehold of fifty acres (or land worth fifty pounds), which cut the number of eligible adult white male voters in half.[52]

In the absence of parties, sectional differences had long been the source of most political conflict in the Old Dominion. Virginia was divided into four geographic sections: the Tidewater and the Piedmont east of the Blue Ridge, the Valley of Virginia, and the trans-Allegheny sections to the west. Following the republican doctrine that voting rights should be based on the ownership of property (land and slaves), the eastern sections, with their large plantations and many slaves, had a voting advantage in the lower house, the House of Delegates. In the 1820s the Tidewater region alone had 26 percent of the white population but 35 percent of the delegates, while the Valley of Virginia and the trans-Allegheny region, with very little slavery, had 44 percent of the white population and only 37 percent of the delegates. As a result, the landed gentry of the east held the political and economic power in Virginia. The center of power was Richmond, located on the fall line between the Tidewater and the Piedmont. This unequal representation stirred up so much resentment in the western counties that between 1816 and 1825 reformers in the west held three large meetings, first asking for constitutional reform and then demanding a statewide referendum on the calling of a constitutional convention.[53]

The sectional patterns of Virginia fit in well with the core and periphery pattern used by Ronald Formisano to explain politics in the Jackson years. As he describes it, political and economic power was often concentrated in a geographic center or core, with the opposition strongest in the outside areas or periphery. In early Massachusetts, for example, the Federalist party, the shipping interests, and the Congregational Church were all concentrated in a center made up of Boston and surrounding counties. The Republican opposition was relegated to regions on the periphery, such as Middlesex County and Cape Cod. Virginia was much the same. Political and economic power based on slavery rested in the central Tidewater and Piedmont regions around Richmond, while the opposition was strongest in the outlying Valley of Virginia and trans-Allegheny in the west and several counties along the Potomac River and Chesapeake Bay in the north and east. In one respect, however, the Virginia pattern was the inverse of that in Massachusetts. In Massachusetts the most forward-looking commercial region was in the center, with the more traditional agrarian interests in the periphery. In Virginia the opposite was true.[54]

Despite the institutional obstacles, the upper-class Virginians of the east developed their own version of party government. As in New York, the election of 1800 provided the incentive. To help Thomas Jefferson, the Republicans in the House of Delegates held a legislative caucus and formed a state central committee of correspondence to work with committees in the counties. Soon afterward Judge Spencer Roane set up the *Richmond Enquirer,* with his cousin Thomas Ritchie as editor. Thus began the Richmond Junto, an unofficial, secretive committee that apparently controlled the Republican caucus in the House of Delegates but whose membership and records were never made public. In fact, its very existence is still the subject of historical debate. Somewhat like the Family party in Pennsylvania, though much less public, membership in the Richmond Junto was determined by family relationships and ownership of landed property close to Richmond.

At the start the most influential members of the Junto were Ritchie; Roane, who sat on the Virginia Supreme Court of Appeals; and Wilson Cary Nicholas, a U.S. senator during Jefferson's first term who later served as governor. Roane set the tone for the Junto with his defense of John Taylor's Old Republicanism and the states' rights doctrines of Jefferson and Madison in the Kentucky and Virginia Resolutions of 1798–1799. In 1819–1820 he produced a series of articles attacking the nationalistic decisions of John Marshall. Although Ritchie was of the Old Republican persuasion, he was moderate in his views and often put the interests of Virginia ahead of the narrow interests of the plantation owners. Despite its roots in the agrarian economy, the Junto did not lose touch with the financial interests in Virginia. Two of the most powerful early members were bankers: Nicholas's brother Philip and Roane's cousin Dr. John Brockenbrough, president of the Bank of Virginia.[55]

Although the Richmond Junto was part of the same political movement that spawned the other regencies and juntos, it operated differently. Instead of being formed, like the New York Bucktails, to gain political power, the Richmond Junto was created to keep power in the hands of the slave-owner establishment of Virginia. Unlike the organizations of Hill, Van Buren, and Kendall, the Richmond Junto did little to develop the new-style political tactics that still influence politics today. To the extent it resembled any of the other organizations, it was most like John Overton's Nashville Junto.

The leaders too were different. Ritchie was not a resentful cripple like Hill, nor the son of a tavern keeper like Van Buren, nor a reclusive old man like Kendall. He was, as one biographer described him, the head of Richmond society, "a tall, lean, quick-moving man . . . always clinging to the old low shoes and silk stockings, secretary of all the public meetings, toastmaster of the dinners, leader of the dances, . . . the state's 'Father Ritchie.'"[56]

But "Father Ritchie" was guiding a state in decline. In the years after the panic of 1819 Virginia was no longer the grand Old Dominion of the colonial and Revolutionary War eras. The deaths of Adams and Jefferson in 1826 marked not only the end of the founding fathers but also the political and economic decline of Virginia. The most populous state in the Union in 1790, it would rank only third by 1830 and seventh in 1860. In part because of the panic, the value of its land plummeted from $206 million in 1817 to $90 million in 1829. Ritchie commented accurately in 1825 that "Virginia [was] rapidly sinking in the scale of the Union."[57]

The end of the grand old age of Virginia was accompanied by the passing of a generation of political leaders. Between 1820 and 1830 John Randolph served his last term in Congress, and death took Wilson Cary Nicholas, Spencer Roane, John Taylor, Thomas Jefferson, and Governor William B. Giles. Replacing them were John Tyler, who became governor in 1825; William C. Rives, who was elected to Congress the same year; Andrew Stevenson, named Speaker of the House in 1827; and John H. Pleasants, who started the anti-Junto newspaper the *Constitutional Whig* in Richmond in 1824. Thomas Ritchie and Senator Littleton Tazewell spanned both generations.

These new men brought a new political era to Virginia. In the 1824 election Ritchie and the Junto came out in favor of William H. Crawford, whose Old Republican views matched theirs. Crawford carried Virginia with 56 percent of the vote, while Adams and Jackson lagged behind with about 20 percent each. The turnout of 12 percent of adult white males was the smallest in the nation. After the election, when it became clear that Crawford could not run again, Ritchie began to look for a presidential candidate he could support. It was obvious from the start that Adams would not do. In March 1825 Ritchie attacked the program of internal improvements in Adams's inaugural address; two months later he expressed his dismay at the nomination of the old Federalist Rufus King; later still he denounced Adams's "Ultra doctrine," particularly his plan for a national university. Ritchie was so hostile to Adams that he became involved in a name-calling battle with the *National Intelligencer,* which was solidly for the president.[58]

Ritchie did not care much for Jackson either. Even though the Jackson party and the Junto were both opposed to Adams, the editor held to the view that the general "was not a qualified statesman."[59] Others, however, thought differently. During the winter of 1825–1826 Senator Randolph joined forces with Van Buren and Calhoun in opposing the Panama Congress and forming an opposition party. Afterward Randolph came home and organized demonstrations for Jackson at several

Fourth of July celebrations. Then in October 1826 Ritchie's close friend Philip N. Nicholas revealed the Junto's interest in the general by writing to Van Buren to ask about Jackson's political views. The turning point came in December 1826 when John Tyler, who was close to Adams, defeated Randolph in the Senate race, alarming Ritchie so much that he quickly accepted Van Buren's proposal of a Jackson party. When Van Buren passed through Richmond on his way home from the South in May 1827, the *Enquirer* ran a series of articles defending the Little Magician from the charge that he was just an ambitious politician.[60] Other politicians, including Tazewell, Stevenson, and Rives, joined Ritchie and Randolph on the Jackson bandwagon. Ritchie continued to attack Adams for abandoning Old Republican views and criticized Clay for his role in the Harrisburg tariff convention. Clay and Adams, he insisted, endangered the Union with their tariff and internal improvements policies.

But Ritchie and the others had a more difficult task justifying their switch to Jackson and convincing their readers and fellow politicians that Jackson represented the Old Republican ideals so many Virginians held dear. Was he indeed "qualified" to be president?[61] The letters of William C. Rives, a committed states' rights Jeffersonian who was elected to Congress in 1823 at age thirty, give some idea of how the new generation of Virginians reacted to Andrew Jackson. Although Rives admitted that Jackson was far from being a devoted republican, he was willing to adjust his definition of republicanism and fit Jackson in. On the tariff, he argued that Jackson was a moderate and Adams was a zealot who would use prohibitive tariff rates to keep cheap foreign goods out of the country. Jackson was a republican because he would make no foreign alliances and would raise no standing army. So, Rives impatiently told another young Virginian, there was no need for any "affected squeamishness & hesitancy in supporting Gen. Jackson." Rives declared himself "most thoroughly satisfied."[62]

Rives's rather lukewarm acceptance of Jackson was typical of the attitude of many other Old Republican Virginians. Ritchie summed up their position. He still believed that Jackson lacked the education to be a "statesman," but he did not question the Old Hero's *republican feeling.* Jackson's temper, he wrote hopefully, was not as bad as it had once been, and in the coming election he would clearly be the lesser evil. Following Ritchie's lead, the Jacksonians called a mixed caucus-convention to meet early in January 1828.[63]

While the Junto party was grudgingly falling in behind Jackson, an

Anti-Jackson party was also taking shape. It began in 1822 when John H. Pleasants became editor of the *Lynchburg Virginian* in the southwestern Piedmont and started to challenge the states' rights views of Ritchie. Pleasants offered a nationalist program of tariffs and internal improvements, defended the rights of Virginians who were not members of the Tidewater-Piedmont planter class, and vigorously supported a referendum on constitutional reform. Pleasants was so delighted when Ritchie's candidate Crawford was defeated in the 1824 election that he wrote a long, gloating editorial announcing "the Death of Thomas Ritchie." Soon afterward Pleasants moved to Richmond and established a new Adams newspaper, the *Constitutional Whig*. Though a nationalist, Pleasants was still influenced by the republican tradition, and he tried to undermine Ritchie's reputation by accusing him and the Junto of being a corrupt court party like the one under King George III. He was so successful that Clay and Webster decided to subsidize him.[64]

Although they constituted a minority party, the Adams men put on an effective campaign. In the summer of 1827 Clay's friend Francis T. Brooke accompanied Samuel Southard on an electioneering "Tour of the [Virginia] Springs." Two of the most prominent supporters of a constitutional convention—Archibald Stuart and Philip Doddridge—joined the campaign. Since the Adams party represented only a minority in the House of Delegates, Pleasants and his supporters decided to call a convention instead of a legislative caucus to kick off their presidential campaign. Early in September 1827 they announced that there would be an Adams convention the first week in January, and by the end of the year, 90 of 102 counties had selected delegates. For a time there was even talk of making Pleasants Adams's running mate. Clay was keeping a close eye on Virginia and was clearly impressed. "Virginia," he told Charles Hammond, "is not idle. A spirit is getting up there worthy of the best days of Rome."[65]

6

POLITICAL PARTIES IN 1828

After a two-month journey from Kentucky to New York City and a side trip to Dunstable, Massachusetts, to see his aging parents, Amos Kendall arrived in Washington on December 14, 1827. Since he had just won an important state election and had revived the bargain charge with his public letter to Clay, he received a warm partisan welcome. Van Buren and Green put together a $2,000 loan and welcomed Kendall and the Kentucky Jacksonians into the national Jackson party.

Kendall found Congress in Jacksonian hands, with Jackson majorities of 26–22 in the Senate and 114–100 in the House. The numbers were a blow to President Adams because it was the first time a president had lost control of both houses. Now with less than a year to go before the election, Adams faced the prospect of losing the presidency as well. His future lay in the hands of the two emerging political parties. The outcome of the election would depend, in large part, on how well each party carried out the many functions of a national political party: controlling Congress, establishing the party's position on important national issues, maintaining a powerful central committee, building a network of state and local parties, connecting with the emerging regencies and juntos, supporting a chain of newspapers, raising money, publishing addresses, dealing with party patronage, selecting a party leader and a compelling message, and, finally, getting out the vote. Americans have exaggerated the role of the election of 1828 in the rise of democracy. The real significance of that election was the rise of national political parties.

The Jacksonians were quick to use their numerical superiority to establish control over Congress. In a remarkable show of punctuality in a less than time-conscious era, all but six Jackson members of Congress arrived on time for the opening session. And as they arrived they found Van Buren, their acknowledged party leader, comfortably settled in Dr. Thornton's boardinghouse near the post office on F Street and issuing party orders. There he shared mess expenses and made political plans with party insiders Louis McLane of Delaware and two of his companions on his southern trip, Churchill C. Cambreleng and William Drayton.

On December 2, the day before Congress was to convene, the Little Magician held a party caucus to choose congressional leaders and decide on party policy. Eager as always to maintain a North-South alliance, he arranged for the nomination of Andrew Stevenson, a member of Thomas Ritchie's Richmond Junto, for Speaker of the House. The next day Stevenson was promptly elected by a party vote of 104 to 94 over incumbent Adams man John W. Taylor of New York. The growing partisanship can be seen in the voting of the New York delegation, which scuttled Taylor's chances by giving him only twelve of the state's thirty-two votes. Southerners also turned against Taylor because of his antislavery position in the Missouri debates.

Stevenson, who had the power to appoint committees, justified Van Buren's confidence by giving the Jacksonians a majority on twenty-one of the twenty-eight House standing committees, including all the important ones. In the Senate, where the committees were elected by vote, the choices were just as partisan, and to cap off the Jackson superiority, Green was voted in as printer. The list of the new committee chairs in the Senate included the names of many future Jackson party leaders— Van Buren, Levi Woodbury, Richard M. Johnson, Mahlon Dickerson of New Jersey, John Branch of North Carolina, Robert Y. Hayne, Thomas H. Benton, and John H. Eaton. The changes did not go unnoticed. Shortly after the committees had been selected the *Albany Argus* printed the list of committee chairmen for both houses and pointed with pride to the names of New Yorkers.[1]

The Jackson men were not above playing dirty tricks on their opponents and glorifying their friends. To weaken Taylor, they spread stories accusing him of immoral behavior, and to keep a new leader from emerging among the Adams congressmen, Stevenson kept John Sergeant from becoming chair of the House Foreign Affairs Committee. In an effort to strengthen Jackson's heroic image, Congressman James

Hamilton Jr. made a motion to add a large depiction of the Old Hero at New Orleans to the historical murals recently installed in the Rotunda. The motion lost by a mostly partisan vote.[2]

Correctly identifying the most compelling economic issue of the day, and certainly of the campaign, the Jacksonians moved directly to the task of passing a tariff bill. They knew that it would be uphill going, for the Adams party had the built-in advantage of Henry Clay's American System. The Jackson men also knew that they would have to consider three major economic interests. The manufacturers of New England were demanding strong protection for their cotton and woolen goods. Southern cotton growers opposed such protection because it forced them to pay high prices for the garments, blankets, and other manufactured items used on their plantations. The farmers of many states, including New York, Pennsylvania, and Ohio, wanted protection for their iron, raw wool, hemp, and flax.

In shaping the bill the Jackson men felt they could ignore the New Englanders, who were likely to vote for Adams regardless of tariff rates. They also had little incentive to please the South, which was generally written off to Jackson. That left the farm states stretching west from New York and Pennsylvania to Missouri, states whose voters strongly supported Clay's American System but had not yet committed themselves on the presidency.

Since the House would send the tariff bill to the Committee of Manufactures, Stevenson and Van Buren were careful in choosing its members. Unwilling to ruffle feathers unnecessarily, they reappointed incumbent chairman Rollin C. Mallary of Vermont, one of the senior members of the House. Mallary, a strong protectionist and Adams man, had been a prominent figure at the Harrisburg tariff convention. To offset Mallary, however, they surrounded him with five Jacksonians representing the key states of New York, Pennsylvania, Ohio, Kentucky, and South Carolina and one other Adams man. The dominant member was Silas Wright of the Albany Regency, who represented the sheep farmers of northwestern New York. A man of good judgment with only one fault— he drank too much—Wright would one day be a leading candidate for president. Now only thirty-two and in his first term in Congress, he was determined to do all he could for "the great interest of agriculture."[3]

Wright had little to fear from the Adams administration. The president could have used his annual message to push for tariff protection but was unwilling to run the risk of losing Virginia and other southern states. From New York a disappointed Jabez Hammond warned Clay that the failure to mention tariff protection would hurt Adams in the Empire State. Another chance came on December 24, when representatives from the Harrisburg convention presented Congress with the resolutions adopted there, but Mallary was unable to find any support in his committee for the high rates for manufactures in the convention schedules.[4]

Instead, the committee lowered the rates on woolen manufactures and raised the rates on raw wool and other raw materials. In raising these rates, the committee carried over the deceptive minimum tariff system from the 1827 bill and introduced another deceptive practice—mixed duties. Importers of cheap raw wool, for example, were asked to pay an ad valorem tariff of only 40 percent, but on top of that they faced a specific tariff of 7 cents. Thus, for the cheapest wool costing 4 cents a pound, the total tariff per pound would be 1.6 cents (40 percent) plus 7 cents, for a total of 8.6 cents, or more than 200 percent. Critics were soon calling the new bill the "tariff of abominations."

But Wright and Van Buren pressed on. Wright resisted all Mallary's efforts to raise the rates on woolen manufactures and lower those on wool and other raw materials. Van Buren frequently wandered over from the Senate side of the Capitol and could be seen looking in on the House Manufactures Committee and twisting arms. The committee brought the bill to the floor of the House on January 31, but it was not passed until April 22 by the narrow vote of 105 to 94. The southern members voted almost unanimously against the bill, the middle and western states almost as unanimously for it. The members from New England, who opposed the reduction in rates for manufactures, voted two to one against it. Without the New York vote of 27–6 for the bill, it would not have passed.

Previous tariff bills had made it through the House only to fail in the Senate. To make sure this did not happen again, the Jacksonians added several amendments to please the manufacturers of New England. One of the amendments, raising the rates on woolens, passed only because Jacksonians Van Buren and Woodbury voted for it. After a number of changes the Senate passed the bill 26 to 21. Again the middle states and the West were unanimously for it, the South against it. In the end the bill passed because New Englanders swallowed the low rates on manufactures as the best they could get and accepted the bill 6 to 5. John Randolph cleverly and maliciously quipped, "The bill referred to manufactures of no sort or kind except the manufacture of a President of the United States."[5] It was too early to tell whether Randolph was correct, but if he was, the kingmaker was Martin Van Buren, who had used a variety of "abominations" to keep rates on manufactures low enough to prevent a rebellion in the South and high enough to salvage key votes from New England.[6]

Each party maintained a central committee in Washington, but neither was especially active. A brief flare-up at the end of December 1827, while Kendall was in Washington, provides some insight into how the committees operated. The Adams central committee had helped Henry Clay gather a large collection of statements denying the bargain charge, but it was not involved in publishing the result. Clay wrote his own defense, Adams edited it, and Peter Force of the *National Journal* published it. That address—a massive pamphlet of ninety-one pages—was more Clay's work than the committee's.[7]

Soon after the address appeared, the Jackson central committee announced in the *Telegraph* that it would respond, but it published nothing until May, when the *Telegraph* carried a long article refuting Clay's arguments. Meanwhile, the Adams central committee kept the controversy alive by placing articles in the press maintaining that Kendall was preparing the response and had made the long trip to Washington to get instructions from his party's central committee. Credit for managing the election campaigns should go to Van Buren, Green, and Clay rather than to the central committees.

The most active central committee was in Nashville, not Washington. After being formed in the spring of 1827 to defend Old Hickory, the Nashville central committee worked well and soon earned the nickname of the "whitewash" committee. Its two leading figures—William B. Lewis and John Overton—knew how to work with Jackson, whose notorious sensitivity and hot temper could easily have destroyed his campaign.

When the committee was first set up, Lewis and Overton had to deal with a tense, frustrated Jackson, who felt as though his hands were "pinioned."[8] He was furious about the efforts to destroy his character, yet he knew that he must let others play the major role in defending his reputation. As the charges mounted—there were at least forty—the relationship between Jackson and the committee grew stronger. The job required great tact and trust on both sides. In one letter that must have angered Jackson, Overton asked him whether Hugh McGary, who had accused Rachel and Andrew of adultery, had actually seen them living together. When Robert Weakley accused Jackson of slave trading, the Old Hero responded with a tough letter grilling him with a number of specific, detailed questions. Showing his confidence in Lewis, he sent the unsealed letter to Lewis first, asking him to make any necessary changes.[9]

A few months before the election the committee and Jackson were working so well together that they were able to cope quite easily with a final series of charges that Jackson had helped Aaron Burr create an independent nation on both sides of the lower Mississippi in 1805 and 1806. The committee took the charges in stride, and one of its members, Alfred Balch, calmly told Jackson that the Burr charge was a very "sm[all] affair."[10]

Below the level of the central committees, both parties were using state and local committees and conventions to build their organizations. Committees had been used in many states since the winning of independence, but nowhere more efficiently than in Kentucky in the 1820s. Arthur Lee Campbell of Louisville, for example, boasted to Andrew Jackson in 1827 that he and "half a dozen, intelligent and zealous friends [had built a] System of Committees" that had "overwhelmed" their "adversaries" in "disgraceful ruin."[11] As the use of committees spread, parties were able to unite members in the smallest villages with those in the state and national party, eventually making a nationwide, mass political party possible.

Conventions were less common than committees, but they were not entirely new. The founding fathers had called a convention to draw up the U.S. Constitution, and the states had called conventions to ratify it. Political parties had called conventions in New Jersey and Maryland as early as 1800. Settlers in Ohio had used conventions to achieve statehood. Religious and reform movements had used them to press their demands. But conventions had not been used regularly for ordinary political tasks such as nominating candidates. Until the 1820s candidates for office either nominated themselves or were nominated by legislative caucuses or special mass meetings.[12]

Conventions became more popular when politicians found that they could be used to solve a specific problem. When parties were first formed, they had a hard time nominating just one candidate for a given district. As a result, two or even three party candidates might divide the vote in that district, allowing a minority outsider to win the election.

Legislative caucuses did not provide the answer because they could not be used in districts where a party had no representative. Imaginative party leaders soon discovered that they could solve the problem by calling conventions, which could decide among multiple candidates. In the run-up to the 1824 election conventions were used to nominate candidates and plan for the state and national elections of that year. As with most political innovations, the Middle Atlantic states (New Jersey and Pennsylvania) led the way, but conventions appeared in Illinois and Virginia as well. The Adams party in Delaware and the Jackson party in Maryland called nominating conventions early in 1827, followed later in the year by both parties in Louisiana and by the Anti-Masons in New York. In the four weeks between mid-December 1827 and mid-January 1828, both parties held conventions in Virginia, Kentucky, Ohio, and Pennsylvania.[13]

As political parties became more acceptable in the 1820s, the use of conventions grew. Conventions were ideal because the parties needed open public meetings at which members could vote on difficult questions. Conventions also blended in nicely with committees. Local committees chose delegates for county conventions, which in turn chose delegates for state conventions. Conventions eventually operated at every level—town, ward, militia company, county, state, and, in time, nation. They chose committees, nominated candidates, printed ballots and handbills, published addresses, and organized parades and other events to bring voters to the polls. But the Jackson and Adams men in 1828 did not go all the way: they did not call a national convention to nominate presidential and vice presidential candidates. The first national nominating convention was held by the Anti-Mason party in September 1831, followed in December by the National Republican party and in May 1832 by the Democratic party.

In the rivalry to set up strong state parties, both sides were tempted by the growing number of state central committees, often called regencies or juntos, that had taken the lead in devising new political techniques. The strongest state committee in New England, and the only one to pose a threat to Adams's supremacy there, was Isaac Hill's Concord Regency in New Hampshire. The alliance of Martin Van Buren's Albany Regency, Thomas Ritchie's Richmond Junto, and John Overton's Nashville Junto provided the framework for the Jackson party. Amos Kendall had committed his Frankfort Junto to Jackson with his long journey from

Kentucky to Washington. And even though Elijah Hayward's organization in southwestern Ohio had not been given a regal name, it matched the others in its accomplishments.

Political parties also relied on an organized party press. Until the 1820s newspaper editors did not rank very high in either the American economy or society. Most often they labored alone, writing articles, setting type, editing, and then printing, folding, and cutting—a dirty job with a meager income. Upper-class Americans such as Samuel Bell, Josiah S. Johnston, and John Quincy Adams looked down on them; they referred to newspapermen scornfully as mere "printers," not editors, and sometimes called them "skunks" or "wretches."[14]

And many of the newspapers they produced were less than impressive. Almost always small, four-page, weekly publications, the entire newspaper was printed on one sheet of paper and then folded and cut. Advertisements filled pages one and four, leaving only the two inside pages for news, editorials, and features. The finished product was expensive (almost a dollar a copy in today's money) and hard to read because the print was so small. Circulation was also small—perhaps an average of 500 copies per issue.

But the years after the War of 1812 brought revolutionary changes in the techniques of printing and publishing and a great increase in the number of newspapers. Daily newspapers became available. The circulation of even the smaller newspapers rose well above 500 and reached 2,000 a year for the better-known papers. The *United States Telegraph* once claimed an annual circulation of 20,000. Even the smallest newspapers reached many more readers than the circulation figures indicated, because nonsubscribers could easily find a copy to read free of charge in taverns, hotels, village stores, post offices, and the homes of family and friends.[15]

Most important, editors no longer worked alone, and the quality of the newspapers improved immensely. The editors had become the respected owners and managers of significant business enterprises, supervising employees and taking political stands. They openly backed political parties. With their growing influence over the spread of ideas and information, these new editors were providing vital links that brought party, voter, and government together and sped up the rise of democracy.

Neither side had a monopoly on capable editors. In Cincinnati, for example, Adamsite Charles Hammond of the *Liberty Hall and Cincinnati Gazette* was a match for Jacksonian Moses Dawson of the *Inquisitor and Cincinnati Advertiser,* although he also had to compete with Elijah Hayward and his *National Republican.* In Philadelphia John Binns of the *Democratic Press* and Robert Walsh of the *National Gazette and Literary Messenger,* both of whom were Adams men, kept pace with John Norvell of the *Aurora and Franklin Gazette* and Stephen Simpson of the *Columbian Observer* (which went bankrupt in 1826). In Washington Peter Force of the *National Journal* and Joseph Gales and William W. Seaton of the *National Intelligencer* had their hands full competing with Duff Green and his *United States Telegraph.*

Other Jackson newspapers included the *Eastern Argus* of Portland, Maine (edited by Francis O. J. Smith); Concord's *New-Hampshire Patriot* (Isaac Hill); the *Statesman* of Boston (Nathaniel Greene); Harrisburg's *Pennsylvania Intelligencer* (Simon Cameron); the *Hartford Times* (John M. Niles); the *New York Evening Post* (William Cullen Bryant); the *New York Enquirer* (Mordecai Noah); the *Albany Argus* (Edwin Croswell); the *Baltimore Republican and Commercial Advertiser* (Dabney Smith Carr); the *Richmond Enquirer* (Thomas Ritchie); the *Star* of Raleigh, North Carolina (Alexander Lawrence); the *Argus of Western America* in Frankfort, Kentucky (Amos Kendall and Francis Preston Blair); and Nashville's *Republican and State Gazette* (John Fitzgerald).

Adams newspapers included Concord's *New Hampshire Journal* (Jacob B. Moore); Boston's *Massachusetts Journal* (Alexander and Edward Everett); the *Literary Cadet* of Providence, Rhode Island (Sylvester S. Southworth); Rochester, New York's *Telegraph* and *Anti-Masonic Enquirer* (both edited by Thurlow Weed); *Niles' Register* (Hezekiah Niles) and the *Patriot* (Isaac Munroe) in Baltimore; the *Constitutional Whig* of Richmond (John H. Pleasants); Columbus's *Ohio State Journal* (John Bailhache); Lexington's *Kentucky Reporter* (Thomas Smith); the *Register* of Raleigh, North Carolina (Joseph and Weston Gales); Louisville's *Focus* (William W. Worsley); and the *Nashville Whig* (John P. Erwin).

To support these newspapers the parties had to find new ways to raise money. Clay and Webster had made some progress by setting up a fund that they used to support struggling Adams newspapers. They hoped to raise additional funds from their wealthy supporters in Boston, Philadelphia, and other northern cities. The Jacksonians also focused on supporting Jackson newspapers and starting new ones. It was rumored that Van Buren had a fund of $30,000 to $50,000 for this purpose, but there was little evidence to confirm the amount. There were other ways to raise money and cover expenses. Toward the end of the 1828 campaign the *United States Telegraph* became so valuable that Jackson congress-men and senators paid Duff Green to send bundles of his newspaper into their districts. Both sides took illegal advantage of the franking privilege of congressmen and senators and mailed not only newspapers but also candidates' biographies, broadsides, election buttons, and other campaign items free of postage. There was also the questionable tactic of lending money to editors; well-timed loans from Van Buren's fund brought Green and Kendall aboard the Jacksonian movement. Robert V. Remini estimates that the parties and individual politicians spent as much as a million dollars in the campaign.[16]

Much of this money went to publish and circulate addresses, which had first appeared in America during the years leading up to the Rev-olution, written by patriots hoping to persuade Americans to revolt. Similar addresses appeared during the wars between Federalists and Anti-Federalists and then between Federalists and Republicans to determine the sort of government America should have. Although the addresses of 1828 were not as graceful or as literary as the earlier ones, they may be just as valuable historically because they offer a convenient way to learn what Americans thought about their society—particularly about the in-teraction of republicanism and democracy.[17]

A few of the addresses were personal in nature or narrow in subject matter, such as Clay's address on the bargain charge and Andrew Er-win's attack on Jackson for speculating in slaves, but most were broad statements by state committees defending their party while denouncing the opposition. Confident that their words would win over the voters, party leaders on both sides published thousands of copies of these docu-ments—30,000 of the Virginia Adams party address alone.

This Virginia address and the Jacksonian address in New Hampshire show how similar in their assumptions and how different in their opin-ions these addresses could be. Both were apocalyptic statements proud of American republicanism and democracy, determined to keep both yet fearful that the two were in great danger. Repeating some of the worst fears of the Old Republicans of the South, the two addresses warned that corruption was endangering the idyllic society left by the found-ing fathers. The New Hampshire men decried "the uniform practice of electing the Secretary of State to the office of President," which was "as-similating our government to a monarchy."[18] The Virginia men replied that the election of a military man as impetuous as Andrew Jackson would undermine "the principle, sacred in every well ordered Republic, which proclaims the military subordinate to the civil power."[19] They both agreed, as the Virginians put it, that "in this hour of danger" they must "save the Temple of Liberty from pollution."[20]

Yet they could not agree on the source of the "pollution." For the Adams men in Virginia it lay in the growing tendency of Americans to transfer their "affections" from "republican simplicity and virtue, to military pomp and glory."[21] For the New Hampshire men the source lay in the corrupt bargain that had brought Adams and Clay into office.

The general tone and style of the two addresses were also quite different. The Virginia address started on a defensive note, first denying that Jackson's plurality in the 1824 popular vote proved that he was more popular than Adams and then denying that Clay had disobeyed the instructions of the Kentucky legislature by backing Adams in the second election. The entire document had an unemotional, constitutional tone. There were at least thirty political science words in the address, half of them the words *constitution* or *constitutional*. The address ended with the promise that the people of Virginia, with their "uniform devotion to civil liberty" and their history of "noble daring in the defense of freedom," would defend the republic. This was followed by a list of resolutions, the first of which stated, almost as an afterthought, that John Quincy Adams was "a fit person to be supported for the Office of President."[22]

In contrast, the Jackson address started aggressively by reviewing the corrupt bargain charge and by giving examples of the "deep grudge" that had once existed between Adams and Clay.[23] It went on to accuse the administration of rewarding western congressmen John Scott and Daniel Cook for voting for Adams in the House runoff. The address ended with a flourish:

Believing that the great mass of the people cannot be corrupted . . . believing that the character of Andrew Jackson as an honest man, as a pure and incorruptible patriot, as a prudent, discreet and sagacious statesman, cannot be shaken—knowing that a great majority of the people are firmly attached to the principles of the revolution—we have full faith that the cause of the people, the cause of truth and freedom, WILL PREVAIL.[24]

The differences between the two statements are revealing. The Adams address defended the constitutionality of the Adams program and promised that the people of Virginia would defend the republic but said little about Adams himself. The Jackson address was much more personal. It attacked the opposition for its violations of republican virtue and promised that Jackson would save the republic.

In dealing with the issue of political patronage the Adams and Jackson parties shared a common problem. In American society *patronage* was a dangerous word. Americans had revolted in 1775 partly because they believed that the king was acting corruptly in dispensing money and jobs to his favorites. Many Americans still felt the same way about patronage, but others were beginning to believe that patronage was a useful tool in the new American politics. The Adams men could not agree on how to distribute jobs. Clay and Webster realistically recognized the value of party patronage, but Adams still thought like a 1775 revolutionary and refused to condone the use of an immoral spoils system. The constant pressure of Federalists looking for positions made the Adams dilemma even greater.

As the opposition party, the Jacksonians had their own problem with patronage. Trying to get into office, they saw two different ways of doing it. The regency-junto types in the party—men such as Kendall, Van Buren, and Green—believed that they must offer their followers the spoils of office, whereas Old Republican idealists such as Ritchie resolutely opposed patronage. Jackson talked like an Old Republican on this subject, but Kendall and Van Buren thought they could win him over. During the campaign the Jacksonians tried to evade the issue of patronage by resorting to the slogan "Jackson and Reform," in which "reform" could be interpreted as either doing away with patronage entirely or removing officeholders who had behaved corruptly.

The presence of John McLean as head of the Post Office, where many of the patronage jobs were located, complicated the issue. McLean was serving under Adams but was devoted to Calhoun, and much like Adams, he refused to dismiss anyone unless he had betrayed the public trust. McLean had outraged Adams men in New Hampshire and nearby Massachusetts by refusing to remove the head of the Concord Regency, Isaac Hill, as the chief mail contractor in the state after he went over to Jackson in 1825. Adams congressman Edward Everett of Massachusetts, who had already had one run-in with the contractor, wrote to McLean in August 1828 to try to convince the postmaster general to remove Hill.

Everett started aggressively by asking why McLean gave Hill the "power" to compose "filthy libel" and then "distribute his venom throughout the community." "The Chief [Mail] Contractor," he added, should never be the "most virulent and unscrupulous foe of the government."

Everett believed that "the government ought to employ its friends," and he used a quotation from Thomas Jefferson to back up his point.[25]

Clearly irritated, McLean replied immediately that "on the subject of patronage we differ essentially." In appointing a man to office the government had no right to insist that he always "sustain the general measures of the Administration." He dismissed the example of Jefferson, arguing that the Virginian had a unique right to demand such loyalty because he had just been voted into office for a noble political cause. Hill, he admitted, was "now engaged in a decided opposition to the Administration," but since he "strictly perform[ed] his duties," he would not be touched.[26]

Everett also replied quickly. Insisting that all presidents were elected on the basis of a special cause, he rejected the idea that Jefferson was an exception. Earlier in the correspondence Everett had said that patronage was crucial to parties because "the hope of office" was what bound "the mass of the parties together."[27] Now he added the corollary that office was more important in America than in England, where business, family, and "overgrown naval and military establishments" offered alternative opportunities for accumulating honors and wealth that were not available in America. If Jackson was elected and refused to use patronage, it would "cost him every vote out of Tennessee." "The great strength of the Executive," said Everett, "is in its patronage."[28]

This exchange of letters suggests that on the eve of the 1828 election there was more support for patronage than historians have generally believed. Recent efforts to paint a picture of persistent hostility to patronage must deal with Everett's spirited defense of it in these letters. Everett's views are all the more significant because of who he was and who he was not. A member of the Boston aristocracy, an orator, scholar, intellectual, and preacher, a close friend of Henry Clay, he was not a member of a political regency or junto. Like the letters between "Onslow" and "Patrick Henry" (or Calhoun and Adams), the Everett-McLean correspondence adds to our understanding of the impact of republican ideas in America more than fifty years after the Revolution. The changes in the economy and society had made republicanism more tolerant of politicians and party patronage than it had been in 1775.

One of the most vital tests of a national party in a democratic society is its ability to take its candidate and its message to the people. Each of the two parties in 1828 had to present the better side of a strong but flawed candidate. The Adams party could be proud of its intellectual, experienced, highly moral and sophisticated president, but it was also defensive about his stubbornness, coldness, and occasional arrogance. Jacksonians conceded that Jackson had a bad temper, had not traveled, and lacked a college education, but they turned this liability into a virtue. Having grown up on the frontier, they argued, he was a man of nature who had the "practical common sense, that power and discrimination of judgment . . . which are more valuable than all the acquired learning of a sage." The big problem for each party was how to present its candidate's better side.[29]

As democracy became more established during the 1830s and 1840s, stump speaking, lecturing, and campaign tours became the standard way of promoting candidates and spreading the party's message, but in 1828 these techniques were not common. One reason was the republican taboo against electioneering. Another was the difficulty of travel, which still kept Americans at home. The third was the lack of precedents. Although Jacksonians Atwater, Eaton, and Green and administration cabinet members Clay, Southard, Barbour, and Rush occasionally went on the road, their efforts were not typical of the campaign.[30]

If stump speaking had been a common method of campaigning, the administration party would have had an advantage, since three of the greatest speakers in American history—Webster, Clay, and Everett—were all Adams men. But none of them made a notable speech. Clay and Webster did go on several campaign tours, but Clay spent most of the time defending himself against the bargain charge, and Webster did most of his speaking in New England, which was already conceded to Adams.

To fill the void the parties turned to mudslinging—a convenient alternative, since each party had a powerful chain of newspapers to circulate its attacks. Throwing mud was not new—Federalists, for example, had tried to discredit Thomas Jefferson with lurid tales of his relationship with Sally Hemings—but there seems to have been an unusual amount of it in 1828. Adams men could blame Jackson: his long career full of violent events had left him vulnerable to attack, and he was unusually suspicious of his enemies. Another cause was the unique set of circumstances that linked the election of 1828 with the preceding election, thus encouraging Americans to look back and assign blame. One could also blame the rise of a new generation of politician-newspapermen, with no established code of behavior. Whatever the cause, political mudslinging became one of the ways the two parties tried to spread their message and define the candidates.

For the Jacksonians the bargain charge was the strongest weapon because it enabled them to align themselves with democracy. By giving Adams the votes to win the election, they insisted, Clay had blocked the will of the people. Kendall was particularly effective on this issue because he knew the Clays so well. He had tutored Clay's children, and in 1823 Clay had paid him to write articles for an Ohio newspaper attacking Adams for making concessions to the British at the Peace of Ghent. In addition Kendall was able to remind his readers that he had read a letter from Clay stating that he planned to support Adams in the House election of 1825.

The charges panicked Clay supporters in the Kentucky legislature into starting an investigation to clear Clay's name. The investigation, which took place in February 1828, had the opposite result, for Kendall used it to reveal his Ohio articles against Adams. Kendall continued to make the charge in a series of public letters to Clay, and on the eve of the election Duff Green repeated all the details in his *Telegraph*. The pressure from the bargain charge was so great that before the campaign was over, Clay had responded with nine formal addresses on the subject, including the one in December 1827 that had commanded so much attention.

Three smaller attacks were keeping Adams on the defensive. In the spring of 1825 the new president bought a billiards table for $50 and set it up in the President's House. An innocent diversion, the table went unnoticed for a year until it was mentioned in a government report in which Adams said he had purchased it with private funds. The table became a campaign issue in the spring and fall of 1826 when both Green and Kendall attacked the president for encouraging gambling by playing billiards. As with the corrupt bargain charge, the administration kept the story alive by issuing a series of weak refutations in Hammond's *Liberty Hall and Cincinnati Gazette*, the *Boston Centinel*, and Walsh's *National Gazette and Literary Messenger* in Philadelphia. When Walsh observed that it was not unusual for people of wealth to have billiards tables, the remark only encouraged the *Charleston Mercury* to label Adams an effete aristocrat.[31]

The story aroused special interest in the West, where billiards tables were little known. One western writer tried to educate his readers by estimating that a table cost as much as a pair of wagon horses. Adams men in Ohio reported ruefully that the billiards story hurt Adams more than any other attack. Thomas Hart Benton mentioned the table in an article describing the supposed regal luxury of the president's parlor.

The *National Journal* and the *National Intelligencer* ignored the story for a year and then tried in vain to brush it off by calling it a trivial matter. The inability to dismiss this rather insignificant story was another setback for the Adams press.

Another, more ludicrous attack was the story relating to the czar of Russia. While Adams was minister to Russia, a young chambermaid on his staff wrote a letter in which she made some casual remarks about the czar. On being informed of the letter, the czar was so amused and curious that he asked to speak to her. So during his next audience with the czar, Adams brought the woman in for a brief (and public) conversation. This humdrum story had no political appeal until it appeared in a short sketch of Jackson published by Isaac Hill in which Hill accused Adams of being a pimp who had procured a woman for the lascivious pleasure of the czar. Once the story appeared in the sketch, it spread throughout the Jackson press.[32]

In both these stories the Jackson newspapers treated Adams badly, but there was also a third story for which Adams must bear full responsibility. On his way back to Washington from Quincy in October 1827, the president stopped in Baltimore to take part in the celebration of the defense of the city against the British in the War of 1812. Asked to give a toast, he rose and said, "Ebony and Topaz, General Ross's posthumous coat of arms, and the republican militia men who gave it."[33] When his listeners appeared confused by the toast, Adams explained that "Ebony and Topaz" came from Voltaire's *Le Blanc et Le Noir:* Ebony stood for the spirit of evil (General Robert Ross, the British commander at Baltimore), and Topaz stood for the good spirit (the American militiamen defending the city). As for Ross's coat of arms, the king had granted a new wording to reward the general, who had died in the battle.

For the Jacksonians, who had been portraying Adams as a stuffy old scholar, the president's supercilious toast was a gift from the gods. It was bad enough for Adams to quote from a sophisticated writer like Voltaire, who was hardly household reading for the average American voter, but it was even worse to throw in the irrelevant coat of arms, something most Americans were barely familiar with. Worst of all was the president's being forced to explain the toast. Realizing that he could add nothing to Adams's discomfiture, Duff Green said he would not comment because he could not match the president's knowledge of "Oriental literature."[34] A dismayed Charles Hammond told Henry Clay that he "wish[ed] Mr. Adams's *ebony and topaz* were Submersed in the deepest profound of the bathos." Then, with a flash of understanding of the special role of famous men in American politics, he added, "You great men have no priviledge [sic] to commit blunders. You belong to others."[35]

There was much less humor and far more hatred in the attacks on Jackson. The most persistent and virulent were the charges that he had murdered six militiamen and that he and Rachel had committed adultery. These attacks, which had so angered Jackson earlier in the campaign, continued even though the Nashville committee challenged them. If anything, they got worse, for Hammond, who had started the adultery stories, combined them in a pamphlet entitled *General Jackson's Domestic Relations.* In January 1828 Hammond began to publish a newspaper extra in Cincinnati entitled *Truth's Advocate and Monthly Anti-Jackson Expositor.* Hammond used the *Truth's Advocate* to spread false stories, one of which called Jackson's father a mulatto and his mother a prostitute. Moses Dawson tried to refute this libel with his own monthly extra, *Friend of Reform & Corruption's Adversary,* also in Cincinnati, but he could not silence Hammond.

Making the same mistake as the Kentucky legislators in dealing with the bargain charge, the administration men in the new Congress demanded an investigation of Jackson's behavior. Unfortunately for the administration, the House Military Affairs Committee, to which the question was sent, was made up of six Jacksonians and only one Adams man and was chaired by James Hamilton Jr. of South Carolina, an ardent Jackson man. Not surprisingly, on February 11, 1828, the committee came in with a report exonerating Jackson.[36]

That report triggered a flurry of anti-Jackson reports from the Adams party, drawn up in a form and language that made them appear to be official congressional documents. The most vicious was the first of a series of "Coffin Handbills" published by John Binns in Philadelphia as a supplement to his *Democratic Press.* The first handbill, which appeared near the end of January 1828, was entitled "Monumental Inscriptions" and featured two rows of three coffins each, with brief attacks on Jackson at the top and bottom. Each coffin was topped by a skull and crossbones and a detailed inscription. About half of these contained the poem "Mournful Tragedy," which called the executions of the militiamen "A dreadful Deed—A bloody Act / Of needless Cruelty."[37]

Shocking as they were, handbills featuring coffins were nothing new. Revolutionaries had used them in England in the seventeenth century, and after the battles of Lexington and Concord, patriots had published a handbill depicting coffins titled "A Bloody Butchery by the British Troops; or the Runaway Fight of the Regulars."[38] Binns's handbill was widely copied and appeared in at least half a dozen different formats, some of which went beyond the six militiamen and attacked Jackson for other misdeeds, such as dueling, slave owning, and slave trading.

That same year artist David Claypoole Johnston produced a print drawn in the shape of a bust of Jackson attacking him for alleged violent misdeeds. Johnston used a theme taken from *King Richard III* (act 5, scene 3) in which the king prepares for the Battle of Richmond and is haunted by the ghosts of the men he has executed. Images of Jackson's victims appeared on his epaulets and face, part of his collar was made up of cannons, and the bust rested on a steaming cauldron, with a smoking chimney protruding from Jackson's head. The cannons and chimney not too subtly conveyed the idea that Jackson lost his temper too quickly and too often and that he invariably resorted to force to settle controversies.

Binns's motif of six coffins spread rapidly. Writing to Jackson on March 4, 1828, barely a month after the first handbill appeared in Philadelphia, John Eaton reported that "Binns 6 militia, & 6 Coffins . . . fairly inundated" New Hampshire before the state election.[39]

An equally dangerous problem for Jackson was his marriage. Americans had been brought up on stories of sexual seduction in which republican virtue invariably won out over immoral behavior. Private immorality, it was assumed, endangered public society. Now the public was faced with the story of a presidential candidate who, the Adams men charged, had stolen another man's wife and lived with her in adultery. It was a major sex scandal. According to the traditionally republican Adams view, acts such as these, especially when committed by a candidate for high office, must be condemned. But the market revolution, with its migration of young men and women into the cities, had disrupted the family and brought gender roles into question. This loosening of social ties had engendered another romantic (Jacksonian) view that such acts were private in nature and that love should be allowed to triumph over legalisms.

These opposing social views blended easily with the political views of each party's supporters. The reformist point of view was drawn from the evangelical Christians, who were moving to the Adams (later Whig) party. Products of the Second Great Awakening, these Adams party men believed that the government had a right to enforce individual discipline and institutional reform. On the other side, however, the Catholics, free thinkers, and others who voted for the Jacksonians had little interest in committing themselves to such stern moralism from the government.

Despite their different positions, each side believed that it was taking the side of republican freedom and virtue against the side of power and corruption—the Adams men by defending the state against immorality, and the Jackson men by defending the couple's right to domestic privacy. Faced with the difficult task of protecting the Jacksons from these accusations, the Jacksonians portrayed the Old Hero as a martyr and condemned the Adams party for destroying his privacy. Using republican language, they accused the Adams party of being engaged in a conspiracy. One of the questions to be answered by the election was whether Jackson should be defeated because he and Rachel had violated the public moral code, or whether he should be elected because the Adams party was interfering in his private life.[40]

Both parties turned enthusiastically to the final duty of a national political party—getting out the vote. Ever since the American Revolution, political groups of one sort or another had shown great ingenuity in developing campaign tactics that entertained the voters and drew them to the polls. In an age when there were no professional sports teams, no movies, no radio or television, politics became the principal source of entertainment, and it was something that could be carried on at the town and county levels. The most common tactic was simply holding a meeting or staging a parade at the same time something important, such as a militia muster or a court session, was taking place. Using the model they knew well—soldiering—party members would march from one part of town to another, advertising the party's goals as they went. They often identified themselves by wearing the party symbol, such as a hickory branch. To punctuate their message they might shoot off rifles or even cannons.

The climax would come when, to celebrate their cause, the marchers performed some dramatic act such as erecting a tall pole or pushing a large ball, sometimes from one town to another. Raising a pole was not a new idea. In 1775 patriots raised liberty poles to denounce the British; half a century later Jackson men or Adams men raised hickory or ash poles to honor their party and attack their opponents. These were not trivial operations; by 1828 the height of the poles had reached one hundred feet.

Even though custom dictated that only men could march, women did not let themselves be excluded. If they were sympathetic with the paraders, the women would illuminate their homes; if not, they left them dark. This practice sometimes invited retaliation: the marchers would not hesitate to stop in front of a hostile house and utter in unison a series of groans. Lighted homes would get a series of cheers.[41]

One of the most successful parades took place in Baltimore during the celebration of the city's defense. What started as a salute to heroic Americans in the War of 1812 was quickly converted into a rally for Andrew Jackson. Many of the seven hundred paraders wore hickory leaves, the crowd gave three cheers for Old Hickory, and the marchers fired off several cannons. Afterward the crowd consumed three bullocks, and the principal speaker gave an address celebrating the heroism of the Old Hero. The organizer of the celebration, former Federalist lawyer Roger B. Taney, would soon become Jackson's attorney general.[42]

Often the party men sang as they marched. The most popular ballad was "The Hunters of Kentucky," which glorified the riflemen defending New Orleans from the British. "Jackson," the ballad went, "was wide awake, and / wasn't scar'd with trifles, / for well he knew what aim we take / with our Kentucky rifles."[43] A French observer several years later compared the parades to Catholic religious processions in Mexico.[44] The parades and the music gave the marchers a sense of belonging to a powerful movement.

To create pride in party membership, both parties encouraged the manufacture and distribution of campaign materials. The fad began in 1824 with the visit of Lafayette, grew during the election of 1824 and after the deaths of Jefferson and Adams in 1826, and became a significant part of the electoral process in 1828. One silk kerchief made in 1824 served to welcome Lafayette to Castle Garden at the foot of Manhattan Island in New York. A John Quincy Adams bandana honored the new president at his inauguration in 1825, and small busts of Andrew Jackson decorated Jackson bandanas in 1828. By then the modest trickle of campaign materials had turned into a torrent of political tickets, portrait prints, circulars, commemorative china, snuffboxes, ribbons, sheet music, political tokens and buttons, whiskey flasks, and pewter goblets, all appropriately inscribed for one candidate or another.[45] When Martin Van Buren traveled through western New York in 1828 to learn about the Anti-Masonic movement, he carried large boxes of these campaign materials to distribute to his followers.

On the eve of the 1828 election neither the Jackson nor the Adams party had become a truly national organization. The variety of their party names gave them away. The Jacksonians indiscriminately called themselves the Democratic party, the Democratic-Republican party, the Republican party, and occasionally even the National Republican party, but they were most commonly known as the Jackson party. The Adams men preferred the Republican party, the National Republican party, or sometimes the People's party, but they were usually known as the Adams party. Until the parties abandoned the names of their candidates, they would be considered personal factions and could not be thought of as political parties as we now know them.

Another indication that these were not yet national parties lay in the voting results of the 1827 and 1828 congressional elections. One important attribute of a vigorous two-party system is a high percentage of close elections. If we assume that a close election is one in which the winner receives 55 percent or less of the vote and the loser 45 percent or more (a differential, or gap, of 10 points or less), the elections in 1827–1828 do not reveal a widespread two-party system. In only 12 percent of the elections was the differential 10 points or less; in contrast, in 1839–1840, when the second two-party system was finally in operation, the differential was 10 points or less in 43 percent of the elections, and that percentage rose to 55 percent in 1849–1850.[46]

But in the context of 1828 the Jackson party had more right to claim national pretensions than did its opponents. In Congress, even though their hold was precarious and party voting was not the norm, the Jackson men had gained enough control to focus on the central issue of the day, the tariff, and pass a tariff bill that promised to help them in the coming election. Both central committees were strong enough to deal with the bargain charge, but there is no clear evidence that they did much more. For the Jackson party the Nashville central committee did more to defend Jackson than the Washington committee, and the most effective central figure in Washington was Duff Green of the *United States Telegraph,* who coordinated the political efforts of the Jackson newspapers, the state organizations, the Nashville committee, and Jackson himself. On the other side, Henry Clay made himself sick working to build a national Adams party.

The Jacksonians were also more successful in building a national network of state and local organizations, even though neither party had much success in the South. The Jacksonians surpassed the Adams men in party building partly because they succeeded in taking over the regencies and juntos in half a dozen states. In annexing these organizations they brought into their party politicians, editors, and in some cases public officials who helped them set up committees, publish newspapers, and raise money.

The Jackson state parties and newspapers were superior to those backing Adams because they were more aggressive and more willing to work with one another than their Adams counterparts were. The relationship between the New York and New Hampshire parties was particularly close. This cooperation among the Jackson parties was most noticeable in their use of the press. According to one Jackson newspaper man, the party was building "a chain of newspaper posts, from the New England States to Louisiana, and branching off through Lexington to the Western States."[47] During the campaign Green worked steadily to increase the circulation of the *Telegraph*. His political ally John C. Calhoun helped him substantially by convincing members of Congress to take responsibility for paying for the distribution of the *Telegraph* in their districts. Led by the enthusiastic cooperation of Congressman Thomas P. Moore of Kentucky, the Jackson congressmen greatly increased the circulation of Green's newspaper. By the end of 1826 Green was exchanging articles with 163 other editors. Cooperation among Jackson newspapers was so great that in some parts of the country there were chains of local newspapers within the larger chain. Hill's *Patriot*, for example, received articles from Green and distributed them to a small chain in Maine and New Hampshire. Hill also circulated local news. On one occasion Jackson resolutions passed in Dover, New Hampshire, were printed within forty hours in five New Hampshire newspapers.[48]

Finally, the Adams men were having much more difficulty than the Jacksonians in taking their message to the people and coming to terms with the question of party patronage. A comparison of the New Hampshire Jackson party address and the Virginia Adams statement shows a bold, confident, aggressive Jackson party and a defensive, constitutional-minded Adams party. And the Jackson party seemed much more united in its approach to party patronage than the Adams men were.

Judged on the criteria for becoming a national party, the Jacksonians seemed far ahead of their rivals for office. Whether this would translate into a Jackson victory was still uncertain as the last few months of the campaign unfolded.

7

ELECTION YEAR

When the New Year dawned on the lower Mississippi River in 1828, Andrew and Rachel Jackson were on board the steamboat *Pocahontas* on their way to New Orleans to take part in the celebration of the thirteenth anniversary of the Battle of New Orleans. Jackson had consistently refused to campaign, but this was an event he believed he could attend, for no one could criticize the hero of New Orleans for returning to the scene of his triumph. Jackson insisted that this was not a political celebration, but everyone knew there were certain to be political advantages. Louisiana was one of the few western states that showed some likelihood of voting for Adams, and it would do Jackson no harm to mingle with the delegations from the important states of New York, Pennsylvania, Ohio, and Kentucky, who would be traveling with him. Furthermore, Jackson's enemies were attacking him so harshly for committing adultery and murdering militiamen that he relished the chance to return to the role of hero. Van Buren thought it was such a good opportunity that he wanted to be in on it, so he sent his friend James A. Hamilton of New York to act as his representative. Also on board were two of Jackson's chief political advisers, William B. Lewis and John Overton.

On the morning of the eighth an enormous crowd of spectators and a large fleet of ships and boats waited impatiently in a thick mist for Jackson to arrive. At ten o'clock, just as the sun broke through, the *Pocahontas* hove into view, and General Jackson, his head uncovered, could be seen standing on the fantail. The crowd cheered wildly, many of the ships fired their cannons, and four days of dinners, parades, and other festivities began. Writing in 1860, James Parton, who relied on Lewis for much of his information, called it "the most stupendous thing of the kind that had ever occurred in the United States . . . surpassed . . . only by the reception [years later] of the orator [and Hungarian patriot Louis] Kossuth in the city of New York."[1]

Two Adams men who were in New Orleans at the time had a somewhat less enthusiastic opinion. According to one, the sale of tickets for the banquet was so slow that the sponsors had to cut the price from $6 to $3 to fill the hall. A friend of Webster wrote that "the famous entrée on the 8th. Jany. last, . . . was an ill omen for the 'Heroites.' It excited no more attention, than [an ordinary] military parade. . . . As the 'Hero' walked along the streets, not a shout of welcome nor a move of a hat or a handkerchief answered his obsequious bows. . . . How different . . . from the visit of Lafayette . . . and the delirium of feeling which every where manifested itself at his presence."[2]

Even so, Jackson's reception was far noisier and warmer than any being experienced by John Quincy Adams. Later, however, during the summer, the president had two opportunities. On the Fourth of July he presided at the ceremonies for the start of construction of the Chesapeake and Ohio Canal. It was a significant event, for on the same day in Baltimore, Charles Carroll, the only surviving signer of the Declaration of Independence, was speaking at a similar celebration for the Baltimore and Ohio Railroad. It was the perfect setting for Adams to take credit for two major contributions to the American movement westward. But as so often happened, he refused to stoop to "electioneering" and let the opportunity slip by with only a few cursory remarks. At the end of his speech, when he tried to dig the traditional first few shovelfuls of dirt, a stubborn root got in the way. Then suddenly a different Adams—one who remembered that he had once been a farmer—took over. He tore off his coat, rolled up his sleeves, cut through the root, and made the dirt fly. The audience loved it and gave him an ovation. This John Quincy Adams would have been a much stronger candidate than the one who was running for reelection.[3]

But Adams could not change. A month later, as he headed north for his usual summer holiday, he spent the first two nights at Baltimore and Philadelphia. In each case he was greeted by large, cheering crowds who wanted to hear the president, but in neither instance did he give a speech. The notations in his diary are most revealing. After his experience in

Baltimore he complained that an unruly Jackson meeting had kept him awake and commented dourly that there were meetings like that taking place "in every part of the Union." "A stranger would think," he added, "that the people of the United States have no other occupation than electioneering."[4] The next night at the Philadelphia dock a similar crowd gave him three cheers and made it difficult for him to proceed up the street to his hotel. When the shouting continued after he went inside, the president came out on the porch and hastily said good night. In his diary he noted unhappily that some of the people had shouted, "Huzza for Jackson." Adams had let two more opportunities to connect with voters pass him by.[5]

During and after Jackson's journey to New Orleans both parties took steps to settle on their candidate for vice president. On January 8, the day Jackson was welcomed at New Orleans, his followers held rallies and conventions in many states to honor the Old Hero and nominate his running mate. Jackson men in New Jersey, Maryland, Ohio, Pennsylvania, Indiana, Kentucky, and Virginia, none of which had yet endorsed a candidate, fell in line and nominated the ticket of Jackson and Calhoun.

There was still, however, some question about Calhoun. A week before the Kentucky convention, Worden Pope, a prominent Jackson supporter in Louisville, received a letter from U.S. Senator John Rowan saying that he and all eight of the Jackson congressmen from Kentucky were supporting the South Carolinian for vice president. Provoked by the news, Pope wrote to one of the congressmen, Charles A. Wickliffe, to raise some questions. The Jackson party's main goal, Pope said, should be to defend republicanism and stop the slide toward corruption, but the nomination of Calhoun would do something quite different. Since both Jackson and Calhoun were slaveholders, it would bring up the question of slavery, and it would anger De Witt Clinton, who wanted the nomination himself. If Jackson and Calhoun won, a struggle would ensue between Clinton and Van Buren for supremacy in New York. The Jacksonians could avoid the problem by making Clinton vice president, thus removing him from New York and leaving Van Buren in control of patronage in the state. Moreover, Clinton would be a much stronger candidate for vice president than Calhoun because of his popularity in northern states such as Maryland, New Jersey, Ohio, Indiana, and Illinois.[6]

Pope's letter laid bare the fundamental problem of slavery, which had the potential to split the Jackson party and the nation. Never before had a political party nominated slaveholders for both president and vice president. The nomination of Clinton, however, might not have been a wise solution. Ever since the debate over slavery in Missouri, southerners had believed, incorrectly, that Clinton stood at the head of the antislavery movement in the North. On balance, his nomination might have triggered more hostility than Calhoun's.

Within the next few weeks a series of events made the issue purely academic. Pope had barely mailed his letter when, on January 8, the Jackson state parties nominated Calhoun for vice president. And a month later, on February 11, Clinton ended all speculation about his political future when he died suddenly at his home in Albany. His unexpected death (Clinton was only fifty-eight) dramatically altered the election scene in New York. Many of the Clintonians who had been supporting Jackson simply because Clinton admired the Old Hero were now free to vote for Adams. Clinton's death worried Van Buren, who now faced the real possibility that Jackson might not carry New York, but it also encouraged the Little Magician because if Jackson won, Van Buren would surely be in control of party patronage in the state.

The story of nominations on the Adams side was far less portentous. Adams had no competition for his party's presidential nomination, and there was no great rush to run for vice president. Instead, the inner circle had to go out and find someone willing to accept the job. Hoping that the nomination of a Pennsylvanian would help them carry the state, they first offered the position to Governor John Shulze, but he lacked the political passion to take on the task. Looking inward, they offered it to Henry Clay, who turned it down supposedly because of ill health, and then to James Barbour, who preferred the position of minister to Great Britain. Finally, returning to the idea of choosing a Pennsylvanian, they convinced Secretary of the Treasury Richard Rush, a strong advocate of Clay's American System, to be the candidate. Starting in January 1828 the Adams and Rush ticket was nominated by the lower house in Vermont and Massachusetts and by conventions in Maine, New York, Pennsylvania, New Jersey, Maryland, Ohio, Kentucky, and Indiana. Aside from the nomination of the Anti-Masonic ticket in New York, the nominations were now complete.

The wave of party conventions and nominations stimulated interest in the presidential election, and predicting the outcome had become a popular pastime. Gamblers were preparing odds, and politicians on both sides were making estimates. Although now almost a year old, the most detailed and thoughtful predictions were those offered by John Eaton and Daniel Webster. "The Presidential question," Eaton told Jackson, depends "entirely upon your health & life." If those are "preserved, . . . the game is over."[7] While conceding all of New England to Adams, he predicted confidently that Jackson would win more than 20 of the 36 votes in New York and all but 5 of the 109 electoral votes in the eastern states from Pennsylvania down to Georgia. All 65 western votes, North and South, would also go to the Old Hero.

Webster painted a different picture. In a letter to his Federalist friend Jeremiah Mason of New Hampshire, he wrote: "I . . . believe confidently, in Mr. Adams's reelection. I set down New England, New Jersey, the greater part of Maryland, and perhaps all Delaware, Ohio, Kentucky, Indiana, Missouri, and Louisiana for him. We must then get votes enough in New York to choose him, and I think cannot fail." "It is not impossible," he concluded, "that Pennsylvania may go for Mr. Adams."[8]

Neither man was quite as confident as he seemed, but each had good supporting evidence. Ever since publishing his "Letters of Wyoming" about Jackson, Eaton had recognized the power of Jackson's image as a republican hero. He understood the resentment felt by many Americans who believed that Adams and Clay had corruptly deprived the Old Hero of the presidency. He also knew that in 1824 Jackson had carried eight of the thirteen southern and western states. And as a senator Eaton had seen firsthand the problems Adams and Clay were facing in dealing with patronage and building a party.[9]

Webster, however, could defend his optimism. The Adams party had more than held its own in the summer and fall congressional elections of 1826. Seen through Webster's Federalist eyes, the better sort of people were bound to rally around the American System of Adams and Clay.[10] Attacks on Jackson's marriage and his behavior as a "military chieftain" were becoming commonplace. Furthermore, the results of the 1824 election were encouraging. In the East Adams had carried New England by a wide margin, had won twenty-seven of the thirty-nine electoral votes in New York and Delaware, and had come close to winning New Jersey and Maryland. Prospects were good in the West, where Clay had carried Ohio, Kentucky, and Missouri, and where the combined vote for Clay and Adams had exceeded the total for Jackson in Indiana.[11]

Both sides were poring over the same numbers: 261 electors would vote in 1828; 131 votes were needed to win. The votes would come from twenty-four states, twenty of which would be using the winner-take-all system; in Maine, New York, Maryland, and Tennessee the votes would be cast in districts. For simplicity's sake, the twenty-four states can be divided into a smaller, more manageable number of regional groups:

Six New England states: 51 votes
New York: 36 votes
Pennsylvania: 28 votes
Three remaining Middle Atlantic states: 22 votes
Virginia: 24 votes
Three remaining southeastern states: 35 votes
Ohio and Kentucky: 30 votes
Seven remaining western states: 35 votes
Total: 261 votes

Assuming that New England (except, perhaps, New Hampshire) would go for Adams and that much of the South and West would vote for Jackson, the closest races seemed likely to take place in New Hampshire, the Middle Atlantic states, Ohio, and Kentucky. Because of the district system, the New York vote would be divided. Pennsylvania, where Jackson and Calhoun were very popular, seemed likely to vote for the Old Hero, but the state had long favored internal improvement and tariffs, Adams's key issues. Ohio and Kentucky were more complex. In 1824 the combined Clay and Adams vote in Ohio far exceeded the vote for Jackson, and Clay had easily carried his home state of Kentucky.[12] Yet the bargain charge had greatly weakened Adams and Clay in both states, and the Yankee Adams had never been popular west of the mountains. The alliance of Van Buren and Ritchie seemed to tie Virginia to Jackson. All in all, the numbers seemed to favor the Old Hero:

Half of New York: 18 votes
Pennsylvania: 28 votes
Half of the other Middle Atlantic states: 11 votes
Southeastern states (including Virginia): 59 votes
Seven western states (without Ohio and Kentucky): 35 votes
Jackson total: 151 votes

Adams, however, could win by getting more than half the votes in New York and the small Middle Atlantic states and by carrying Missouri and Louisiana as well as Ohio and Kentucky in the West. Clay had carried Missouri in 1824, and Louisiana now seemed to be leaning toward

Adams. The congressional delegation in the state was four to one in favor of the administration.[13] If the votes fell this way, Adams would have an electoral majority:

New England: 51 votes
New York: 26 votes
Small Middle Atlantic states: 18 votes
Ohio and Kentucky: 30 votes
Missouri and Louisiana: 8 votes
Adams total: 133 votes

Or if Webster was correct and Adams managed to carry Pennsylvania, he could win even without the increase in New York and the other Middle Atlantic states:

New England: 51 votes
New York: 18 votes
Pennsylvania: 28 votes
Remaining Middle Atlantic states: 11 votes
Ohio and Kentucky: 30 votes
Missouri and Louisiana: 8 votes
Adams total: 146 votes

But the presidential election was not the only one on the political calendar. Before the ballots for president and vice president were actually cast in the fall, several dozen state elections to choose state officeholders and congressmen were scheduled to take place. These elections commanded attention; they were important not only in their own right but also as a useful source of information about the likely outcome of the presidential election. Voting data from these elections were readily available. Local newspapers carried the returns from nearby townships and counties, and national newspapers such as *Niles' Register* and the *United States Telegraph* published the results from all the states. There was so much franking and exchanging of newspapers that readers had access to a wide range of information. By following the state elections, historians and readers can put themselves in the shoes of Americans living in 1828.

The elections began in New Hampshire with the end of the snow in March and continued until November, with clusters of elections coming in April, August, and October:

March: New Hampshire

April: Connecticut, Rhode Island, Massachusetts, Virginia

July: Louisiana

August: Kentucky, North Carolina, Indiana, Illinois, Missouri,
Alabama

September: Maine, Vermont

October: Pennsylvania, Ohio, New Jersey, Delaware, Maryland,
Georgia

November: New York[14]

MARCH

Because New Hampshire was the first state to hold an election, and because it was tied closely to two other states—Maine and Vermont—it drew much attention. John Eaton was there to see for himself whether Isaac Hill could pull off an upset and start the ball rolling for Old Hickory. He found it less than reassuring when he saw so many coffin handbills. An anxious Daniel Webster was more comfortable with his prediction when he received a letter from his brother Ezekiel saying that the administration would carry the state by some 3,000 to 5,000 votes. Vermont governor Cornelius P. Van Ness learned from his brother John, chair of the Jackson central committee in Washington, that the Jackson leaders were "intense[ly] anxious" about the New Hampshire election and "actually trembled" for fear of the outcome.[15]

The Jacksonians had good reason to be concerned. The Adams convention had reconciled Federalists and Republicans so well that the delegates chose a former Federalist, Samuel Bell's brother John, as the candidate for governor. Several days later conventions in Rockingham and Hillsborough counties endorsed the nomination. With money coming in from the Websters' Federalist friends and the circulation of the Adams *New Hampshire Journal* tripling, the Adams party was able to launch a strong campaign.[16]

Hill responded on January 8 by sponsoring eight Jackson celebrations, the largest at Concord, where six hundred Jacksonians marched to the Old North Church to listen to Hill compare Adams's "polished education" unfavorably with Old Hickory's frontier training. To counteract these events the Adams party distributed more coffin handbills and published a booklet entitled *The Wise Sayings of the Honorable Isaac Hill*, reminding voters that Hill had once preferred Adams to Jackson.

The Adams men also tried to rebut Jacksonian claims that Jackson represented lowly mechanics and farmers against haughty aristocrats, but their own condescending remarks about the "ignorant" workers undercut their message.[17]

The outcome was a decisive victory for the Adams men. Their aggressive campaign and new liberal policy toward Federalists brought an additional 10,000 voters (mostly Federalists) to the polls and enabled Bell to win the election by a vote of 21,149 to 18,672. The voting patterns were similar to those in the early years: old Federalist towns in the Old Colony and along the Connecticut River were now for Adams, while towns in the central part of the state and in the mountains to the north, once Republican, were now for Jackson. Of the two hundred towns voting both in 1814 and in 1828, all but forty-two fell into the old pattern. And, even more conspicuous, the Adams leaders—the Bells, the Websters, and Jeremiah Mason—were either Federalists or former Federalists. The heavy hand of the past rested on the state.[18]

Shifting to the presidential campaign, Hill used the anti-Federalist theme to his advantage. Sounding like Van Buren, he accused a "wealthy" Federalist elite of trying to rule the state. In most towns, he said, teams of Federalist lawyers and Congregational ministers were trying to rule over honest mechanics and farmers. As November drew near he published a short work, *Letter from a Farmer,* in which he pursued Van Buren's theme of political continuity.[19]

Hill also pulled his party together. When the legislature met in June he called a Jackson party convention, the first of its kind in New Hampshire. The two hundred delegates set up a new committee of correspondence with Hill as chairman, nominated presidential electors, and drafted the Jackson election address. During the summer Hill and his party press were forced to spend a large part of their time defending the Old Hero. Hill's most memorable comment came when he was refuting the charges, one after another. Suddenly in mock exasperation he shouted, "Pshaw! Why don't you tell the whole truth? On the 8th of January, 1815, [Jackson] murdered in the coldest blood 1,500 British soldiers for merely trying to get into New Orleans for Booty and Beauty." Like his czar story, this remark won national attention.[20]

Encouraged by the success of their policy toward the Federalists, the administration men became increasingly more willing to accept a new party system. When the Jackson men accused them of creating a new Federalist party, the Adams men pointed out that the Federalists were moving into both parties. One Adams man conceded that the two old parties had reorganized as "the Administration & Jackson parties."[21]

Webster, who heartily agreed, believed that the only way to defeat the Jackson party was to keep up the fight. Smugly convinced, like the Adams men in other states, that the Adams party had the backing of the best and most intelligent men in New Hampshire, he urged Samuel Bell to bring administration ideas to the backward towns that had not yet received them. These were the hill and mountain towns in "the remote parts of the State, farthest from the sources of intelligence," where Hill's *Patriot* was the only source of information, and where the people lacked the "truth & the enjoyment of its light." The presidential election would determine whether the state was actually divided that way.[22]

APRIL

Federalism lasted longer in Massachusetts than in any other state except Delaware. When the Federalist party finally disappeared in Massachusetts in 1827, the Republican party was left with the same problem plaguing the Republicans in New Hampshire and Pennsylvania—whether to amalgamate with Federalists. Choosing to amalgamate, Republicans in the spring of 1827 combined with Federalists to elect Daniel Webster to the U.S. Senate. A year later, in April 1828, they reelected an Adams man, Levi Lincoln, for governor by a wide margin over Marcus Morton, who represented a small faction of Jacksonians. The state also elected a solid delegation of Adams men for Congress. Rhode Island and Connecticut followed suit. The news of the three Adams victories in southern New England and the Jackson setback in New Hampshire reinforced the conventional wisdom that Adams would sweep New England in the fall.[23]

In Virginia the year began with large Jackson and Adams conventions. The "Anti-Jackson" men, as the Adamsites called themselves, demonstrated that two-party politics had arrived in the Old Dominion. Two hundred delegates attended their convention and agreed to contribute $5 each to pay for the publication of 30,000 copies of their address. However, the most important result in the April elections did not concern national affairs or state offices, which remained, as usual, in the hands of the Junto, but the decision whether to hold a convention to revise the state constitution. The voters decided in favor of holding a convention by the convincing margin of 5,000 votes. Again the pattern was the inverse of Formisano's center-periphery pattern. The planters of the Tidewater and the Piedmont voted conservatively against holding a convention (which might lead to a change in representation), while voters from the west and along the Potomac River and Chesapeake Bay voted in favor of the convention.

Since the vote was a setback for the Tidewater-Piedmont Jackson party, it gave some encouragement to the Adams, Anti-Jackson men, whose strength came from the same counties that had voted for the convention.[24]

JULY

The Louisiana election offered more evidence that the Jacksonians might be in some trouble. Despite Jackson's great military victory there in 1815, his authoritarian martial rule after the battle had soured the feelings of many Louisianans toward the general. In the state election in July the Adams party won control of the legislature, elected the governor, and took two of the three seats in the U.S. House of Representatives. Jackson's triumphant return in January had apparently not secured the state. Halfway through the summer the state elections seemed to augur well for Adams.[25]

AUGUST

The administration party hoped that Kentucky would treat Old Hickory with the same disrespect Louisiana had shown. One of the most common themes running through the correspondence of Henry Clay was his belief that the Adams party had to carry Kentucky to win the presidential election. He was confident that it would do both. After all, Kentucky was Clay's state. He had carried it in 1824, he had revived his defense against the bargain charge in Kentucky, and he had personally drawn up an organizational plan for the state party. Late in the winter of 1827–1828 Clay's friend and Adams congressman Robert P. Letcher told the president confidently that their party would certainly win the Kentucky gubernatorial election, which would take place on August 4–6. But the pessimistic Adams was not convinced. That evening he wrote in his diary that "the face of [Letcher's] hopes [was] much fairer than that of his expectations."[26]

Just as in New Hampshire, the Kentucky gubernatorial campaign was new style and partisan. Both parties chose their candidates at conventions, and for the first time the candidates campaigned in many parts of the state. Ironically the candidates were the opposite of what their parties were alleged to be. The "democratic" Jackson party ran former Federalist and college-educated William T. Barry, while the supposedly "aristocratic" Adams party ran the self-made, little-educated stonemason Thomas Metcalfe, known as "Old Stone Hammer." But what really made the state election of 1828 so new style and partisan was the importance of national issues. The newspapers were full of references to the bargain charge, the militiamen, and Jackson's adultery.[27]

Since Metcalfe, a congressman, was tied up in Congress until early May, Barry had a head start in the campaign. By the time Metcalfe returned, Barry had spent several weeks speaking in previously ignored counties in central and western Kentucky. Under great pressure to win the election, Clay came back to Lexington and spent all three days of the election at the Fayette County courthouse, shaking hands with the voters. The campaign turned personal, with the Adams men calling Barry a Federalist, a defaulter, and a Relief man, and the Jackson men attacking Metcalfe for dueling and voting for Adams in 1825.[28]

The national significance of the election brought out 74 percent of the voters, higher than the turnout during the Relief war. Metcalfe defeated Barry by more than a thousand votes, but the Jacksonians won a sixteen-vote majority in the lower house of the legislature and a two-vote majority in the upper house. Three of the four candidates for governor and lieutenant governor failed to carry their home counties, suggesting that party meant more to the voters than personality. Although the Adams candidate won the governor's seat, as Letcher had predicted, the rest of the election went so badly that Adams, Clay, and Letcher could take little comfort.[29]

Wasting no time on recriminations, the Jacksonians took steps to improve their party organization and campaign tactics for the presidential election. One of the best campaigners in the Jackson camp, Congressman Thomas P. Moore, bragged, "We organized, & brought out our force, & electrified them." According to Francis P. Blair, he and Kendall had "almost every Jackson man ticketed & riveted to the polls." Kendall wrote another of his public letters to Clay, denouncing the corrupt bargain, and he completed the life story of Jackson that had been running in the *Argus of Western America*. Help from the outside poured in—circulars and other campaign items from Gulian Verplanck of the

Albany Regency, and a steady flow of copies of the *Telegraph* from Duff Green.[30]

The presidential election was a serious affair for both sides. A few days before the voting began, an upbeat *Argus* told its readers that "the eyes of the world" were upon them, that the "fate of the Republic [would be] decided" by the way they voted, and that they must make a choice between "Liberty or monarchy." Binding it all together was the theme of "Jackson and Reform," which looked back longingly at a republican world free from patronage and corruption.[31]

In contrast, the administration party, like its counterparts in New York and Ohio, was much less positive. Members were beginning to write to Clay complaining about the political situation. They were particularly exercised about voter fraud in the gubernatorial contest, in which the number of votes in six counties—four won by Barry and two by Metcalfe—exceeded the number of eligible voters. Fearing more such corruption in November "if Tennessee disgorges 1,000 voters upon us," iron manufacturer David Trimble spent $250 publishing his own election address to advance the Adams cause. Letcher repeated the same complaint heard in other states—that the Jacksonians had "their force better disciplined." The Adams men were contending, he feared, with an untiring eninmy [sic]" that will "stop at nothing."[32]

During the rest of August five other states held elections. The two in the Old Northwest—Indiana and Illinois—and the one in the Old Southwest—Alabama—offered few clues about the presidential election because these states had been slow to develop political parties. In Indiana a group of Jackson men met on January 8, 1828, chose electors, and discussed the possibility of a Jackson state party, but nothing came of it. Governor James B. Ray was reelected governor in August, but after the election he declared that he was opposed to "partyism."[33]

A similar series of events took place in Illinois, where the early history of the territory and state revolved around Ninian Edwards, who had served as territorial governor, then senator, and in 1826 state governor. In the congressional elections Illinois elected a Jackson man, and Indiana elected two Adams men and one Jackson man. Although Jackson was popular in the West, there was no groundswell for him in these two states.[34]

Although Jackson won the 1824 election in Alabama with 70 percent of the popular vote, no durable political party was organized, and for the rest of the decade a coalition of newspaper editors and bankers ran the state. The group won considerable popular support by establishing a state bank that held interest rates down and promising to protect the voters from so-called aristocrats, a populist theme that later became Jacksonian dogma.[35]

In the other two August elections partyism was more advanced. The history of political parties in Missouri centered around the rivalry between senators Thomas Hart Benton, a strong Jackson man, and David Barton, who had engineered the decision to give Missouri's votes in the 1825 runoff election to Adams. After Benton and the Jackson men held a convention on January 8, 1828, to prepare for the presidential election, Barton and the Adams men followed suit on March 3. In the August state election the Jackson candidates won so easily that the Adams newspaper the *Missouri Intelligencer* referred to the next state assembly as a "Jackson legislature"—encouraging news for the national Jacksonians.[36]

But Missouri had only three electoral votes. A much more valuable indicator would be the state election in North Carolina, which had fifteen. Although Jackson had carried North Carolina in 1824, the congressional delegation had turned to Crawford in the runoff. When Crawford retired, many North Carolinians first considered Adams but were soon disturbed by the nationalism in his annual message, his sympathy for the Georgia Indians, and his unwillingness to send patronage their way.

North Carolinians then turned to Jackson. After meetings at New Bern and Fayetteville in November 1827, at which they set up a committee of correspondence and published an address, they met again at Raleigh to organize a central committee and endorse the ticket of Jackson and Calhoun. At about the same time Adams admirers were holding an ambitious convention at Raleigh, where they chose electors, wrote an address, and arranged to have 10,000 copies of it published.

The North Carolina presidential campaign was the national campaign in microcosm. The Adams party accused the Jacksonians of abusing the franking privilege and preferring military rule to civil rule. They abused Jackson personally for murdering the six militiamen, showing a violent temper, aiding Aaron Burr's conspiracy, and committing adultery with Rachel. And they spread Charles Hammond's story that Jackson's mother had been a "common prostitute." Adams, who got off rather easily, was condemned for his extravagance, his corrupt bargain, and his failure to open the British ports in the West Indies.[37]

Harry L. Watson's study of Cumberland County in North Carolina portrays southern farmers facing severe economic change. As exporters of raw materials, they understood the need for internal improvements, yet they feared the size of the program Adams had laid out. They opposed an all-powerful central government not because it might do away with slavery but because they sincerely believed in republican states' rights. Although there were no avowed presidential parties in North Carolina, Jackson men prevailed over Adams supporters in the August state election.[38]

SEPTEMBER

The last two states to hold elections in the summer of 1828 were Maine and Vermont. Like their neighbor New Hampshire, these two northern New England states were generally loyal to the old Republican party and John Quincy Adams, but factions were beginning to emerge that sought to move in other directions. The first to break away was the faction led by young editor Francis O. J. Smith of the Portland, Maine, *Eastern Argus,* which had come out in favor of Andrew Jackson. Aided by a young men's organization, the *Argus* faction offered a serious threat to the Adams party. In Vermont a Jackson faction emerged in June at the state capital at Montpelier, and Anti-Masonry was moving into the state. Stimulating the move toward Jacksonianism was Isaac Hill's *New-Hampshire Patriot,* which was read in both Maine and Vermont. Although the Adams party carried the two states in the September elections, the Adams men were apprehensive about losing voters to Jackson in November.

OCTOBER

Early in October the three small Middle Atlantic states—New Jersey, Delaware, and Maryland—held their state elections. Although offering a total of only twenty-two electoral votes, these states were important because, together with their much larger neighbors New York and Pennsylvania, they had been pioneers in shaping the early Republican and Federalist parties and the first American party system. Willing to experiment with party conventions, less averse than other states to partyism and party patronage, they had fashioned evenly balanced state party systems that produced close elections. In the presidential election of 1824, for example, which produced competitive races in very few states, Adams defeated Jackson in Maryland by only 109 votes (Adams, 14,632; Jackson, 14,523).[39]

Delaware, where the legislature chose the presidential electors, was the last bastion of the Federalist party. Federalists had dominated the state during the first party system and were still in power as late as the summer of 1827, when both the Jackson and the Adams movements held state conventions to prepare for the presidential election. Most Federalists shifted into the Adams party, but significant numbers followed Senator Louis McLane into the Jackson ranks. The Adams victory in the 1828 state election guaranteed that Delaware's three electoral votes would go to Adams.

Neither New Jersey nor Maryland, where the people voted for president, was likely to be that clear-cut. In the 1824 election the New Jersey Republicans, who were almost as strong as the Federalists in Delaware, split into Jackson and Adams factions. Led by the unscrupulous Colonel Samuel Swartwout and strengthened by a number of former Federalists, the Jackson party won a narrow victory over the Adams faction in 1824. During the 1828 campaign Swartwout continued to lead the Jackson party, while Secretary of the Navy Samuel Southard played a growing role in the Adams party. The Adams party won the 1828 state election and increased its number of congressmen from five out of six to six out of six. Perhaps Adams would do as well in New Jersey a few weeks later.

He would not do as well in Maryland because voting there was by districts and would likely produce a divided vote. Maryland was one of several states in which both sides supported internal improvements and a protective tariff. Presidential parties, which appeared in the election of 1824, did not move into Maryland state politics until 1826. In the congressional election that fall the Adams party won five seats and the Jackson party four, with the Federalists dividing equally between the two parties. By May 1827 the Jackson party was strong enough to hold a convention and establish a strong central committee of correspondence, and the Adams party followed with a convention of its own. The Adams party won control of the House of Representatives that fall and added to its majority in the October election of 1828. With those victories behind them, the Adams men in Maryland were confident that they would win a majority of the electoral votes in November.[40]

On October 6, the day the people of Maryland voted, the state of Georgia was also holding an election, but since there was no opposition to Jackson in Georgia, it went largely unnoticed. The Georgia legislature had taken the democratic step of shifting the election from the legislature to the people, but the voting was likely to be a farce.[41]

The two most anxiously awaited state elections were those scheduled to take place on October 14 in the Jackson stronghold of Pennsylvania and the Adams stronghold of Ohio. In Pennsylvania the most crucial political controversy was the bitter struggle between the postmaster of Philadelphia, Richard Bache, and the strongest Adams voice in the state, editor John Binns of the *Democratic Press*. Binns, now notorious because of his militiamen handbills, was furious because Bache still refused to give him the lucrative post office printing contract. The patronage continued to go to a supporter of the opposition, the *Franklin Gazette,* a Philadelphia newspaper edited by Jacksonian John Norvell and partly owned by the Jacksonian Bache family and Jackson congressman Samuel D. Ingham. Binns wanted Bache removed for being behind in his accounts with the U.S. government, but Postmaster General McLean and Adams refused to act.

In early April 1828 a way out of the morass seemed attainable when McLean finally lost patience with Bache and dismissed him. But instead of replacing him with an Adams man who would give the printing contract to Binns, McLean gave the postmastership to Thomas Sergeant, who was Bache's brother-in-law and had a "pecuniary interest" in the *Franklin Gazette.* Thus the printing contract remained with the Jacksonian *Franklin Gazette.* In a supreme bit of irony, McLean thought he was doing the Adams party a favor because Thomas Sergeant was the brother of the leading Adams man in the state, Congressman John Sergeant, who would be running for Congress in the fall for the third time in two years. Actually, by stirring up more controversy, the appointment put Sergeant's reelection in doubt.[42]

John Sergeant was not the only noteworthy person running for office in the state election. Late in 1827 several of the trade associations in Philadelphia had started a strike for a ten-hour workday. The strike was unsuccessful, but it led to the formation of the Mechanics' Union of Trade Associations, the first city labor union in the United States. On July 1, 1828, the Mechanics' Union formed the Working Men's party, the first American labor party, and nominated candidates for city offices. Eager to get the labor vote, special committees of vigilance of the Adams and Jackson parties nominated a number of Working Men's candidates, who then had the advantage of running on two tickets. The ease with which these candidates were brought into the state election spoke well for the popularity and flexibility of the new political system. Over a very short period, labor candidates had been nominated twice—once by the newly established Working Men's party, and once by one of the two major parties.[43]

Because the Jacksonians nominated many of the labor candidates, some historians have used this to argue that Jacksonian democracy was a liberal pro-labor movement. This does not seem to be so. First, the membership of the Working Men's parties often included nonlaborers such as master craftsmen and other upper-class professionals; second, the Jackson program showed little interest in the basic wage and work-hour demands of the workers. The important point, however, is that the new party system gave labor a chance to be heard, first in Philadelphia and soon afterward in other labor centers such as New York, Boston, and Baltimore.[44]

The Pennsylvania state election was a disaster for the Adams men. In Philadelphia, where they had done so well in 1827, the Jackson candidates for the city assembly and common council defeated their opponents by an average margin of 1,000 votes. The twenty-one candidates who represented both the Working Men's party and the Jackson party were all elected, but none of the Adams–Working Men's candidates won their races. Across the state the Jackson machine won in almost every county. The congressional elections were even worse; only one of the twenty-six Adams candidates won a seat, and John Sergeant, whose election meant so much, was defeated by 557 votes. In reporting to Henry Clay, Sergeant laid the blame on "illegal voters . . . local dissensions," and Adams's failure to get higher tariffs for manufacturers. Apparently, the Federalists, the governor, the Germans, and the press, on whom the Adams party had depended, had not done what was expected of them.[45]

The Ohio political campaign in 1828 was one of the most hard fought of all the state campaigns waged that year. Old protests of antiparty-ism were put aside, and both parties showed that they were far better organized than in the past. Frightened by the Jacksonians' surprising success in the previous October election, the Adams men called a party convention for December 1827 and were gratified by the good turnout. Meanwhile, the Jacksonians started holding county conventions to select delegates for a statewide convention at Columbus on the anniversary of the Battle of New Orleans. They too were successful. When the convention opened on January 8 at least fifty of the sixty-four counties were represented.[46]

During the winter and spring the Adams men seemed to be regaining control. They gave new powers to their central committee, published 10,000 copies of their convention address, and maintained their five-to-two advantage in newspapers over the Jackson party; they even added two new papers in Cincinnati—the *Truth's Advocate and Monthly Anti-Jackson Expositor* (previously mentioned) and, later in the summer, the *Hamilton Intelligencer*. The greatest Adams success came in April when the party won the municipal election in Cincinnati and dismissed a large number of Jacksonian officials.

The Jackson party reacted quickly with Moses Dawson's *Friend of Reform & Corruption's Adversary*. In strategic places such as Zanesville, at the end of the completed portion of the National Road, and in some of the lightly settled northwestern counties, party activists distributed copies of Duff Green's *Telegraph*. As in other western states, they found that the billiards and corrupt bargain charges carried more weight against Adams than did serious attacks on his position on substantive issues.

Coming only two weeks before the presidential election, the Ohio state elections took on special importance as political harbingers, but they were also important in their own right because they would be two of the first western elections to be contested over national as well as local issues. The gubernatorial election would be partisan, pitting the Adams candidate, incumbent Allen Trimble, against the Jackson candidate, five-term congressman John W. Campbell. The Adams party was expected to win the elections, but the outcome was as indecisive as that in Kentucky. The Adams men retained control of the state government, but Trimble barely defeated Campbell (53,981 to 51,861), and the Jacksonians increased their share of the congressional delegation from four to eight out of fourteen.[47] The Adams men were shocked and frightened by the outcome. They realized that the presidential election was only two weeks away and that losing Ohio's sixteen electoral votes would represent a thirty-two-vote swing in the final tabulation.

NOVEMBER

Back in New York, where the state and presidential elections would be held at the same time, three political parties had been maneuvering for position. Van Buren's Bucktail party, now committed to Jackson, moved first. On January 31 it met in a legislative caucus in Albany, where it formally nominated the Old Hero but made no effort to nominate anyone for governor. When the legislature adjourned in April the Adams party held its own caucus, at which it nominated Adams but also made no gubernatorial nomination.

This indecision by the two parties was increased by the unexpected death of Governor De Witt Clinton and the lack of stature of his successor, Lieutenant Governor Nathaniel Pitcher. But it was also a product of the Anti-Masonic movement, for Thurlow Weed and others were trying to combine the Adams and Anti-Masonic parties. During the previous winter Weed had traveled to Washington and discussed the subject with Henry Clay. When he returned in January 1828 Weed and the administration reached an informal agreement to support Adams for president and the Anti-Masonic candidates for governor and lesser state offices. Weed, who had already sold his *Rochester Telegraph,* also secured enough administration backing to start a new newspaper in Rochester, the *Anti-Masonic Enquirer.*

On June 10 the Adams men convened in Albany and published addresses, but they postponed nominations until they had heard from the Anti-Masons. Finally on July 22 they met again and nominated a ticket that brought them partway toward a united front with the Anti-Masons. For governor they selected the rather dull but safe U.S. Supreme Court justice Smith Thompson, who had managed to keep himself out of the Anti-Masonic controversy. But for lieutenant governor they chose the much more popular young assemblyman Francis Granger, who was now committed to the Anti-Mason cause.

Granger was so popular that when the Anti-Masons met in Utica on August 5 they angrily rejected the administration's proposed joint ticket and insisted on nominating Granger for governor on their own ticket. Granger, who did not want to give up his ties with the Adams party, rejected the nomination, and hopes for a merger died. The Anti-Masons then turned to Solomon Southwick for governor. This was a strange decision because Southwick, who had once been an influential Clintonian editor, had recently become involved in wild, unsuccessful financial schemes that had left him and his clients bankrupt.[48]

Somewhat relieved by Weed's failure to unite the Bucktails' two opponents, yet realizing that a difficult election lay ahead, Van Buren sought the right man for governor to create a strong Jackson ticket. After taking another tour of western New York and consulting with his colleagues in the Albany Regency, he decided that he himself would be the best candidate. The formal nomination took place on September 24 at a Jackson convention held, significantly, not in Albany, the Bucktail center of power, but close to Anti-Masonic country in the town of Herkimer. For lieutenant governor the party passed over Pitcher and chose circuit judge Enos Throop, who had treated the Anti-Masons well in court and came from western New York. The lieutenant governor decision was important because it was commonly believed that if Jackson and Van Buren won, Van Buren would move on to Washington. To avoid any trouble with Pitcher, the ever-tactful Van Buren reassured him that he had been left out only because the party needed a westerner on the ticket to balance Van Buren, who lived in Albany. Pitcher, who lived close to Albany, would not do.[49]

The 1828 elections in New York were just as partisan and new style as those in New Hampshire and Kentucky. All the parties nominated their candidates at conventions held along the newly completed Erie Canal rather than in the traditional centers of Albany and New York. The parties showed no hesitation at taking their campaigns to the people. To win the votes of youthful New Yorkers both parties held special conventions for young men and published young men's addresses. For the first time the people, rather than the legislature, would vote for the presidential electors.

The *Albany Argus* also took a new position in defending Jackson against the charge that he was a harsh "military chieftain." Up until 1824 the Jacksonians had accepted the republican thesis that power, especially military power, was a dangerous threat to liberty, a position that put them on the defensive when dealing with Jackson's military behavior. Now they reversed republicanism. Adopting an argument introduced by John Eaton in the "Letters of Wyoming," the *Argus* maintained that the Old Hero had used his military power to preserve, not destroy, order and liberty, especially when enforcing martial law in New Orleans after the battle. Like Washington, Jackson had used his military power to carry out republican ends. This argument spread to other states, including New Hampshire, where Isaac Hill brought it into his January 8 address.[50]

Buoyed by the end of Clintonianism and the rise of Anti-Masonry, the Adams men entered the last weeks of the campaign anticipating victory. In the older, traditional parts of the state—New York City and the lower Hudson River area, where Tammany Hall stood in their way—they had ties with several movements that could help them carry the state. One was the temperance movement, which appealed to the Yankee moralists in their party but turned off the German, Irish, and other elements of the Jackson party. Another was the American Institute, a protectionist movement organized in New York City in December 1827. The heavy concentration of votes in the city made these movements crucial to the success of the Adams party.

The temperance movement never became a political issue, but the question of tariff protection flared up several times. Ever since the War of 1812, merchants in New York and other ports had been importing goods from Europe under the auction system, which allowed them to bid for foreign goods and pay no tariffs until the goods had been resold. State governments, which benefited from the fees, promoted the system, but domestic manufacturers opposed it because it put them in direct competition with foreign companies that were flooding the markets. In December 1827 James Tallmadge and other Adams men in New York took the lead in founding the American Institute to oppose the auction system and promote tariff protection. The following spring the institute held a successful rally that attracted workers as well as manufacturers. A few weeks later, when Jacksonian congressmen, including Churchill C. Cambreleng, refused to sign an antiauction memorial to Congress, the Adams party had another opportunity to make a political issue out of tariff protection. Again it failed to act. Although the institute succeeded in passing resolutions supporting protection, it stuck with its nonpartisan status, removing any possible political advantage for the Adams party. Instead, the Adams men in New York took the same snobbish position as their colleagues in other states—that the best and the brightest in the state were Adams men.[51]

The results of the state elections in 1828 offered hope to the Adams party but ran counter to the general feeling of optimism in the Jackson camp and the downright pessimism on the Adams side.

8

ELECTION DAY

In 1828 there was no uniform presidential election day. Voting for president took place over a period of two weeks, beginning on Friday, October 31, in Pennsylvania and Ohio and ending on Thursday–Friday, November 13–14, in Tennessee. The great majority of the states limited the voting to one day, but five states allowed two or even three. The busiest day in 1828 was Monday, November 3, when twelve states held elections; next busiest was the following Monday, when four states called their voters to the polls.[1]

With two weeks between the first elections and the last, some historians have assumed that news from the early elections arrived in time to influence those that came later. This is highly unlikely. First of all, no one complained about it. There were many complaints about illegal voting and other forms of corruption, but the question of timing was not among them. Second, the first fifteen of the twenty-two states that held a popular vote (the legislature voted for president in Delaware and South Carolina) had their elections so close together (between October 31 and November 5) that it would have been impossible for the early results to influence the later ones. In the remaining seven states, which voted between November 10 and 14, results might have been influenced by the early vote, but the contest was so one-sided in all but two states (Maryland and Indiana) that the influence would have been minimal.

The process of collecting and recording election returns in 1828 was a slow one, for there was no express mail or telegraph to send the results quickly. The first returns to appear in *Niles' Register*, centrally located in Baltimore, were partial returns from Pennsylvania, Ohio, New York, Virginia, and Connecticut five to seven days after the elections in those states.[2] Jackson at the Hermitage heard nothing about the election until returns from a number of counties arrived from nearby Kentucky and Ohio seven and ten days after the votes had been cast. When Duff Green reported to Jackson from Washington on November 12, all Green knew was that the Portland district in Maine and sixteen districts in New York had voted for the Old Hero.[3]

Nonetheless, several historians have assumed that word spread quickly enough to affect the voting. According to one, "around the second week in October returns came dribbling out of Pennsylvania," and "hard on the heels came word from Ohio that Jackson had scored a second triumph." Green then "swiftly notified . . . all those states where the polls had not yet opened." This would have been impossible, because the Pennsylvania and Ohio presidential elections did not take place until October 31. The writer must be referring to news of the state elections there, which were held on October 14. Yet the writer goes on to say that Jackson told William B. Lewis to "pass the information along to the other Western states so that they could use it to advantage."[4]

Another historian maintains that the "balloting began in September" and that Pennsylvania and Ohio "broke for Jackson . . . in mid-October." Then, according to this writer, the New York Jackson committee held the information back until just before the voting began in that state. This is incorrect, because there was no presidential voting in September, and the mid-October elections in Pennsylvania and Ohio were state, not presidential.[5]

Isolated, therefore, by geography, the candidates and the party leaders waited anxiously for the election results. They were much more unsure about who would win than they should have been, for the outcomes never seem as certain to contemporaries as they do to historians one or two hundred years later. In late October 1828 no one was sure how Ohio, Kentucky, and New York would vote, and many thought that even Pennsylvania, strongly Jacksonian, might swing to Adams if the Germans voted as a bloc. One Pennsylvanian promised Clay that "if we get the dutch we are safe." The leaders (still the men to be reckoned with) were particularly anxious, for they knew that their careers were at stake. Adams, always harder on himself than on his fellow countrymen, and never willing to "electioneer," had already given up any hope of winning. When unfavorable news began to arrive in Washington, he reacted in his usual way. "I have," he wrote on December 3, "only to submit [to defeat] with resignation." He talked vaguely about giving up politics and writing a history of the United States or the memoirs of his father and himself. Clay, usually an optimist but now sick and exhausted, no longer had the energy to fight. The sharp-eyed Margaret Bayard Smith noted sadly that he was "much thinner, very pale, his eyes sunk in his head and his countenance sad and melancholy. . . . His voice was feeble and mournful." The last year of the campaign had also been difficult for Webster, who had to stand by helplessly and watch his wife Grace die from cancer and many of his Federalist friends move over to the Jackson side. Yet as late as October 1, he could still reassure Clay that "Mr. Adams [would] be elected."[6]

Charged up by a realistic anticipation of victory, Jackson waited expectantly at the Hermitage. His recent correspondence, on which he continued to rely for news of the campaign, had taken a frightening turn. Letters arrived before the election pleading with him to beware of assassination plots and to "be always prepared to give [himself] a vomit" should he be poisoned. Others feared that the administration would announce his death to discourage people from voting for him. A less macabre letter urged Jackson to take a tour through Kentucky and Indiana, timing his ride so that he would reach each state while people were voting. Jackson may have prepared himself to vomit, but he rejected the idea of a tour.[7]

Calhoun was already looking ahead. After four difficult years as vice president in the opposition's administration, he could only anticipate another four engaged in two more conflicts. One concerned the tariff. The other was a potential fight with Jackson over some critical remarks Calhoun had made about the general's questionable behavior in his invasion of Spanish Florida. Both conflicts had already begun. Van Buren's confidant James A. Hamilton was secretly collecting evidence about the behavior of Calhoun and Jackson during the Florida campaign, and hotheads in South Carolina were denouncing the policy of protective tariffs. After Congress adjourned in late May 1828, Calhoun returned to South Carolina and went to work preparing the *Exposition and Protest,* which was published by the state legislature in December. The *Exposition* was a long essay on the tariff, outlining the grievances of South Carolina and proposing state interposition (veto or nullification) as the solution, while the *Protest* was the legislature's formal repudiation of the tariff of abominations.

Of all the men to be reckoned with, Van Buren was the only one still engaged in the campaign. A few days before the start of the voting he had to deal with the false rumor that he had tried to shift the election back to the state legislature in New York and a letter from William H. Crawford, who was still opposing Calhoun for vice president.

On Monday evening, November 10, Jackson's biographer, the notorious Henry Lee, rode into Nashville bearing the good news that Jackson's majority in twenty-four of sixty-four counties in Ohio was 9,724 and that his majority in four of twelve congressional districts in Kentucky was 5,759. When Jackson heard the news the next morning he sat down at once and sent the information on to his old friend John Coffee in Alabama. "It appears," he chortled, that "Ky. & ohio are safe." A few days later the letter arrived from Green with the heartening information that Jackson had won the district around Portland, Maine, and half of the voting districts in New York State.[8]

At the same time Clay was receiving similar bits of information from Philemon Beecher of Ohio. With almost half the returns counted, Jackson's margin in the Buckeye State was 8,330. Clay was also getting unfavorable reports from Kentucky and Virginia. Sad and depressed, he could only reply that Adams might still win if he carried all five of the "disputed states"—Ohio, Indiana, Illinois, Louisiana, and Kentucky. But Clay was only bluffing. Jackson carried all the "disputed states" and won the election.[9]

Jackson had not only won; he had won so decisively that the victory could be called a landslide. In a great national decision he had carried all sections except New England. Eaton's optimistic prediction of a year ago had come true (see Table 8.1).

These voting returns and the story of the 1828 election campaign offer a rich body of information about the political culture of the young republic. They show, first of all, that the people had won the struggle over who should vote for presidential electors. Only two of the twenty-four states—Delaware and South Carolina—still entrusted that power to the legislature. The returns also show that the electoral system had the potential to override the popular vote. Despite winning 56 percent of the popular vote (the largest majority in the nineteenth century), Jackson came close to losing in the electoral vote. As political scientist Svend

Table 8.1. Results of the 1828 Election

State	Electoral Votes Jackson	Electoral Votes Adams	Popular Votes Jackson	Popular Votes Adams
Maine	1	8	13,927	20,773
New Hampshire	...	8	20,922	24,124
Vermont	...	7	8,385	24,365
Massachusetts	...	15	6,019	29,837
Connecticut	...	8	4,448	13,838
Rhode Island	...	4	821	2,754
New York	20	16	140,763	135,413
New Jersey	...	8	21,951	23,764
Pennsylvania	28	...	101,652	50,848
Delaware	...	3	Legislature	
Maryland	5	6	24,565	25,527
Virginia	24	...	26,752	12,101
North Carolina	15	...	37,857	13,918
South Carolina	11	...	Legislature	
Georgia	9	...	19,362	642
Ohio	16	...	67,597	63,396
Indiana	5	...	22,237	17,052
Illinois	3	...	9,560	4,662
Missouri	3	...	8,272	3,400
Kentucky	14	...	39,394	31,460
Tennessee	11	...	44,293	2,240
Alabama	5	...	17,138	1,938
Mississippi	3	...	6,772	1,581
Louisiana	5	...	4,605	4,097
Total	178	83	647,292	507,730

Source: Svend Petersen, *A Statistical History of American Presidential Elections* (New York: Frederick Ungar, 1963), 20.

Petersen later demonstrated, a switch of only 11,517 votes in five states (slightly less than 1 percent of the total) would have brought Adams a very close victory in the electoral college and made him president for four more years (see Table 8.2).

This speculation is fanciful, but it helps explain why there was so much concern in the late 1820s about the electoral college. The Jacksonians already believed that the system had cheated them out of a victory in 1824–1825. Old-timers remembered the thirty-six ballots needed to elect Thomas Jefferson in the House of Representatives in 1801. Many felt strongly that the president should never again be elected by the House.

Table 8.2. 1828 Presidential Election: Hypothetical Outcome with Less than 1 Percent Switch in Popular Votes

		Actual Electoral College Vote	
		Adams	Jackson
		83	178
	Hypothetical Shift in Votes	Hypothetical Electoral Change	
Ohio	2,101	+16	−16
Kentucky	3,968	+14	−14
New York (7 districts; 2 at large)	2,600	+9	−9
Louisiana	255	+5	−5
Indiana	2,593	+5	−5
Total	11,517	+49	−49
New totals		132	129

Source: Svend Petersen, *A Statistical History of American Presidential Elections* (New York: Frederick Ungar, 1963), 19. Sean Wilentz outlines a similar scenario in *The Rise of American Democracy: Jefferson to Lincoln* (New York: Norton, 2005), 308–309.

If Jackson had lost again in the electoral vote after winning such a high percentage of the popular vote, his followers would have been more convinced than ever that the will of the people had been thwarted.

Americans have interpreted the election in various ways. In the mid-nineteenth century, when antipartyism still existed and the first great national historian, George Bancroft, was glorifying the providential spread of American democracy, biographers of Jackson gave his election credit for the rise of democracy. They pointed out with pride that the numbers voting for president had risen from 356,000 in 1824 to 1,156,000 in 1828. In his 1860 classic the *Life of Andrew Jackson*, James Parton explained the election: "The scepter," he wrote, "was about to be wrested from the hands" of the upper classes. "Nearly all the talent, nearly all the learning, nearly all the ancient wealth, nearly all the business activity, nearly all the book-nourished intelligence, nearly all the silver-forked civilization of the country, united in opposition to General Jackson, who represented the country's untutored instincts."[10] In a later biography economist William Graham Sumner agreed that the election led to the rise of democracy.[11]

Progressive-period historians who dominated American historiography in the first half of the twentieth century added another dimension to the democratic theme. They postulated a persistent economic struggle between the vested interests and the common people—the farmers and laborers. According to Frederick Jackson Turner, after the panic of 1819 the western Relief movement "found its leader in Andrew Jackson." Turner believed that democracy had grown up in the West and that Jackson had been elected by an agrarian coalition of new democratic states. In *The Age of Jackson* the last of the Progressives, Arthur M. Schlesinger Jr., argued that it had grown up in the East and that Jackson was a nineteenth-century FDR fighting the battles of urban workers.[12]

A combination of political scientists and historians filled in the Progressive interpretation by introducing the concept of party systems. According to their analysis, the first two-party system occurred between 1790 and 1815 and a second between 1828 and 1856, with the election of 1828 serving as an all-important election of realignment. In time, third, fourth, and fifth two-party systems were added.[13]

Neither the democratic, economic struggle in the Progressive interpretation nor the concept of successive party systems escaped unscathed. The first was far too simplistic. Although the Jacksonians did talk and write continually about democracy and the rise of the common man in the 1828 campaign, they ignored the evidence that democracy had already emerged and that many of the Jackson leaders—men such as Thomas Ritchie, Levi Woodbury, John C. Calhoun, Louis McLane, John Randolph, and even Jackson himself—were hardly from the ranks of the common man. As Richard Hofstadter put it, "Jackson's election was more a result than a cause of the rise of democracy." Historians also began to question whether the Federalists and Republicans had developed a true two-party system.[14]

Not until 1960, however, was evidence introduced demonstrating that democracy had preceded Jackson's election and that the election of 1828 did not greatly increase the percentage of Americans voting. In an influential article that year, Richard P. McCormick showed that states had routinely drawn large percentages of adult white males to the polls well before 1828. In only six states—New York, Maryland, Virginia, Ohio, Indiana, and Louisiana—was the percentage of voting in the presidential election of 1828 higher than in any previous election in that state. It should be noted, however, that there was indeed a great increase in the rate of voting for president between 1824 and 1828. And the trend continued. The average national turnout for presidential elections rose from 26.5 percent of eligible voters in 1824 to 56.3 percent in 1828 to 78 percent in 1840.[15]

McCormick also questioned the existence of a two-party system in 1828. Pointing out that a two-party system is characterized by close elections, he found that, based on that criterion, the election of 1828 fell far short. In only six of the twenty-two state presidential elections that year (New Hampshire, New York, New Jersey, Maryland, Ohio, and Louisiana) was the differential, or gap, between winner and loser less than 10 percentage points. Not until 1840, when the number of states with close elections had risen to sixteen out of twenty-six, could it be said that the United States had a true two-party system. The average differential of 36 points in 1828 dropped to 11 points in 1840.[16]

Since the middle of the twentieth century, when the Progressive view went out of favor, other schools of thought have tried to explain the election of 1828. The consensus interpretation maintained that neither Jackson nor his followers seriously challenged the business interest and that Americans were united in their support for liberal capitalism. In his chapter on Jackson, Hofstadter pointed out that the Bank of the United States, supposedly the center of controversy between the powerful rich and the Jackson democrats, was never an issue in the election of 1828. The ethnocultural school argued that in the election of 1828 (and in other elections) men voted not for democratic or economic reasons but because of their religious, ethnic, or other social affiliations. The market revolution interpretation, which was best presented by Charles Sellers in 1991, argued that the election was a fight between the Adams men, who welcomed the rise of a capitalist economy, and the Jackson men, who opposed it. Donald J. Ratcliffe once commented that this interpretation was "a more sophisticated version of the old Progressive view."[17]

A persistent theme running through many analyses of the election is the argument that Jackson was elected by the votes of southern slave owners, who assumed that because Jackson was a slave owner himself, he would be loyal to the peculiar institution. The leading advocate of this interpretation was Edward Channing, a Progressive historian from New England who produced a scholarly six-volume history of the United States soon after World War I. Channing protested that Jackson would not have won had it not been for the support of the solid South. He put the blame on the three-fifths clause in the Constitution, which, he said, unfairly increased the representation of the slaveholding states. As a result, the 2.5 million whites in the South had almost as many electoral votes (105) as the 4.75 million free people in the North (137). "Jackson was raised to the presidency," he wrote, "by the over-representation of the South."[18]

The returns from the 1828 election in Virginia bear out Channing's thesis. Primarily because of the state's restrictive suffrage laws, only 28 percent of adult white males in Virginia voted, and thanks to the three-fifths clause, the number of electoral votes they produced was greatly magnified. As a result, 38,853 Virginia voters accounted for 24 electoral votes, or one for every 1,618 voters; in contrast, Ohio's 130,993 voters accounted for only 16 electoral votes, or one for every 8,187 voters. An even more glaring discrepancy occurred in New York, where, because of the district system, 276,176 voters accounted for only 4 electoral votes, or one for every 69,044 voters.

The slavery interpretation has been hotly contested, but it has never died. In 1935 Turner attacked it in his final book, *The United States 1830–1850*. First of all, Turner wrote, there was no "solid South." The residents of several states that Channing called southern, such as Missouri and Kentucky, thought of themselves as western. He conceded that the southern states backing Jackson had an advantage in the three-fifths rule, but he pointed out that the fast-growing western states had to overcome the disadvantage of an apportionment system based on the out-of-date census of 1820. Furthermore, the small New England states that supported Adams so loyally had the constitutional advantage of a provision assigning two electors to each state regardless of its size.[19]

Richard H. Brown forthrightly endorsed Channing's position. In an influential article he observed that "the concrete measure of difference between defeat [for Jackson] in 1824 and victory in 1828 was the Old Republican strength of the South Atlantic states and New York, brought to the Jackson camp, carefully tended and carefully drilled by Van Buren." The article went on to trace the influence of slavery on the Jackson party from the Missouri Compromise to the Dred Scott decision.[20]

In 1978 William J. Cooper carried the slavery thesis a few steps further. Noting that Jackson won 81.4 percent of the popular vote in the South in 1828, Cooper argued that the Jacksonians turned to the Old Hero as the "new apostle of the South, the new Jefferson." Cooper used the ideological words of South Carolina novelist William Gilmore Simms to explain why the South so resolutely backed the Old Hero. Jackson was, wrote Simms, "a States' Rights man, opposed to Tariffs, Banks, Internal Improvements, American Systems, Fancy Railroads,

Floats, Land Companies, and every Humbug East and West, whether of cant or cunning." Using the words of another southern idealist, Cooper quoted Thomas Ritchie, who said that there must be "no tampering with slavery."[21]

Harry L. Watson thought differently. In his 1981 study of Cumberland County, North Carolina, Watson dismissed several arguments that linked the Jackson victory to the defense of slavery. In particular he rejected the thesis that opponents who attacked Adams for a "broad construction" of the Constitution were really accusing him of wanting to use that broad construction to abolish slavery.[22]

By the end of the twentieth century the slavery interpretation of the election was strengthened by a revisionist trend in the interpretation of Jacksonian democracy. Rejecting the economic notion that Jackson was a liberal democrat defending the common man, the revisionists pointed out that during his era, advances for white males were more than off-set by increased restrictions on women, blacks, and Native Americans. These critics insisted that the Jacksonians showed little inclination to fight for social reforms. Richard John argued that instead of organizing their party from the bottom or common man up, the Jacksonians built it from the top down. Led by Martin Van Buren and Duff Green, they united the slave owners of the South with party men in the North on a platform that defended slavery. Despite opposition within the party, Van Buren and Green insisted on nominating a ticket of two slave own-ers, and once in office, the Jackson men continued to defend slavery by using riots and post office restrictions to oppose abolitionism. Robert Pierce Forbes expanded on this thesis in his recent work on the Missouri Compromise.[23]

The election returns for the six representative states in this study support a number of these interpretations. In four of the six states— New Hampshire, Kentucky, Ohio, and Virginia—there were echoes of the Progressive–market revolution point of view that the election was a democratic struggle between economic groups.

The Jackson men in New Hampshire came close to carrying the state but fell short by a narrow margin, with 20,922 votes for Jackson (46 percent) to 24,124 for Adams (see Table 8.3). A town-by-town study of the election shows that economic differences played a significant role in determining the outcome. Although the number of towns voting for each candidate was about the same (99 for Jackson, 103 for Adams), well over half the Jackson towns had a low tax apportionment (below $3.50

Table 8.3. 1828 Presidential Vote in New England

State	Jackson	Adams
New Hampshire	20,922 (46%)	24,124 (54%)
Maine	13,927 (40%)	20,773 (60%)
Remaining New England States	19,673 (22%)	70,794 (78%)
Vermont	8,385	24,365
Massachusetts	6,019	29,837
Connecticut	4,448	13,838
Rhode Island	821	2,754
New England total	54,522 (32%)	115,691 (68%)

Source: Svend Petersen, *A Statistical History of American Presidential Elections* (New York: Frederick Ungar, 1963), 20.

per 1,000 population), compared with 38 percent of the Adams towns. Among the more prosperous towns, 35 percent of those voting for Adams were in the higher rankings ($4 and above), compared with only 21 percent of the towns voting for Jackson. Two-thirds of the wealthiest towns voted for Adams, one-third for Jackson.[24]

Webster's assumption that the townspeople in the remote, hilly, often mountainous regions of New Hampshire favored Jackson proved to be sound. Of the sixty-four towns in the White Mountains of northern New Hampshire, forty-six voted for Jackson; in the southern hill towns, Jackson towns outnumbered Adams towns thirty-nine to fourteen. In contrast, Adams towns predominated (sixty-five to nineteen) in the accessible, developed valleys of the Connecticut and Merrimack rivers, the Old Colony seacoast region, and the towns along the Massachusetts border.

The relationship between counties' growth rates and voting records shows similar correlations. Counties with slow rates of growth were generally long-settled counties with well-established economies where the best land had already been taken. Newer, younger, poorer settlers were likely to pass them by and migrate to less accessible counties where land was cheaper, giving those counties high rates of growth. Between 1820 and 1830 New Hampshire grew at the rather sluggish rate of 10 percent. The two extremes were the mountainous and most remote Coos County, which grew at the extraordinary rate of 70 percent, and long-settled Cheshire County on the Massachusetts border, which lost 3 percent of its population. Not surprisingly, fast-growing Coos County voted

65 percent for Jackson, while shrinking Cheshire County gave Jackson only 26 percent of its vote. The settlers moving north into Coos County were younger, poorer, and more likely to vote for Jackson than were those living in Cheshire County. Jacksonianism flourished in the remote parts of New Hampshire, far from the more highly developed state of Massachusetts. The Jackson men tended to be less well-off and younger than the Adams men. Economic pressures were at work.[25]

They were also at work in Kentucky. As in New Hampshire, Kentucky voters turned out in large numbers for the election—70.7 percent of those eligible, fourth highest in the nation. The pattern of the vote was the same as in the state election in August, with centers of Jackson support in the outer tier of the Bluegrass, the counties along the Ohio River and the lower Green River. The Adams party remained strong in the heart of the Bluegrass and in a vast, less-populated region in southeastern Kentucky along the Wilderness Road.

Lynn Marshall used data from this election to discover whether there was any correlation between the 1828 vote for Jackson in Kentucky and various economic, social, and political patterns in the state. He first examined the quality of soil in Kentucky to see whether Jackson supporters were predominantly tilling poor soil or good soil. There was no correlation. Then he analyzed the type of counties where most Jackson men lived to see whether they were predominantly farming or mercantile regions, but again there was no correlation. He finally found three correlations. There was a negative correlation between counties that voted strongly for Jackson and those with a large slave population. Counties with large, southern-style plantations such as Fayette County in the heart of the Bluegrass favored Adams. He also discovered a positive correlation between the Jackson counties and, as in New Hampshire, the fast-growing counties. The strongest connection was the positive correlation between Jackson counties and counties that had supported the Relief acts. Jackson won eight of the ten consistent Relief counties and nine of ten with the fastest rates of growth.[26]

Marshall now had a clear picture of the Jacksonians in Kentucky. They were men on the make, ordinarily in debt, who chose to live in underdeveloped counties where land was cheap and their neighbors were like them. Amos Kendall had decided to live with such people when he moved from the rich upper-class life of Lexington in the heart of the Bluegrass to Georgetown and later Frankfort, in the fast-growing yet still backward fringes of the Bluegrass. In so doing he had fled from the world of Henry and Lucretia Clay, and later the Adams party, to the world of future Jackson men Richard M. Johnson and Francis Preston Blair.

Although the Progressive, conflict-of-interests interpretation was not the main theme of Donald J. Ratcliffe's study of Ohio, he too found economic correlations. After ranking the Ohio counties according to the per capita value of real estate, he correlated the results with the counties' presidential vote. Seven of the eight counties with the highest valuation voted for Adams, and eleven of the top fifteen. Eight of the ten poorest counties were for Jackson, and eleven of the poorest fifteen.[27]

A final state in which democracy and economic interests were at stake was Virginia. In the Old Dominion the Jackson-Junto party represented the conservative planters of the Tidewater-Piedmont center, who supported states' rights Old Republicanism. Opposing them were democratic reformers from the underrepresented, often commercial outer reaches of the state (the periphery), where the Adams party was strong. Although the reformers had won a victory in April when the referendum for a constitutional convention carried, the Jackson party won easily in the presidential election by a vote of 26,752 to 12,101. Of the 102 counties in Virginia, the Adams party carried only 29: 7 in the west, 6 in the Valley of Virginia, 13 in the Chesapeake-Potomac region, and only 3 in the Tidewater-Piedmont.[28]

The economic pattern of backward, relatively poor, often remote Jackson counties and prosperous, highly developed Adams counties was repeated in many other parts of the country. Adams tended to do well in the counties along the Erie Canal; the shores of Lake Ontario, Lake Erie, and Chesapeake Bay; the commercial valleys of the Hudson, Delaware, Potomac, Ohio, Wabash, and Illinois rivers; the prosperous trading areas along the North Carolina coast; and the lower Mississippi River at New Orleans.

This democratic, economic interpretation has been challenged by evidence that regional religious, ethnic, and cultural differences also played an important role. In New Hampshire the Toleration Act of 1819, which allowed town tax funds to be used for any Christian church, had ended the dominance of Congregationalism and encouraged the growth of Baptist and Methodist churches. By 1828 the number of Baptist and Methodist churches exceeded the number of Congregational churches 173 to 149. The shift away from Congregationalism benefited the Jackson party, which lacked Congregational support. Only 38 percent of the Congregational churches were in Jackson towns, compared with 62 percent in Adams towns.[29]

One of the best ways to understand the influence of ethnocultural differences is to follow the track of the "Universal Yankee Nation," which Webster counted on to elect John Quincy Adams. Anti-Masonry, which played such an important role in the New York election, would not have flowered had it not been for the moral New Englanders who had settled in western New York and turned it into the reform-minded "Burned-Over District." Far more committed to social and political equality than their fellow New Yorkers, the transplanted Yankees promoted reforms such as public education, abolition of the militia, and the end of imprisonment for debt. As historian Lee Benson has pointed out, the rise of Anti-Masonry caused an abrupt change in New York voting patterns. In Genesee County, the heart of the Anti-Masonic movement, Van Buren's Bucktails won only 30 percent of the vote in 1828, down from 48 percent in 1826. In central and eastern New York, which resisted Anti-Masonry, the opposite took place. The Ulster County Bucktails, for example, increased their vote from 46 percent to 63 percent. The enthusiasm for reform in the voting districts west of Lake Cayuga gave Adams a margin of nearly 12,500 votes and almost allowed him to carry the state (see Table 8.4).[30]

The influence of the Yankee Nation and New England culture swept into Ohio in the 1828 election. The settlements of the New England–based Ohio Company along the Ohio River in the southeastern corner of the state were reliably for Adams. And in seven counties in the Western Reserve on Lake Erie, transplanted settlers from Connecticut, mostly of English stock, voted for Adams. The influence of migrants can also be seen in the Miami Purchase and the Virginia Military District in southwestern Ohio. These areas had been settled by a mixture of Pennsylvanians and southerners, who made Cincinnati the center of the Jackson movement in the West. The counties constituting much of this part of Ohio gave Jackson two-thirds of their votes in 1828. Farther north in the "Backbone" section of eastern Ohio, former Pennsylvanians in a number of counties, including Wayne and Holmes, had brought their enthusiasm for Jackson across the border.[31]

German migrants played a major part in the politics of both Ohio and Pennsylvania. Counties with German settlements, mostly in northeastern Ohio south of the Western Reserve, were solidly for Jackson. Six of the top ten Jackson counties in Ohio had substantial enclaves of German immigrants. A few counties near or along the National Road with Scotch-Irish populations were also Jacksonian. The German vote was

Table 8.4. 1828 Presidential Vote in Western New York Anti-Mason Districts

District Number	Adams	Jackson
26	9,119	7,011
27	7,079	4,631
29	6,832	3,256
30	7,983	3,660
Total	31,013	18,558

Source: Svend Petersen, *A Statistical History of American Presidential Elections* (New York: Frederick Ungar, 1963), 19.

even more important in Pennsylvania, which had a German governor. The Adams party hoped to get valuable support from the Pennsylvania Germans, who had the reputation of voting as a bloc. In 1828 they lived up to this reputation, but the bloc voted for Jackson. Despite all the attention lavished on them by the Adams men, the eight leading German counties gave Jackson an average of 70 percent of their votes and contributed nearly 13,000 to the large Jackson majority (see Table 8.5).

Tradition should not be overlooked in studying the election. In New Hampshire the traditional voting pattern, in which the Federalists controlled the main lines of trade and communication—the Connecticut and Merrimack river valleys and the Old Colony coastal settlements—was repeated in 1828 by the Adams party. In New York Martin Van Buren stubbornly looked back at the election of 1800 and insisted that "the old Federalist manor influence" along the Hudson River was responsible for making the election so close. In some ways the comparison was meaningless, for in 1800 there had been no Battle of New Orleans, no Erie Canal, and no Anti-Masonic party, and hardly anyone had heard of Andrew Jackson. Yet it is not surprising that Van Buren, whose goal was to restore the old party system, insisted on looking back. There was some truth in what he said. The voting districts on the upper Hudson, the home of Stephen Van Rensselaer and earlier patroons, and the districts between Albany and Lake Champlain, all of which had been reliably Federalist in 1800, gave Adams a majority of almost 3,000 votes in 1828.[32]

The Adams majorities on the manor lands and in western New York almost won him the state, but large Jackson majorities in New York City and central New York were enough to give the state to the Jacksonians. The presidential vote was remarkably close: Jackson, 140,783 (20 electoral votes); Adams, 135,413 (16 electoral votes). Van Buren's decision to

Table 8.5. 1828 Presidential Vote in Pennsylvania German Counties

County	Jackson	Adams
Berks	4,583	894
Dauphin	1,974	1,140
Lancaster	5,186	3,719
Lebanon	1,417	597
Lehigh	2,000	516
Northampton	3,028	889
Schuylkill	863	220
York	3,645	1,864
Total	22,696	9,839

Source: *Philadelphia Democratic Press*, November 19, 1828, cited in Philip S. Klein and Ari Hoogenboom, *A History of Pennsylvania* (New York: McGraw-Hill, 1973), 409.

run for governor proved to be a wise one, for he won the election by a substantial margin, but only because the nomination of an Anti-Masonic candidate split the opposition vote. In the end he fell 1,498 votes short of winning a majority of the votes. The final tally was Van Buren 136,794 (49.5 percent), Thompson (Adams party) 106,444 (38.5 percent), and Southwick (Anti-Mason) 33,345 (12.1 percent). If the Adams and Anti-Masonic parties had run a coordinated campaign, it is quite likely that Thompson and Adams would have carried New York, but the change in electoral votes would not have altered the outcome of the presidential election.[33]

Another determinant in the election was the role of one individual—Andrew Jackson. In very few elections has the personality of one candidate played such an important role. Jackson was the first candidate to have nicknames, the first to be born poor and to grow up on the frontier, the only candidate who could be compared to George Washington, the only president to fight a duel (and kill a man in the process), and the only general to defeat the British in a face-to-face battle. Jackson was such a violent, charismatic person that he dominated the election and his era. In comparison, John Quincy Adams was a pale, far less dominant figure.

Throughout the election campaign the Old Hero held the center of the stage. From the moment the Jacksonians accused Adams of stealing the presidency with a corrupt bargain until the very end, when many of Jackson's followers feared his assassination, the campaign was about Andrew Jackson. In past elections the candidates had followed the republican pattern of staying out of the limelight, but Jackson ended all that by issuing at least sixty addresses, speeches, or public writings of some sort during the campaign.

Even more striking were the quarrels and controversies involving Jackson to which the Jacksonians felt obliged to respond during the campaign. The editors of the Jackson papers cite more than two hundred references to some forty different controversies for the years 1825 to 1828. Some of the conflicts, such as those involving the execution of the six militiamen and Jackson's alleged adultery, continue to be well known; others, such as his entanglement with the Allison family over land deals, his use of bribes in treaty negotiations with the Chickasaws, and his role in the death of his slave Gilbert, have not received as much attention. These and other charges dogged Jackson throughout the campaign. They kept him on the defensive and forced him to depart from the republican doctrine that presidential candidates must not campaign. His decisive victory was in many ways a vindication for Old Hickory.

The sheer volume of Jackson's publications, correspondence, and controversies was so central to the campaign on both sides that it has led some historians to argue that Jackson was not just a candidate but also the leader of the Jackson party. According to Robert V. Remini, for example, "From the very beginning of the attempts to organize an opposition, the Hero was the head of the party—without question and without doubt."[34] It is true that Jackson gradually assumed the leadership of his party, but most of his work and letter writing during the campaign were devoted to defending himself, not his party, against the many charges being leveled against him. Credit for creating and building the Jackson (later Democratic) party must go to Martin Van Buren, John C. Calhoun, Thomas Ritchie, Duff Green, and state leaders such as Amos Kendall and Isaac Hill.

There were two policy issues powerful enough to influence the election. One was the tariff. At the start of the campaign it looked as if each party would have to support tariff protection in order to win. Americans from all walks of life and all regions—workers, manufacturers, and farmers in New England, the Middle Atlantic states, and the Northwest—believed that they would benefit immensely from tariff protection. The Adams party easily could have exploited this issue, since Henry Clay was already trumpeting it in his American System.

When Clay departed for Kentucky in June 1827, it looked as if the Adams party had decided to make the tariff and Clay's American System its central theme, but that issue was soon lost in the revelations and responses of Beverley, Buchanan, Jackson, Kendall, and Clay. The Harrisburg tariff convention offered another opportunity, and later, in New York State, the Adams men could have taken a stand in favor of the protective antiauction movement. But each time Adams held back. He was never a committed tariff man, and he was eager to gain support in Virginia and other southern states that were opposed to the tariff. Although he offered dozens of federal programs in his first annual message, he ignored the tariff and continued to ignore it in the next two messages. One of the most loyal Adams men, Jabez Hammond of New York, was furious when he learned of the omission in the December 1827 message. When John Sergeant lost his seat in Congress in 1828, he blamed it on Adams's failure to support high tariff protection. Meanwhile, the Jacksonians were evading the question as much as possible and finally rode to victory on Van Buren's carefully crafted tariff of abominations.

The other powerful issue was the definition of republicanism—whether to follow the newer version, with its emphasis on democracy and acceptance of change, or the traditional version, with its stress on personal and public virtue. The Adams party offered a candidate with great personal virtue and ability, but Adams forfeited that advantage when his first annual message called for a dizzying array of "improvements" and a redefinition of republicanism.[35] Adams, so easy to caricature as a Massachusetts intellectual and aristocrat, never had a chance to appear democratic in comparison to the self-made man of the frontier. The Jacksonians won the battle over traditional republicanism at the start of the campaign with John Eaton's portrait of Jackson as a virtuous Cincinnatus; they added to their advantage with their attacks on Adams for corruption and their well-chosen slogan of "Jackson and Reform." The Jackson party had correctly measured the pulse of Americans, who were more comfortable supporting the ideals of the past, even though they might be willing to try new forward-looking institutions such as capitalism, democracy, and party government.

There is no doubt that much of the election was about Andrew Jackson and that it reflected a number of crucial social, economic, and cultural issues, including republicanism, democracy, slavery, religious beliefs, and the market revolution. Even though some version of these issues influenced the outcome in many counties and states, the election did not turn on them. Instead, the major theme of the election, the one that left the most enduring mark on the United States, concerned the institution that John Quincy Adams scornfully called "electioneering." This was the story of the rise of mass political parties and the origins of a two-party political system that still exists today. These were, of course, just beginnings—neither the parties nor the system would be fully developed until the election of 1840.[36] Only half a dozen states—New Hampshire, New York, New Jersey, Maryland, Ohio, and Kentucky—had a two-party system in 1828, and national parties were still a decade away, but the roots of a modern two-party system were firmly in place.

The origins of this system go back to the Era of Good Feelings, when the panic of 1819 and the debates over slavery in Missouri led some, like Van Buren, to call for a return to the old party system. The three years between Adams's first annual message in 1825 and Jackson's election in 1828 saw the birth of the Jackson-Democratic party and the Adams–National Republican–Whig party. At the presidential level the Democrats were more successful, winning six of the eight elections between 1828 and 1856, but the Whigs offered strong competition. In the 1840s they won two of the three presidential elections, and had it not been for the Liberty party in 1844, they might have won three straight. In those three presidential elections the differential between the two parties in the states averaged only 10 percentage points. Furthermore, the Whigs kept close to the Democrats in the state elections. In the five years from 1840 to 1844 the Whigs won control of both houses of state legislatures in forty-one elections, the Democrats won control in forty-five, and the two parties broke even in fifteen. In the nine years from 1840 to 1848 the Whigs won a median of 45 percent of the congressional seats and 43 percent of the gubernatorial seats. Between the late 1830s and the early 1850s politics became a popular pastime in America. Large numbers of eligible voters came out to vote—78 percent in 1840 and 75 percent in 1844. Some regard the era as the golden age of party politics.[37]

The new, well-organized system of political parties was all the more popular because it was so necessary. In drawing up the Constitution the founding fathers had paid no attention to the need for political parties. Instead, they left the United States with the awkward electoral college system, under which the states choose electors who then vote for president and vice president. The republican assumption that candidates would somehow rise up fresh from the people was unrealistic in the democratic, capitalist world that was emerging. Therefore, the new political party system developed in the election of 1828 was more than simply a political movement. It was an extraconstitutional reform made necessary by omissions in the original Constitution. Institutions such as the Democratic and Republican parties, which have shown great durability; their national committees and party conventions; and the system of presidential primaries are essential additions to the Constitution.[38]

The success of the new party system in 1828 stemmed from the willingness of the party founders to spend time and money on organization. No one was more aware of the need for this than Henry Clay, who told Charles Hammond: "Where there is system on the one side" and none or little on the other, "defeat [for the latter] is inevitable."[39] Although the party system was designed to work from the bottom up, it was built from the top down. The two main builders, especially during the 1828 campaign, were Martin Van Buren, who went to Washington in 1821 determined to rebuild the party system, and Henry Clay, whose contributions to party building have not been adequately recognized. Andrew Jackson and later Abraham Lincoln became indispensable symbols.

During the 1828 campaign politicians on both sides explored innovative ways of using committees and conventions to unite their town and county parties. The high point for conventions came between December 1827 and January 1828, when both parties in more than half a dozen states held state conventions at which they published addresses and nominated presidential, congressional, and local candidates. Van Buren even offered to call a national nominating convention in his letter to Ritchie but pulled back when he realized that the campaign was going his way without such a convention.

The Jacksonians started out ahead because they organized better than their opponents; they paid more attention to detail and recruited a broader range of workers. Nothing was too small to command their attention, no one too low socially to hold a position. These "faceless functionaries," as Lynn Marshall dubbed them, spread the party line and got more voters out on election day than their often more prominent opponents. One of the differences between the upper levels of the two parties was that the Adams party depended on the upper-class friends of Clay, while the Jackson party followed the lead of socially marginal professional politicians such as Van Buren, Hill, and Kendall. (It was ironic that Kendall had been an employee of the Clays before rising to the top of the emerging Jackson party in Kentucky.) Finally, the Jacksonians were more willing to fight. There is no better expression of this attitude than the advice Kendall gave to his Kentucky friend and fellow Jackson man Francis Preston Blair. Kendall instructed Blair to "be up and doing

. . . organize, organize [and] a fig for the fainted [sic] hearted men who are ready to surrender."[40]

The Jacksonians secured the services of many of these new-style editor-politicians when they brought the Albany Regency, the Frankfort Junto, and other such state organizations into their party. None of the Jacksonians—Van Buren, Hill, Ritchie, Kendall, Green, and Hayward—were particularly successful men when Adams took office in 1825. Van Buren's Bucktails had suffered heavy losses; Hill had committed himself unwisely to William H. Crawford; John H. Pleasants had written Ritchie's political obituary after the Crawford disaster; Kendall's Relief party had lost two straight elections; Green was stuck on the frontier of Missouri; and Hayward faced the task of overcoming a large Adams lead in Ohio.

Once they joined the Jackson party, however, they played important roles. They provided leadership, built organizations, raised funds, publicized party dogma, and smeared the opposition. Three years later, as Jackson took office, all of them had become well-established, prominent American political figures. Many had moved into the Jackson administration. Within a few months Van Buren went from senator to governor to secretary of state. Hill moved from second comptroller to senator to governor. Kendall became fourth auditor, then postmaster general, and soon rivaled Van Buren as the most influential man in Jackson's administration. As Jackson's commissioner of the General Land Office, Hayward presided over one of the greatest land booms in American history. Ritchie fought off Pleasants's attacks and continued to reign in Richmond. More loyal to Calhoun than to Jackson, Green became the South Carolinian's spokesman in Washington.

The smaller group of editors on the Adams side enjoyed the same upward mobility. In 1825 Thurlow Weed had just returned from an unsuccessful job-seeking trip to Washington. By 1829 he had become editor of the *Albany Evening Journal* and would soon be recognized as the political head of the Whig and later Republican parties. Charles Hammond, who was uncertain about his future in 1825, rose to the top of the Ohio bar. John Binns was not so fortunate. Immediately after the 1828 election an unruly Jackson mob came close to murdering him and tearing down his printing shop. But even he recovered and served for twenty-five years as an alderman in Philadelphia.

Another reason why the Jackson party rose more quickly than its rival was its ability to come to terms with the question of patronage. At the start of the campaign both parties roundly condemned patronage as the corrupt use of government funds, and the Jacksonians spent two sessions of Congress attacking Adams for corruption. The Adams party was also losing ground because Adams refused to appoint many Federalists to office. Determined to do better, and realizing that patronage was the glue that held parties together, the Jacksonians adopted their ambiguous slogan of "Jackson and Reform." By the eve of the election Green's *Telegraph* was promising openly that Jackson would "reward his friends and punish his enemies."[41]

The Jacksonians also outdid the Adams men with the zealotry, violence, and overwhelming force of their campaigning. Clay's brother Porter had compared the force to the "currant [*sic*] of the Mississippi." This, together with the equally powerful, violent image of Andrew Jackson, who had killed a man in a duel and had threatened to cut the ears off another, made the Jacksonians formidable opponents. In the eyes of the Adams men the Jacksonians were "artful," "clamorous" men who would do anything, including lie, to elect Old Hickory. The Adams party was particularly critical of junto leaders such as Isaac Hill, whom it described as "traversing [New Hampshire] like a flying dragon . . . trying to revolutionize the state." In contrast, they considered their own leaders and themselves to be "pure patriotic, uncorrupted and incorruptible republican and accomplished statesmen." Daniel Mallory of New York described his Adams compatriots as "mostly quiet moral people—men of wealth and influence."[42]

This behavior and these attitudes, which were characteristic of the politicians in all the representative states except Virginia, had unfortunate consequences for the Adams cause. They lent credence to the Jacksonian charge that their opponents were rich, aristocratic, class-conscious, and undemocratic. They also frightened the Adams men so much that they came to believe that the Jackson men were stronger than they actually were. In all the representative states the Adams men conceded that their opponents were better organized than they were. Clay received report after report that the Adams men were "paralised" by fear and were responding timidly.[43] That was not a good formula for victory.

Waiting for Jackson to arrive in Washington, Daniel Webster summed up the anxiety of the American people, who wondered what the new president would bring. "Nobody knows what he will do," wrote Webster to his brother Ezekiel, but "when he comes, he will bring a breeze."

Webster and the people must have been disappointed by the inaugural address. In one of the shortest inaugural speeches in American history, talking in a barely audible voice, the Old Hero pledged himself to a vague, democratic, Old Republican platform of government "for the good of the people," states' rights, the end of corruption, and a balanced budget. They really had no right to be disappointed, however, because the address accurately reflected a campaign in which Jackson had avoided taking a stand on most issues and allowed Eaton, Green, and Van Buren to present him as an Old Republican hero who would return from his farm and restore republican virtue.[44] Nor should anyone have been surprised by the tumultuous riot that followed the inauguration. The wild celebrators were the same "clamorous" Jacksonians whose power had been compared to the "currant" of the Mississippi and who had used their enthusiasm to make Jackson president.

The "breeze" that Webster expected finally arrived in December when the president sent Congress his first annual message. Two of his proposals—Indian removal and moderate tariff reduction—were pleasing to slave owners; three others—direct election of the president, rotation in office, and a new national bank—were efforts at democratization.[45] Congress pleased Jackson and the South by passing the Indian Removal Act, forcing the Indians out of Georgia, Alabama, and Mississippi. Efforts to satisfy southern demands for tariff reductions failed, however, leading to an abortive attempt in South Carolina to nullify the tariffs. Congress also failed to support any of Jackson's democratic proposals.

Rebuffed by Congress, Jackson turned to the new officers in the executive branch to bring democracy to Washington. During the long nine-month period between the inauguration and the annual message, the president's men moved rapidly to set up a spoils system—called rotation in office—which they believed would make the government more democratic (and also strengthen the Jackson party). By the time Congress convened in December 1829, Green, Van Buren, and the others had removed so many officeholders that critics began to accuse them of "sweeping" their opponents out of office. Although defenders of Jackson have demonstrated that the overall number of removals was far less than what the critics charged, one careful study of the subject revealed that Jackson removed more than 40 percent of all officials who had received a presidential appointment, a very high rate. More important, this was just the beginning. From then on, every time the government changed from one political party to another, the percentage of presidential removals went steadily upward (see Table 8.6). It is apparent that Jackson's party men had instituted a new, lasting policy of patronage that they considered democratic and indispensable to the new party system.

Critics of the Jacksonians have deplored the rise of this spoils system. They point with scorn at the lowering of standards in the Post Office, where a succession of spoils men—William T. Barry, Amos Kendall, and John M. Niles—replaced Postmaster General John McLean, who had refused to remove anyone who was doing his duty. These critics have a point. Considerable damage was done to morale at the Land Office and the federal armory at Harpers Ferry as well as the Post Office. But for the many party men who had inadequate incomes, a government job was a necessity, and public support for a patronage system was more widespread than the critics have admitted. When highly moral public servants such as Edward Everett and Jabez Hammond defended, even demanded, party patronage, it suggests that support for the policy was growing.[46]

The Jackson spoils system brought new people into the government, but there is some dispute over how democratic it was. Critics of the Jacksonians have used a study of federal appointments at the upper levels to show that the Jackson appointees were socially no different from those appointed by Thomas Jefferson. But a closer look at this study reveals that Jackson was expanding on a trend started by Jefferson to broaden the social base of appointments. Although there is no comparable study of appointments at lower levels, usually referred to as clerks, there is ample evidence that the Jacksonians broadened that base. Certainly contemporaries thought they had, for there were many complaints about the lowering of social standards in Washington after the Jacksonians took office. Two other statistics stand out. Jackson appointed more than seventy of the once lower-class newspaper editors to office, and at least forty editors were elected to Congress during the administrations of Jackson and Van Buren. This in itself was democratization. In addition, the party organizations became so adept at bringing voters to the polls that the percentage of adult white males voting for president rose from 56 percent in 1828, remained stable for two elections, and then hit the all-time high of 78 percent in 1840. In fifteen states that year, the turnout was over 80 percent.[47]

The most significant and, in some ways, most democratic event of Jackson's first term was his veto of the bill to recharter the Bank of the United States. The veto message was significant because Jackson was

Table 8.6. Removals of Presidential Appointees

President	Number of Officials at Start of Administration	Number of Removals	Percent Removed
Jackson	610	252	41
Harrison/Tyler	924	458	50
Polk	924	342	37
Taylor/Fillmore	929	628	68
Pierce	929	823	89
Lincoln	1,520	1,457	96

Source: Carl R. Fish, "Removal of Officials by the Presidents of the United States," in *Annual Report of the American Historical Association for the Year 1899*, 2 vols. (Washington, D.C.: Government Printing Office, 1900), 1:84.

the first president to take advantage of the veto power, and his use of it greatly strengthened the presidency. It was democratic because it was aimed at the common people, not the elite stockholders, and the message was written by Amos Kendall in the new populist writing style rather than in the traditionally ponderous style of the past. There was very little connection, however, between the bank veto and the election campaign, because there had been almost no references to the Bank of the United States during the campaign.

But there was one democratic change that was directly related to the campaign and continued to gain momentum during and after Jackson's two terms in office. It was the rise of a durable two-party political system. The election of 1828 put the United States on the track of a political party system that helped make democracy work—although its neglect of women, African Americans, and Native Americans cannot be excused. However flawed, today's system enables the people to express their opinions, elect a government, and, when operating at its best, ensure that their will is carried out.

So how should the election of 1828 be remembered? It did not bring democracy to America, but it did much to enhance it. Important issues such as slavery, tariff protection, the Bank of the United States, and the power of the presidency were not debated, yet the new administration made efforts to deal with all of them. The Jackson party won because it offered a more charismatic candidate, a more vigorous campaign, a more acceptable recipe for preserving the past, and a more forthright acceptance of a new political system. It was an election in which campaigning outweighed issues. In the nearly two centuries following the election of 1828, the American people would produce many more like it.

ANDREW JACKSON'S FIRST
INAUGURAL ADDRESS, MARCH 4, 1829

Fellow-Citizens: About to undertake the arduous duties that I have been appointed to perform by the choice of a free people, I avail myself of this customary and solemn occasion to express the gratitude which their confidence inspires and to acknowledge the accountability which my situation enjoins. While the magnitude of their interests convinces me that no thanks can be adequate to the honor they have conferred, it admonishes me that the best return I can make is the zealous dedication of my humble abilities to their service and their good.

As the instrument of the Federal Constitution it will devolve on me for a stated period to execute the laws of the United States, to superintend their foreign and their confederate relations, to manage their revenue, to command their forces, and, by communications to the Legislature, to watch over and to promote their interests generally. And the principles of action by which I shall endeavor to accomplish this circle of duties it is now proper for me briefly to explain.

In administering the laws of Congress I shall keep steadily in view the limitations as well as the extent of the Executive power, trusting thereby to discharge the functions of my office without transcending its authority. With foreign nations it will be my study to preserve peace and to cultivate friendship on fair and honorable terms, and in the adjustment of any differences that may exist or arise to exhibit the forbearance becoming a powerful nation rather than the sensibility belonging to a gallant people.

In such measures as I may be called on to pursue in regard to the rights of the separate States I hope to be animated by a proper respect for those sovereign members of our Union, taking care not to confound the powers they have reserved to themselves with those they have granted to the Confederacy.

The management of the public revenue—that searching operation in all governments—is among the most delicate and important trusts in ours, and it will, of course, demand no inconsiderable share of my official solicitude. Under every aspect in which it can be considered it would appear that advantage must result from the observance of a strict and faithful economy. This I shall aim at the more anxiously both because it will facilitate the extinguishment of the national debt, the unnecessary duration of which is incompatible with real independence, and because it will counteract that tendency to public and private profligacy which a profuse expenditure of money by the Government is but too apt to engender. Powerful auxiliaries to the attainment of this desirable end are to be found in the regulations provided by the wisdom of Congress for the specific appropriation of public money and the prompt accountability of public officers.

With regard to a proper selection of the subjects of impost with a view toward revenue, it would seem to me that the spirit of equity, caution, and compromise in which the Constitution was formed requires that the great interests of agriculture, commerce, and manufactures should be equally favored, and that perhaps the only exception to this rule should consist in the peculiar encouragement of any products of either of them that may be found essential to our national independence.

Internal improvement and the diffusion of knowledge, so far as they can be promoted by the constitutional acts of the Federal Government, are of high importance.

Considering standing armies as dangerous to free governments in time of peace, I shall not seek to enlarge our present establishment, nor disregard that salutary lesson of political experience which teaches that the military should be held subordinate to the civil power. The gradual increase of our Navy, whose flag has displayed in distant climes our skill in navigation and our fame in arms: the preservation of our forts, arsenals, and dockyards, and the introduction of progressive improvements in the discipline and science of both branches of our military service are so plainly prescribed by prudence that I should be excused for omitting their mention sooner than for enlarging on their importance. But the bulwark of our defense is the national militia, which in the present state of our intelligence and population must render us invincible. As long as our Government is administered for the good of the people, and is regulated by their will; as long as it secures for us the rights of person and property, liberty of conscience and of the press, it will be worth defending; and so long as it is worth defending a patriotic militia will cover it with an impenetrable aegis. Partial injuries and occasional mortifications we may be subjected to, but a million of armed freemen, possessed of the means of war, can never be conquered by a foreign foe. To any just system, therefore, calculated to strengthen this natural safeguard of the country, I shall cheerfully lend all the aid in my power.

It will be my sincere and constant desire to observe toward the Indian tribes within our limits a just and liberal policy, and to give that humane and considerate attention to their rights and their wants which is consistent with the habits of our Government and the feelings of our people.

The recent demonstration of public sentiment inscribes on the list of Executive duties, in characters too legible to be overlooked, the task of *reform,* which will require particularly the correction of those abuses that have brought the patronage of the Federal Government into conflict with the freedom of elections, and the counteraction of those causes which have disturbed the rightful course of appointment and have placed or continued power in unfaithful or incompetent hands.

In the performance of a task thus generally delineated I shall endeavor to select men whose diligence and talents will insure in their respective stations able and faithful cooperation, depending for the advancement of the public service more on the integrity and zeal of the public officers than on their numbers.

A diffidence, perhaps too just, in my own qualifications will teach me to look with reverence to the examples of public virtue left by my illustrious predecessors, and with veneration to the lights that flow from the mind that founded and the mind that reformed our system. The same diffidence induces me to hope for instruction and aid from the coordinate branches of the Government, and for the indulgence and support of my fellow-citizens generally. And a firm reliance on the goodness of that Power whose providence mercifully protected our national infancy, and has since upheld our liberties in various vicissitudes, encourages me to offer up my ardent supplications that He will continue to make our beloved country the object of His divine care and gracious benediction.

Source: James D. Richardson, ed., *A Compilation of the Messages and Papers of the Presidents, 1789–1897,* 10 vols. (Washington, D.C.: U.S. Congress, 1897–1899), 2:436–438.

EXCERPTS FROM ANDREW JACKSON'S FIRST
ANNUAL MESSAGE, DECEMBER 8, 1829

. . . To the people belongs the right of electing their Chief Magistrate; . . .

Let us, then, endeavor so to amend our system that the office of Chief Magistrate may not be conferred upon any citizen but in pursuance of a fair expression of the will of the majority.

I would therefore recommend such an amendment of the Constitution as may remove all intermediate agency in the election of the President and Vice-President. . . .

The duties of all public officers are, or at least admit of being made, so plain and simple that men of intelligence may readily qualify themselves for their performance; and I can not but believe that more is lost by a long continuance of men in office than is generally to be gained by their experience. I submit, therefore, to your consideration whether the efficiency of the Government would not be promoted and official industry and integrity better secured by a general extension of the law which limits appointments to four years. . . .

The proposed limitation would destroy the idea of property now so generally connected with official station, and although individual distress may be sometimes produced, it would, by promoting that rotation which constitutes a leading principle in the republican creed, give healthful action to the system.

. . . I invite your attention to the existing tariff, believing that some of its provisions require modification. . . . When we reflect upon the difficulty and delicacy of this operation [setting tariff rates], it is important that it should never be attempted but with the utmost caution. . . .

All attempts to connect [the tariff laws] with the party conflicts of the day are necessarily injurious, and should be discountenanced. . . . The great mass of legislation relating to our internal affairs was intended to be left where the Federal Convention found it—in the State governments. . . .

The condition and ulterior destiny of the Indian tribes within the limits of some of our States have become objects of much interest and importance. It has long been the policy of Government to introduce among [the Indians] the arts of civilization, in the hope of gradually reclaiming them from a wandering life. This policy has, however, been coupled with another wholly incompatible with its success. Professing a desire to civilize and settle them, we have at the same time lost no opportunity to purchase their lands and thrust them farther into the wilderness. By this means they have not only been kept in a wandering state, but been led to look upon us as unjust and indifferent to their fate. Thus, though lavish in its expenditures upon the subject, Government has constantly defeated its own policy, and the Indians in general, receding farther and farther to the west, have retained their savage habits. . . .

. . . [T]he people of those [southern] States and of every State, . . . submit to you the interesting question whether something can not be done, consistently with the rights of the States, to preserve this much-injured race.

As a means of effecting this end I suggest for your consideration the propriety of setting apart an ample district west of the Mississippi . . . to be guaranteed to the Indian tribes. . . .

The charter of the Bank of the United States expires in 1836, and its stockholders will most probably apply for a renewal of their privileges. . . . Both the constitutionality and the expedience of the law creating this bank are well questioned by a large portion of our fellow-citizens, and it must be admitted by all that it has failed in the great end of establishing a uniform and sound currency.

Under these circumstances, if such an institution is deemed essential to the fiscal operations of the Government, I submit to the wisdom of the Legislature whether a national one, founded upon the credit of the Government and its revenues, might not be devised which would avoid all constitutional difficulties and at the same time secure all the advantages to the Government and country that were expected to result from the present bank.

Source: James D. Richardson, ed., *A Compilation of the Messages and Papers of the Presidents, 1789–1897*, 10 vols. (Washington, D.C.: U.S. Congress, 1897–1899), 2:442–462.

NOTES

ABBREVIATIONS

AHR   *American Historical Review*

AJP   Andrew Jackson, *The Papers of Andrew Jackson,* ed. Harold D. Moser, Daniel Feller, et al., 7 vols. to date (Knoxville: University of Tennessee Press, 1994–)

ANB   *American National Biography,* ed. John A. Garraty and Mark C. Carnes, 24 vols. (New York: Oxford University Press, 1999)

DAB   *Dictionary of American Biography,* ed. Allen Johnson, 10 vols., 2 vols. in 1 (New York: Charles Scribner's Sons, 1936)

DWP   Daniel Webster, *The Papers of Daniel Webster: Correspondence,* ed. Charles M. Wiltse et al., 7 vols. (Hanover, N.H.: University Press of New England, 1974–1986)

HCP   Henry Clay, *The Papers of Henry Clay,* ed. James F. Hopkins et al., 11 vols. (Lexington: University Press of Kentucky, 1959–1992)

JCCP   John C. Calhoun, *The Papers of John C. Calhoun,* ed. Robert L. Meriwether, Clyde N. Wilson, et al., 28 vols. (Columbia: University of South Carolina Press, 1959–2003)

JQAM   John Quincy Adams, *Memoirs of John Quincy Adams,* ed. Charles Francis Adams, 12 vols. (Philadelphia: J. B. Lippincott, 1875)

LC   Library of Congress

INTRODUCTION

1 James Parton, *Life of Andrew Jackson,* 3 vols. (New York: Mason Brothers, 1860), 3:1–173.

2 William Nisbet Chambers and Walter Dean Burnham, eds., *The American Party Systems: Stages of Political Development* (New York: Oxford University Press, 1967).

3 Stephen Skowronek, *The Politics Presidents Make: Leadership from John Adams to Bill Clinton* (Cambridge, Mass.: Harvard University Press, 1997), 130–133.

4 Gordon S. Wood, *The Radicalism of the American Revolution* (New York: Knopf, 1991), 234. For other good discussions of the definition of democracy, see Sean Wilentz, *The Rise of American Democracy* (New York: Norton, 2005), xvii–xxiii; and Robert H. Wiebe, *Self-Rule: A Cultural History of American Democracy* (Chicago: University of Chicago Press, 1995), 1–11.

CHAPTER 1 THE SPRING OF 1825

1   Heinrich Heine, "Vitzliputzli," prelude, stanza 1, in *The Complete Poems of Heinrich Heine: A Modern English Version*, trans. Hal Draper (Cambridge, Mass.: Suhrkampf/Insel Publishers, 1982), 599.

2   George Canning, "The King's Message," December 12, 1826, quoted in George Dangerfield, *The Awakening of American Nationalism* (New York: Harper & Row, 1965), 194.

3   Andrew Burstein, *America's Jubilee: How in 1826 a Generation Remembered Fifty Years of Independence* (New York: Knopf, 2001).

4   For the most recent study of Bancroft, see Lilian Handlin, *George Bancroft: The Intellectual as Democrat* (New York: Harper & Row, 1984).

5   Robert V. Remini, *Daniel Webster: The Man and His Times* (New York: Norton, 1997), 184.

6   Daniel Webster, *The Great Speeches and Orations*, ed. Edwin P. Whipple (Boston: Little, Brown, 1879), 135.

7   Lilian Handlin, "George Bancroft," in *ANB* 2:99.

8   Remini, *Daniel Webster*, 251.

9   Frank Monaghan, "Marquis de Lafayette," in *DAB* 5 (pt. 2):538; Stanley J. Idzerda et al., *Lafayette, Hero of Two Worlds: The Art and Pageantry of His Farewell Tour of America* (Hanover, N.H.: University Press of New England, 1989).

10 Webster, *Great Speeches*, 127, 135.

11 Harry L. Watson, *Liberty and Power: The Politics of Jacksonian America* (New York: Hill & Wang, 1990), 42–51.

12 Jeremy Belknap, *The History of New Hampshire*, 2d ed., 3 vols. (Boston: Bradford & Read, 1813), 3:251.

13 Gordon Wood, *The Radicalism of the American Revolution* (New York: Knopf, 1992), 7, 232, passim.

14 Henry Steele Commager, ed., *America in Perspective: The United States through Foreign Eyes* (New York: Random House, 1947), 25.

15 David Waldstreicher, *In the Midst of Perpetual Fetes: The Making of American Nationalism, 1776–1820* (Chapel Hill: University of North Carolina Press, 1997).

16 In this discussion of suffrage requirements I have drawn on Alexander Keyssar, *The Right to Vote: The Contested History of Democracy in the United States* (New York: Basic Books, 2001).

17 Richard P. McCormick, "New Perspectives on Jacksonian Politics, *AHR* 65 (1960): 292, 294; Sean Wilentz, *The Rise of American Democracy* (New York: Norton, 2005), 138–139.

18 Edward Stanwood, *A History of the Presidency* (Boston: Houghton, Mifflin, 1898), 93, 103; Noble E. Cunningham Jr., "Election of 1800," in *History of American Presidential Elections 1789–1968*, ed. Arthur M. Schlesinger Jr., 4 vols. (New York: Chelsea House, 1971), 1:129.

19 McCormick, "New Perspectives," 294.

20 Richard Franklin Bensel, *The American Ballot Box in the Mid-Nineteenth Century* (Cambridge: Cambridge University Press, 2004).

21 Robert H. Wiebe, *Self-Rule: A Cultural History of American Democracy* (Chicago: University of Chicago Press, 1995), 55.

22 For the antiparty view, see Richard Hofstadter, *The Idea of a Party System: The Rise of Legitimate Opposition in the United States, 1780–1840* (Berkeley: University of California Press, 1969), 1–73. Belknap, *History of New Hampshire*, 3:251; Alan Taylor, "'The Art of Hook & Snivey': Political Culture in Upstate New York during the 1790s," *Journal of American History* 79 (1993): 1371.

23 Daniel Walker Howe, *What Hath God Wrought: The Transformation of America, 1815–1848* (New York: Oxford University Press, 2007), 202–242.

24 Donald B. Cole, *The Presidency of Andrew Jackson* (Lawrence: University Press of Kansas, 1993), 7–8; Howe, *What Hath God Wrought*, 213–222; George R. Taylor, *The Transportation Revolution, 1815–1860* (New York: Holt, Rinehart & Winston, 1951), 77.

25 Richard R. John, *Spreading the News: The American Postal System from Franklin to Morse* (Cambridge, Mass.: Harvard University Press, 1995), 1, 51.

26 *The Statistical History of the United States from Colonial Times to the Present* (Stamford, Conn.: Fairfield Publishers, 1947), 302.

27 Hofstadter, *Idea of a Party System*, 212–271; Jeffrey L. Pasley, *"The Tyranny of Printers": Newspaper Politics in the Early American Republic* (Charlottesville: University Press of Virginia, 2001), 348–349, 460n36.

28 For the impact of the Second Great Awakening on the rise of democracy in America, see Howe, *What Hath God Wrought*, 164–202.

29 Emil Pocock, "Popular Roots of Jacksonian Democracy: The Case of Dayton, Ohio, 1815–1830," *Journal of the Early Republic* 9 (1989): 489–516; Andrew R. L. Cayton, "The Fragmentation of 'A Great Family': The Panic of 1819 and the Rise of a Middling Interest in Boston, 1818–1822," ibid., 2 (1982): 143–167.

30 William W. Freehling, *Prelude to the Civil War: The Nullification Controversy in South Carolina, 1816–1836* (New York: Harper & Row, 1965), 109.

31 Samuel Flagg Bemis's *John Quincy Adams and the Foundations of American Foreign Policy* (New York: Knopf, 1949) and *John Quincy Adams and the Union* (New York: Knopf, 1956) are classics.

32 *JQAM* 6:520–525, 546–547.

33 For the most recent and most complete study of Henry Clay, see Robert V. Remini, *Henry Clay: Statesman of the Union* (New York: Norton, 1991).

34 Remini, *Daniel Webster*, 239.

35 Jackson to John Coffee, January 6, 1825, Jackson to John Overton, January 10, 1825, in *AJP* 6:8, 14.

36 Jackson to Samuel Swartwout, February 22, March 6, 1825, ibid., 40–43, 47–48.

37 John C. Calhoun, "Speech at Abbeville, S.C.," May 27, 1825, Calhoun to Joseph G. Swift, June 27, 1825, in *JCCP* 10:24, 33.

38 Martin Van Buren, "The Autobiography of Martin Van Buren," ed. John C. Fitzpatrick, in *Annual Report of the American Historical Association for the*

Year 1918, 2 vols. (Washington, D.C.: Government Printing Office, 1920), 2:149.

39 For more on Kendall, see Donald B. Cole, *A Jackson Man: Amos Kendall and the Rise of American Democracy* (Baton Rouge: Louisiana State University Press, 2004).

40 See W. Stephen Belko, *The Invincible Duff Green: Whig of the West* (Columbus: University of Missouri Press, 2006).

41 See Glyndon G. Van Deusen, *Thurlow Weed: Wizard of the Lobby* (1947; reprint, New York: Da Capo, 1969).

CHAPTER 2 TAKING SIDES, 1825–1826

1 John Quincy Adams, "Inaugural Address," in *A Compilation of the Messages and Papers of the Presidents 1789–1897*, ed. James D. Richardson, 10 vols. (Washington, D.C.: U.S. Congress, 1897–1899), 2:294–299.

2 George Dangerfield, *The Awakening of American Nationalism* (New York: Harper & Row, 1965), 240.

3 James M. Garnett to John Randolph, September 2, 1825, John Randolph Papers, LC, quoted in Thomas M. Coens, "The Formation of the Jackson Party, 1822–1825" (doctoral diss., Harvard University, 2004), 275; Calhoun to Samuel Southard, August 16, 1825, in *JCCP* 10:38.

4 Clay to Charles Hammond, November 6, 1825, in *HCP* 4:794.

5 Coens, "Formation of the Jackson Party," 242–243.

6 Jackson to Samuel Swartwout, February 22, 1825, in *AJP* 6:41. For an analysis of this letter, see Coens, "Formation of the Jackson Party," 222–228.

7 Charles Tutt to Jackson, June 1, 1825, in *AJP* 6:78–79.

8 Jackson to Robert Coleman Foster and William Brady, October 12, 1825, ibid., 108–111.

9 Jackson to the Tennessee General Assembly, October 14, 1825, ibid., 113–114. For rotation in office, see Gordon S. Wood, *The Radicalism of the American Revolution* (New York: Knopf, 1991), 304.

10 Clay to Charles Hammond, November 1, 1825, in *HCP* 4:780–784.

11 Perry M. Goldman and James S. Young, eds., *The United States Congressional Directories 1789–1840* (New York: Columbia University Press, 1973), 168–181.

12 *JQAM* 7:64–65.

13 John Quincy Adams, "First Annual Message," December 6, 1825, in Richardson, *Messages and Papers*, 2:299–317.

14 Ibid.; Stephen Skowronek, *The Politics Presidents Make: Leadership from John Adams to Bill Clinton* (Cambridge, Mass.: Harvard University Press, 1997), 110–127.

15 *Richmond Enquirer*, December 8, 1825.

16 *JQAM* 7:77–78; *Niles' Weekly Register* 29 (1825–1826): 225.

17 Calhoun to Ingham, September 9, 1825, in *JCCP* 10:41.

18 John Niven, *Martin Van Buren: The Romantic Age of American Politics* (New York: Oxford University Press, 1983), 105–107; Martin Van Buren, "The Autobiography of Martin Van Buren," ed. John C. Fitzpatrick, in *Annual Report*

of the American Historical Association for the Year 1918, 2 vols. (Washington, D.C.: Government Printing Office, 1920), 2:199–201.

19 Register of Debates in Congress, 19th Cong., 1st sess. (1825–1827), 401.

20 For Calhoun's duties as president of the Senate, see JCCP 10:xxx–xxxiv.

21 Clay to John J. Crittenden, March 10, 1826, in HCP 5:158.

22 For the "Patrick Henry"–"Onslow" debate and the controversy over the identity of "Patrick Henry," see JCCP 10:xix–xxx.

23 Calhoun to Jackson, June 4, 1826, ibid., 110–111.

24 Jackson to Calhoun, July 18, 1826, ibid., 158–160. Jackson's reference to "98 and 1800" was to the Republican states' rights protest against the Alien and Sedition Acts between 1798 and 1800.

25 Calhoun to Littleton W. Tazewell, June 13, 1826, ibid., 128–129; Arthur P. Hayne to Jackson, July 20, 1826, in AJP 6:188–190.

26 W. Stephen Belko, The Invincible Duff Green: Whig of the West (Columbia: University of Missouri Press, 2006), 157–161.

27 JCCP 10:xiv.

28 William Nisbet Chambers, Old Bullion Benton, Senator from the New West (Boston: Little, Brown, 1956), 137.

29 Jabez Hammond to Clay, March 16, 1826, in HCP 5:175.

30 Charles King to Clay, March 21, 1826, ibid., 186.

31 Calhoun to Van Buren, July 7, 1826, in JCCP 10:156–157.

32 Jackson to William Stoddert and the Citizens of Jackson, Tennessee, September 19, 1825, in AJP 6:102–103.

33 Jackson to Thomas P. Moore, July 31, 1826, Jackson to William P. Keene, June 16, 1827, Jackson to Robert Paine et al., September 30, 1826, ibid., 194–195, 343–344, 220.

34 Jackson to John Coffee, August 20, 1826, ibid., 198–199.

35 Jackson to James Monroe, October 23, 1816, November 12, 1816, ibid., 4:69–71, 73–75.

36 Mary W. M. Hargreaves, The Presidency of John Quincy Adams (Lawrence: University Press of Kansas, 1985), 51.

37 Jackson to Sam Houston, April 15, 1826, Jackson to Richard Keith Call, September 30, 1826, in AJP 6:164–165, 217–219.

38 Henry R. Warfield to Clay, July 5, 1826, Richard Peters Jr. to Clay, October 24, 1826, in HCP 5:523–526, 819–821.

CHAPTER 3 ORGANIZING AT THE TOP, 1827

1 James K. Polk to William Polk, December 14, 1826, Jackson to James K. Polk, December 24?, 1826, in Correspondence of James K. Polk, ed. Herbert Weaver et al., 9 vols. to date (Nashville: Vanderbilt University Press, 1969–), 1:56–60, 60–65.

2 Mary W. M. Hargreaves, The Presidency of John Quincy Adams (Lawrence: University Press of Kansas, 1985), 111.

3 F. W. Taussig, The Tariff History of the United States, 6th ed. (New York: G. P. Putnam's, 1914), 79–84.

4 Donald B. Cole, *Martin Van Buren and the American Political System* (Princeton, N.J.: Princeton University Press, 1984), 160–161.

5 *JQAM* 7:201, 222, 224.

6 Ibid., 208, 235.

7 Ibid., 219–253.

8 Ibid., 235.

9 Ibid., 216–217.

10 Culver H. Smith, *The Press, Politics, and Patronage: The American Government's Use of Newspapers 1789–1875* (Athens: University of Georgia Press, 1977), 256–258.

11 The statistics for Clay's correspondence are based on the letters in *HCP* 7:1–503.

12 Markley to Clay, March 11, 1827, Johnson to Clay, March 12, 1827, Whittlesey to Clay, March 13, 1827, Crowninshield to Clay, March 14, 1827, Clay to Crowninshield, March 18, 1827, ibid., 6:283–284, 290–292, 300–301, 319–320.

13 Webster to Clay, March 25, 1827, ibid., 354–358.

14 Clay to Webster, April 14, 1827, ibid., 444–445.

15 Webster to Clay, April 14, 1827, Clay to Webster, April 20, 1827, ibid., 445–447, 467–468.

16 Robert V. Remini, *Andrew Jackson and the Course of American Freedom, 1822–1832* (New York: Harper & Row, 1981), 125; Jackson to Carter Beverley, June 5, 1827, in *AJP* 6:330–332.

17 Clay, "Pittsburgh Response, June 20, 1827," in *HCP* 6:700–703.

18 Clay, "Lexington Address, June 29, 1827," ibid., 728–730.

19 Donald B. Cole, *A Jackson Man: Amos Kendall and the Rise of American Democracy* (Baton Rouge: Louisiana State University Press, 2004), 88, 100–101, 106–108.

20 Daniel Webster to Ezekiel Webster, June 11, 1827, Webster to Taylor, June 19, 1827, in *DWP* 2:218, 222–223.

21 Degrand to Clay, June 1, 1827, in *HCP* 6:633–634; Hargreaves, *Presidency of Adams*, 274–275.

22 Taussig, *Tariff History of the United States*, 82–86.

23 Webster to John C. Wright, April 20, 1827, Wright to Webster, May 24, 1827, in *DWP* 2:195–197, 208–210.

24 Clay to Webster, August 19, 1827, Webster to Clay, September 28, 1827, in *HCP* 6:929–930, 1084–1086.

25 Clay to Webster, October 25, 1827, ibid., 1187–1188; Everett to Webster, November 18, 1827, in *DWP* 2:253–254.

26 Jabez Hammond to Clay, March 16, 1826, in *HCP* 6:175–176.

27 Martin Van Buren, "The Autobiography of Martin Van Buren," ed. John C. Fitzpatrick, in *Annual Report of the American Historical Association for the Year 1918*, 2 vols. (Washington, D.C.: Government Printing Office, 1920), 2:514.

28 Van Buren to Thomas Ritchie, January 13, 1827, in *Papers of Martin Van Buren* (Alexandria, Va.: Chadwyck-Healey, Microfilm, 1987).

29 For two views on the letter favorable to Van Buren, see Sean Wilentz, *The Rise of American Democracy* (New York: Norton, 2005), 295–296; and Joel H. Silbey, *Martin Van Buren and the Emergence of American Popular Politics* (Lanham, Md.: Rowman & Littlefield, 2002), 49–51. For two views attacking Van Buren, see Richard H. Brown, "The Missouri Crisis, Slavery, and the Politics of Jacksonianism," *South Atlantic Quarterly* 65 (1966): 55–70; and Robert Pierce Forbes, *The Missouri Compromise and Its Aftermath: Slavery & the Meaning of America* (Chapel Hill: University of North Carolina Press, 2007), 213–215.

30 In his first letter to Jackson, Van Buren was bold enough to warn Old Hickory against writing letters in his own defense. In the second he opposed a plan to bring Jackson to Washington. Van Buren to Jackson, September 14, November 4, 1827, in *AJP* 6:392–393, 399–400. The Little Magician was determined to exercise leadership in the Jackson party.

31 *Niles' Weekly Register*, March 10, 17, 1827; Robert V. Remini, *Martin Van Buren and the Making of the Democratic Party* (New York: Columbia University Press, 1951), 140.

32 Robert V. Remini, *The Election of Andrew Jackson* (Philadelphia: J. B. Lippincott, 1963), 68–71.

33 Nathan Sargent, *Public Men and Events from the Commencement of Mr. Monroe's Administration, in 1817, to the Close of Mr. Fillmore's Administration, in 1853*, 2 vols. (Philadelphia: J. B. Lippincott, 1875), 1:110.

34 W. Stephen Belko, *The Invincible Duff Green: Whig of the West* (Columbia: University of Missouri Press, 2006), 144.

35 Ibid., 138.

36 John Niven, *John C. Calhoun and the Price of Union* (Baton Rouge: Louisiana State University Press, 1988), 86–87, 124–126.

37 James Hamilton Jr. to Jackson, February 16, 1827, in *Correspondence of Andrew Jackson*, ed. John Spencer Bassett and John Franklin Jameson, 7 vols. (1926–1935; reprint, New York: Kraus Reprint, 1969), 3:344.

38 *National Intelligencer*, March 12, 1827.

39 *Charleston Southern Patriot*, March 30, 1827, cited in Remini, *Van Buren and the Making of the Democratic Party*, 142.

40 *JQAM* 7:272, 9:119.

41 Eaton to Jackson, January 27, February 4, 1827, in *AJP* 6:267–269, 277–283.

42 Eaton to Jackson, February 8, 1827, ibid., 286–287.

43 Ibid., 314.

44 Ibid., 315.

45 Remini, *Election of Jackson*, 63–64, 209n6.

46 Francis Johnson to Clay, April 29, 1827, in *HCP* 6:497.

47 Clay to Edward Everett, May 22, 1827, ibid., 579–580.

48 Belko, *Invincible Duff Green*, 115.

49 *JQAM* 7:219. For an excellent article on the Southard affair, see Michael Birkner, "The General, the Secretary, and the President: An Episode in the

Presidential Campaign of 1828," *Tennessee Historical Quarterly* 42 (1983): 243–253.

50 Jackson to Southard, January 5, 1827, in *AJP* 6:255.

51 Jackson to Southard, March 6, 1827, ibid., 296–299.

52 *JQAM* 7:253.

53 *AJP* 6:228.

CHAPTER 4 ORGANIZING AT THE BOTTOM: THE EAST

1 Webster to Clay, June 2, 1827, in *HCP* 6:641.

2 For the history of New Hampshire from the colonial period to the middle of the nineteenth century, see Jere R. Daniel, *Experiment in Republicanism: New Hampshire Politics and the American Revolution, 1741–1794* (Cambridge, Mass.: Harvard University Press, 1970); Lynn W. Turner, *The Ninth State: New Hampshire's Formative Years* (Chapel Hill: University of North Carolina Press, 1983); Donald B. Cole, *Jacksonian Democracy in New Hampshire, 1800–1851* (Cambridge, Mass.: Harvard University Press, 1970).

3 Jeremiah Mason to Daniel Webster, February 20, 1825, in *DWP* 2:28–30; David L. Morril to Clay, September 18, 1826, in *HCP* 5:692–693.

4 Ezekiel Webster to Daniel Webster, January 27, 1827, in *DWP* 2:151–154.

5 Thomas L. Gaffney, "Maine's Mr. Smith: A Study of Francis O. Smith, Politician and Entrepreneur" (doctoral diss., University of Maine, 1979), 1–2.

6 Clay to Webster, May 28, 1827, in *HCP* 6:603–604; Cole, *Jacksonian Democracy in New Hampshire*, 62–63.

7 Ezekiel Webster to Daniel Webster, June 17, 1827, in *DWP* 2:219–221; Shaw Livermore, *The Twilight of Federalism: The Disintegration of the Federalist Party 1815–1830* (Princeton, N.J.: Princeton University Press, 1962), 223–226.

8 Samuel Bell to Daniel Webster, November 8, 1827, in *DWP* 2:251–252.

9 Van Buren to Ritchie, January 13, 1827, in *Papers of Martin Van Buren* (Alexandria, Va.: Chadwyck-Healey, Microfilm, 1987).

10 Silas Wright to Van Buren, December 17, 1828, ibid.; *Register of Debates in Congress*, 22d Cong., 1st sess. (1831–1833), 1325–1327.

11 Duff Green to William Berkeley Lewis, September 2, 1827, Duff Green Papers, LC, quoted in W. Stephen Belko, *The Invincible Duff Green: Whig of the West* (Columbus: University of Missouri Press, 2006), 89. For analyses of the Albany Regency, see Donald B. Cole, *Martin Van Buren and the American Political System* (Princeton, N.J.: Princeton University Press, 1984), 86–98; and Robert V. Remini, "The Albany Regency," *New York History* 39 (1958): 341–355.

12 The other election decided in the House of Representatives was the election of 1800, when Thomas Jefferson and Aaron Burr tied in the electoral college. It took thirty-six ballots in the House of Representatives to break the deadlock and elect Jefferson. Because of this election the Constitution was amended (Twelfth Amendment; 1804) to provide for separate elections for president and vice president.

13 Rudolph Bunner to Gulian Verplanck, March 6, 1827, Gulian C. Verplanck Papers, courtesy of the New-York Historical Society.

14　For the memorials, see *American State Papers: Documents, Legislative and Executive*, vol. 5, *Finance* (Washington, D.C.: 1832–1861), 613–614, 680, 697–701, 723, 745, 750, 847–848, 862, 864–869, 895–897, 899–900, 992–994, 1023–1024; William L. Marcy to Van Buren, January 29, 1828, Martin Van Buren Papers, LC.

15　Martin Van Buren, "The Autobiography of Martin Van Buren," ed. John C. Fitzpatrick, in *Annual Report of the American Historical Association for the Year 1918*, 2 vols. (Washington, D.C.: Government Printing Office, 1920), 2:171.

16　*Albany Argus*, July 24, 1827.

17　For two different treatments of the Anti-Masonic movement, see William P. Vaughn, *The Antimasonic Party in the United States 1826–1843* (Lexington: University Press of Kentucky, 1983); and Ronald P. Formisano and Kathleen Smith Kutolowski, "Antimasonry and Masonry: The Genesis of Protest, 1826–1827," *American Quarterly* 29 (1977): 139–165.

18　Van Buren to Churchill C. Cambreleng, October 23, 1827, Van Buren Papers, LC.

19　Jerome Mushkat, *Tammany: The Evolution of a Political Machine, 1789–1865* (Syracuse, N.Y.: Syracuse University Press, 1971), 75–108.

20　Peter B. Porter to Clay, April 5, 1827, in *HCP* 6:405.

21　Peter B. Porter to Clay, January 3, 1827, ibid., 6.

22　Jabez Hammond to Clay, January 28, 1827, ibid., 130.

23　Clay to Stephen Van Rensselaer, March 21, 1827, ibid., 334.

24　Jabez Hammond to Clay, January 28, 1827, ibid., 130.

25　Jabez Hammond to Clay, April 11, 1827, ibid., 433.

26　Jabez Hammond to Clay, March 22, 1827, ibid., 337.

27　Ibid.

28　Austin L. Moore, "Thomas Jackson Oakley," in *DAB* 7 (pt. 1): 604.

29　Clay to Webster, April 20, 1827, Webster to John C. Wright, April 30, 1827, in *DWP* 2:194, 196.

30　Joseph Story to Webster, June 10, 1827, ibid., 217.

31　Webster to Clay, June 2, 1827, in *HCP* 6:639–641.

32　Ibid.

33　Peter B. Porter to Clay, May 1, 1827, ibid., 503.

34　Webster to Taylor, June 19, 1827, in *DWP* 2:222.

35　Thurlow Weed, *Autobiography of Thurlow Weed*, ed. Harriet A. Weed (1883; reprint, New York: Da Capo Press, 1970), 319.

36　Jabez Hammond, *The History of Political Parties in the State of New-York*, 2 vols. (Albany, N.Y.: C. Van Benthuysen, 1842), 2:258.

37　Ibid., 259.

38　Ibid., 258–259.

39　Peter B. Porter to Clay, January 3, May 1, October 26, 1827, Webster to Clay, November 5, 1827, in *HCP* 6:6, 502, 1190, 1233–1235.

40　Daniel Mallory to Clay, September 28, 1827, ibid., 1083–1084.

41　De Alva Stanwood Alexander, *A Political History of the State of New York*, 2 vols. (Port Washington, N.Y.: Ira J. Friedman, 1909), 2:358.

42 The New York legislature did not take back the power to choose electors. John Sergeant to Clay, October 24, 1827, in *HCP* 6:1185.
43 Webster to Clay, November 5, 1827, ibid., 1235.
44 Alexander, *Political History of New York*, 2:358–359.
45 Peter B. Porter to Clay, November 6, 22, 1827, in *HCP* 6:1240, 1303.
46 Philip S. Klein and Ari Hoogenboom, *A History of Pennsylvania* (New York: McGraw-Hill, 1973), 182–194.
47 Kim T. Phillips, "The Pennsylvania Origins of the Jackson Movement," *Political Science Quarterly* 91 (1976): 489–508.
48 Buchanan to Jackson, September 21, 1826, in *AJP* 6:212.
49 Jackson to William Moore, January 4, 1827, ibid., 251.
50 Peter P. F. Degrand to Joseph E. Sprague, July 4, 1826, Adams Family Papers, Massachusetts Historical Society, quoted in Mary W. M. Hargreaves, *The Presidency of John Quincy Adams* (Lawrence: University Press of Kansas, 1985), 273; Benjamin W. Crowninshield to Clay, March 14, 1827, John Binns to Clay, April 28, 1827, in *HCP* 6:304, 492.
51 Webster to Richard Peters Jr., April 10, 1827, in *DWP* 2:186.
52 Calhoun to Littleton W. Tazewell, July 1, 1827, in *JCCP* 10:292–293.
53 Michael Durey, "John Binns," in *ANB* 2:801–802.
54 Richard J. Purcell, "Robert Walsh," in *DAB* 10 (pt. 1): 391–392.
55 Webster to Adams, March 27, 1827, in *DWP* 2:179.
56 Adams to Clay, August 23, 1827, in *HCP* 6:953.
57 Asa Earl Martin, "John Andrew Shulze," in *DAB* 9 (pt. 1): 140–141.
58 Markley to Clay, May 19, 1827, in *HCP* 6:571.
59 Binns to Clay, April 28, 1827, ibid., 492–493.
60 Markley to Clay, May 19, 1827, ibid., 571.
61 Crowninshield to Clay, March 14, 1827, ibid., 304.
62 Binns to Clay, April 28, 1827, ibid., 492–493.
63 Binns to Clay, May 10, 1826, ibid., 5:352–353.
64 *JQAM* 7:262.
65 Hopkinson to Webster, April 13, 1827, in *DWP* 2:188–189.
66 Thomas I. Wharton to Clay, August 3, 1827, in *HCP* 6:846–847.
67 *JQAM* 7:297.
68 Josiah H. Johnston to Clay, September 13, 1827, in *HCP* 6:1030.
69 Sergeant to Clay, August 23, 1827, ibid., 954.
70 Sergeant to Clay, August 13, 17, 1827, ibid., 897–898, 919–920.
71 Ibid., 955n3.
72 Ibid.
73 Sergeant to Clay, August 23, 1827, ibid., 955.
74 Clay to Webster, April 14, 1827, ibid., 444.
75 Sergeant to Clay, October 5, 1827, ibid., 1112.
76 Ibid., 1023n4.
77 Sergeant to Clay, October 14, 1827, ibid., 1148.
78 *JQAM* 7:333.
79 Sergeant to Clay, October 14, 1827, in *HCP* 6:1148.

CHAPTER 5 ORGANIZING AT THE BOTTOM: THE WEST AND THE SOUTH

1 *The Statistical History of the United Sates from Colonial Times to the Present* (Stamford, Conn.: Fairfield Publishers, 1965), 685.

2 Donald J. Ratcliffe, "Voter Turnout in Early Ohio," *Journal of the Early Republic* 7 (1987): 223–251; Emil Pocock, "Popular Roots of Jacksonian Democracy: The Case of Dayton, Ohio, 1815–1830," *Journal of the Early Republic* 9 (1989): 489–515.

3 Merton L. Dillon, "Benjamin Lundy," in *ANB* 14:137–138.

4 Charles Hammond to John C. Wright, December 20, 1822, quoted in Harry R. Stevens, *The Early Jackson Party in Ohio* (Durham, N.C.: Duke University Press, 1957), 55.

5 Ted D. Stahly, "Caleb Atwater," in *ANB* 1:728–730.

6 *Cincinnati National Republican and Ohio Political Register*, November 8, 1825, quoted in R. Carlyle Buley, *The Old Northwest: Pioneer Period 1815–1840*, 2 vols. (Bloomington: Indiana University Press, 1950), 2:160n2.

7 Webster to Wright, October 12, 1826, in *DWP* 2:133–134.

8 Buley, *Old Northwest*, 2:162.

9 Donald J. Ratcliffe, *The Politics of Long Division: The Birth of the Second Party System in Ohio, 1818–1828* (Columbus: Ohio State University Press, 2000), 229.

10 Moses Dawson to Clay, May 24, 1827, in *HCP* 6:587–588.

11 Robert V. Remini, *The Election of Andrew Jackson* (Philadelphia: J. B. Lippincott, 1963), 95.

12 Caleb Atwater to Jackson, September 4, 1827, in *AJP* 6:389.

13 Hammond to Clay, November 5, 1827, in *HCP* 6:1232.

14 Ratcliffe, *Politics of Long Division*, 196–197.

15 *Liberty Hall and Cincinnati Gazette*, April 27, 1827, quoted in Buley, *Old Northwest*, 2:162n10.

16 Hammond to Clay, September 27, November 26, 1826, in *HCP* 5:723, 955.

17 Hammond to Clay, March 28, 1827, ibid., 6:370.

18 John C. Wright to Daniel Webster, May 24, 1827, in *DWP* 2:208.

19 Ibid.

20 Ratcliffe, *Politics of Long Division*, 178–179.

21 Hammond to Clay, January 4, 1826, October 18, 1827, in *HCP* 5:7, 6:1160–1162.

22 Clay to Hammond, October 30, 1827, ibid., 6:1204.

23 Samuel Finley Vinton to Clay, June 14, 1827, ibid., 682.

24 *HCP*, 6:797.

25 Ratcliffe, *Politics of Long Division*, 186–190.

26 Ibid., 178–180.

27 Hammond to Clay, October 29, 1827, in *HCP* 6:1199–1201.

28 Clay to Hammond, November 16, 1827, ibid., 1269–1271.

29 Hammond to Clay, October 29, 1827, ibid., 1199.

30 Hammond to Clay, August 10, October 18, November 5, 1827, ibid., 876, 1160, 1232.

31 Clay to Hammond, November 16, 1827, ibid., 1270.

32 Alexis de Tocqueville, *Democracy in America*, ed. Phillips Bradley, 2 vols. (New York: Knopf, 1945), 1:362.

33 For a good example of the new, popular writing style that was taking over American politics, see Kendall's editorials in the *Argus of Western America* concerning the 1824 election, later published as *The Wictorian Dinner* (Frankfort, Ky.: *Argus of Western America*, 1824). The word "Wictorian" was an allusion to Robert Wickliffe, a wealthy Anti-Relief lawyer from Lexington. Recent studies of the democratic writing style are Kenneth Cmiel, *Democratic Eloquence: The Fight over Popular Speech in Nineteenth-Century America* (New York: William Morrow, 1990); and Andrew W. Robertson, *The Language of Democracy: Political Rhetoric in the United States and Britain* (Ithaca, N.Y.: Cornell University Press, 1995).

34 *Argus of Western America*, February 18, May 5, 1824, cited in Donald B. Cole, *A Jackson Man: Amos Kendall and the Rise of American Democracy* (Baton Rouge: Louisiana State University Press, 2004), 86.

35 *Argus of Western America*, October 4, 1826.

36 Francis Johnson to Clay, April 8, 1827, in *HCP* 6:412–414.

37 Porter Clay to Henry Clay, February 22, 1827, ibid., 222–223.

38 Clay to John W. Taylor, April 4, 1827, ibid., 394–395.

39 John J. Crittenden to Clay, November 15, 1827, ibid., 1264.

40 William W. Worsley to Clay, April 17, 1827, ibid., 452.

41 Crittenden to Clay, November 15, 1827, ibid., 1264.

42 John Harvie to Clay, January 10, 1827, ibid., 38.

43 Crittenden to Clay, November 19, 1827, ibid., 1286.

44 Amos Kendall to Francis P. Blair, January 9, 1829, Blair and Lee Family Papers, Manuscripts Division, Department of Rare Books and Special Collections, Princeton University Library, Princeton, N.J.

45 *Argus of Western America*, September 12, 19, 26, 1827.

46 Kendall to William T. Barry, September 17, 1827, Andrew J. Donelson Papers, LC.

47 Kendall to Jackson, August 22, 27, 1827, in *AJP* 6:381–384; *Argus of Western America*, September 26, 1827.

48 Clay to John F. Henry, September 27, 1827, in *HCP* 6:1073–1076.

49 Ibid.

50 Crittenden to Clay, November 15, 1827, ibid., 1265.

51 Ibid., 1287.

52 Richard P. McCormick, *The Second American Party System: Party Formation in the Jacksonian Era* (Chapel Hill: University of North Carolina Press, 1966), 178–181; William G. Shade, *Democratizing the Old Dominion: Virginia and the Second Party System* (Charlottesville: University Press of Virginia, 1996), 50–77.

53 Although the inequities do not seem unbearably large, they were large enough to give the eastern planters of Virginia control of the house. William

W. Freehling, *The Road to Disunion*, vol. 1, *Secessionists at Bay 1776–1854* (New York: Oxford University Press, 1990), 169–170.

54 Ronald P. Formisano, *The Transformation of Political Culture: Massachusetts Parties, 1790s–1840s* (New York: Oxford University Press, 1983), 14–15; Shade, *Democratizing the Old Dominion*, 70–77.

55 Harry Ammon, "The Richmond Junto, 1800–1824," *Virginia Magazine of History and Biography* 63 (1955): 395–419, and Joseph H. Harrison Jr., "Oligarchs and Democrats in the Richmond Junto," ibid., 78 (1970): 184–198, accept the existence of the Junto. The chief doubter is F. Thornton Miller in "The Richmond Junto. The Secret All-Powerful Club; or Myth," ibid., 99 (1991): 63–80, especially 64–65. Miller argues that the myth of the Junto began when Ritchie's rival editor, John H. Pleasants, attacked Ritchie in republican terms as the head of a corrupt organization similar to those around King George III at the time of the Revolution.

56 C. C. Pearson, "Thomas Ritchie," in *DAB* 8 (pt. 1): 628.

57 *Richmond Enquirer*, October 11, 1825; Robert P. Sutton, "Nostalgia, Pessimism, and Malaise: The Doomed Aristocrat in Late-Jeffersonian Virginia," *Virginia Magazine of History and Biography* 76 (1968): 41–65.

58 *Richmond Enquirer*, January 6, March 8, May 19, 1825, November 10, 24, December 7, 1826.

59 Ibid., April 1, 1825.

60 Charles Henry Ambler, *Thomas Ritchie: A Study in Virginia Politics* (Richmond, Va.: Bell, Book and Stationery Co., 1913), 106; *Richmond Enquirer*, March 20, 23, April 13, 24, 1827.

61 Raymond C. Dingledine, "The Political Career of William Cabell Rives" (doctoral diss., University of Virginia, 1947); *Richmond Enquirer*, August 7, 1827.

62 William C. Rives to Thomas Walker Gilmer, July 20, 22, 1827, in "Letters of William C. Rives, 1823–1829," *Tyler's Quarterly Historical and Genealogical Magazine* 5 (1924): 230–237.

63 *Richmond Enquirer*, November 27, 1827.

64 Ambler, *Thomas Ritchie*, 95–97.

65 Brooke to Clay, September 21, November 17, 20, 23, 1827, Clay to Brooke, November 24, 1827, Clay to Hammond, November 16, 1827, in *HCP* 6:1270; Shade, *Democratizing the Old Dominion*, 88; Ambler, *Thomas Ritchie*, 116.

CHAPTER 6 POLITICAL PARTIES IN 1828

1 Perry M. Goldman and James S. Young, eds., *The United States Congressional Directories 1789–1840* (New York: Columbia University Press, 1973), 193–204.

2 *JQAM* 7:399–400.

3 Goldman and Young, *U.S. Congressional Directories*, 199; Silas Wright to Azariah Flagg, April 7, 1828, Flagg-Wright Correspondence, Azariah C. Flagg Papers, New York Public Library, Astor, Lenox, and Tilden Foundations.

4 Jabez Hammond to Clay, December 11, 1827, in *HCP* 6:1350–1351.

5 F. W. Taussig, *The Tariff History of the United States* (New York: G. P. Putnam's Sons, 1892), 101–102.

6 Many contemporary politicians, especially John C. Calhoun, believed that Van Buren engineered the tariff bill with high rates for raw materials so that New England would oppose it and be blamed when it was defeated. Robert V. Remini overturned this interpretation with his article "Martin Van Buren and the Tariff of Abominations," *AHR* 63 (1958): 903–917. I agree with Remini that Van Buren wanted the bill to pass in order to gain the support of farmers in New York, Ohio, Pennsylvania, Kentucky, and other states.

7 *An Address to the Public Containing Certain Testimony in Refutation of the Charges against Him Made by Gen. Andrew Jackson, Touching on the Last Presidential Election* (Washington, D.C.: *National Journal*, 1827). A brief summary of the address and a list of the statements in it are in *HCP* 6:1394–1396.

8 Jackson to Richard Keith Call, May 3, 1827, in *AJP* 6:315.

9 Overton to Jackson, May 14, 1827, Jackson to Lewis, August 5, 1828, Jackson to Weakley, August 5, 1828, ibid., 319, 486–488, 488–490.

10 Alfred Balch to Jackson, September 3, 1828, ibid., 503.

11 Arthur Lee Campbell to Jackson, February 4, 1827, ibid., 276.

12 For the rise of the national nominating convention, see James S. Chase, "Jacksonian Democracy and the Rise of the Nominating Convention," *Mid-Atlantic* 45 (1963): 229–249; and James S. Chase, *Emergence of the Presidential Nominating Convention, 1789–1832* (Urbana: University of Illinois Press, 1973).

13 For a good discussion of the convention system in Illinois, see Thomas Ford, *A History of Illinois*, 2 vols. (New York: 1854), 1:313–315, 316–322, cited in Robert V. Remini, ed., *The Age of Jackson* (New York: Harper & Row, 1972), 7–12.

14 Josiah S. Johnston to Clay, April 13, 1830, in *HCP* 8:191–192; *JQAM* 8:215.

15 For a description of the *Argus of Western America*, see Donald B. Cole, *A Jackson Man: Amos Kendall and the Rise of American Democracy* (Baton Rouge: Louisiana State University Press, 2004), 60–61; for the *United States Telegraph*, see W. Stephen Belko, *The Invincible Duff Green: Whig of the West* (Columbia: University of Missouri Press, 2006), 98–102. For the number of newspapers published in the United States, see Jeffrey L. Pasley, *"The Tyranny of Printers": Newspaper Politics in the Early American Republic* (Charlottesville: University Press of Virginia, 2001), 403.

16 Robert V. Remini, *The Election of Andrew Jackson* (Philadelphia: J. B. Lippincott, 1963), 86.

17 Bernard Bailyn used these addresses to illustrate the belief in republicanism that stirred Americans to revolt. See Bernard Bailyn, ed., *Pamphlets of the American Revolution, 1750–1776*, 2 vols. (Cambridge, Mass.: Harvard University Press, 1965).

18 "The New Hampshire Address," in *The American Party Battle: Election Campaign Pamphlets, 1828–1876*, ed. Joel H. Silbey, 2 vols. (Cambridge, Mass.: Harvard University Press, 1999), 1:71.

19 "The Virginia Address," ibid., 92.

20 Ibid., 96.

21 Ibid., 95.

22 Ibid., 96.

23 "New Hampshire Address," ibid., 69.

24 Ibid., 83.

25 Edward Everett to John McLean, August 1, 1828, in "Use of Patronage in Elections," ed. Worthington C. Ford, *Proceedings of the Massachusetts Historical Society*, 3d series, 1 (1908): 360–363.

26 McLean to Everett, August 8, 1828, ibid., 363–370.

27 Everett to McLean, August 1, 1828, ibid., 360–363.

28 Everett to McLean, August 18, 1828, ibid., 370–377.

29 *Address of the Republican General Committee of Young Men of the City and County of New York Friendly to the Election of Gen. Andrew Jackson* (New York: 1828), 38, cited in John William Ward, *Andrew Jackson: Symbol for an Age* (New York: Oxford University Press, 1955), 52.

30 Remini, *Election of Jackson*, 131.

31 Edwin A. Miles, "President Adams' Billiard Table," *New England Quarterly* 45 (1972): 31–43.

32 Isaac Hill, *Brief Sketch of the Life, Character and Services of Major General Andrew Jackson* (Concord, N.H.: Manahan, Hoge, 1828), 49–50.

33 *HCP* 6:1233.

34 Remini, *Election of Jackson*, 123.

35 Hammond to Clay, November 5, 1827, in *HCP* 6:1232–1233.

36 Robert Tinkler, *James Hamilton of South Carolina* (Baton Rouge: Louisiana State University Press, 2004); William C. Cook, "The Coffin Handbills— America's First Smear Campaign," *Imprint: Journal of the American Historical Print Collectors Society* 27 (2002): 24–25.

37 Cook, "Coffin Handbills," 26.

38 Ibid.

39 Eaton to Jackson, March 4, 1828, in *AJP* 6:431.

40 Norma Basch, "Marriage, Morals, and Politics in the Election of 1828," *Journal of American History* 80 (1993): 890–918.

41 Jean H. Baker, "The Ceremonies of Politics: Nineteenth-Century Rituals of National Affirmation," in *A Master's Due*, ed. William J. Cooper Jr., Michael F. Holt, and John McCardell (Baton Rouge: Louisiana State University Press, 1985), 161–178; Arthur M. Schlesinger Jr., ed., *Running for President: The Candidates and Their Images*, 2 vols. (New York: Simon & Schuster, 1944).

42 Remini, *Election of Jackson*, 109.

43 "The Hunters of Kentucky" (broadside, LC), cited in Ward, *Andrew Jackson*, 217–219.

44 Michel Chevalier, *Society, Manners, and Politics in the United States: Letters on North America* (Garden City, N.Y.: Doubleday, 1961), 304–308.

45 Bill Cook, "Random Jottings of a Collector on the Presidential Election of 1828" (unpublished paper, 2005).

46 *Congressional Quarterly's Guide to U.S. Elections*, 4th ed., ed. John L. Moore, John P. Preimesberger, and David R. Tarr, 2 vols. (Washington, D.C.: CQ Press, 2001), 2:834–836, 838, 855–857, 872–875.

47 Remini, *Election of Jackson*, 77.

48 Donald B. Cole, *Jacksonian Democracy in New Hampshire, 1800–1851* (Cambridge, Mass.: Harvard University Press, 1970), 168.

CHAPTER 7 ELECTION YEAR

1 James Parton, *Life of Andrew Jackson*, 3 vols. (New York: Mason Brothers, 1860), 3:138.

2 Samuel Jaudon to Webster, May 21, 1828, in *DWP* 2:350.

3 *JQAM* 8:49–50; Henry A. Hawken, *Trumpets of Glory: Fourth of July Orations, 1786–1861* (Granby, Conn.: Salmon Brook Historical Society, 1976), 94, 125–126.

4 *JQAM* 8:76.

5 Ibid.

6 Anthony M. Brescia, ed., "The Election of 1828: A View from Louisville," *Register of the Kentucky State Historical Society* 74 (1976): 51–57.

7 Eaton to Jackson, February 4, 1827, in *AJP* 6:280.

8 Webster to Jeremiah Mason, April 10, 1827, in *DWP* 2:184. For class lines in New Hampshire, see Donald B. Cole, *Jacksonian Democracy in New Hampshire* (Cambridge, Mass.: Harvard University Press, 1970), 72.

9 For details on the elections of 1824 and 1828, see Edward Stanwood, *A History of the Presidency* (Boston: Houghton Mifflin, 1898), 125–165; and Svend Petersen, *A Statistical History of American Presidential Elections* (New York: Frederick Ungar, 1963), 18–20.

10 Webster to Samuel Bell, July 29, 1828, in *DWP* 2:356.

11 Stanwood, *History of the Presidency*, 136.

12 Ibid.

13 Kenneth C. Martis, *The Historical Atlas of Political Parties in the United States Congress 1789–1989* (New York: Macmillan, 1989), 88–89.

14 For election dates and a comprehensive study of state political parties in the Jacksonian era, see Richard P. McCormick, *The Second American Party System: Party Formation in the Jacksonian Era* (Chapel Hill: University of North Carolina Press, 1966).

15 Eaton to Jackson, March 4, 1828, in *AJP* 5:431; Ezekiel Webster to Daniel Webster, March 1, 1828, in *DWP* 2:307; C. P. Van Ness to Isaac Hill, April 6, 1828, Isaac Hill Papers, New Hampshire Historical Society.

16 Cole, *Jacksonian Democracy in New Hampshire*, 68–69.

17 Ibid., 69–72.

18 Ibid., 72–73.

19 Ibid., 77–78; Martin Van Buren, *Inquiry into the Origin and Source of Political Parties in the United States* (1867; reprint, New York: Augustus M. Kelley, 1967).

20 Cole, *Jacksonian Democracy in New Hampshire*, 74–76.

21 Estwick Evans to Daniel Webster, October 28, 1828, in *DWP* 2:372–373.

22 Webster to Samuel Bell, July 29, 1828, ibid., 356–357.

23 Arthur B. Darling, *Political Changes in Massachusetts, 1824–1828* (New Haven, Conn.: Yale University Press, 1925), 40–65; Ronald P. Formisano, *The Transformation of Political Culture: Massachusetts Parties, 1790s–1840s* (New York: Oxford University Press, 1983), 190–196, 246–249, 351–352.

24 William G. Shade, *Democratizing the Old Dominion: Virginia and the Second Party System* (Charlottesville: University Press of Virginia, 1996), 50–77.

25 McCormick, *Second American Party System,* 310–315; John M. Sacher, *A Perfect War of Politics: Parties, Politicians, and Democracy in Louisiana, 1824–1861* (Baton Rouge: Louisiana State University Press, 2003).

26 *JQAM* 7:484.

27 Donald B. Cole, *A Jackson Man: Amos Kendall and the Rise of American Democracy* (Baton Rouge: Louisiana State University Press, 2004), 107–109.

28 Leonard P. Curry, "Election Year—Kentucky, 1828," *Register of the Kentucky State Historical Society* 55 (1957): 201–203.

29 Ibid., 203; Frank F. Mathias and Jasper B. Shannon, "Gubernatorial Politics in Kentucky, 1820–1851," *Register of the Kentucky State Historical Society* 88 (1990): 253–256.

30 Thomas P. Moore to Gulian C. Verplanck, May 29, 1828, Gulian C. Verplanck Papers, courtesy of the New-York Historical Society, cited in Robert V. Remini, *The Election of Andrew Jackson* (Philadelphia: J. B. Lippincott, 1963), 210; Francis P. Blair to Joseph Desha, October 30, 1828, Joseph Desha Papers, LC; T. P. Moore to [John C.?] Rives, November 11, 1828, Frank Johnson to John J. Crittenden, April 12, 1828, John J. Crittenden Papers, LC, cited in Lynn L. Marshall, "The Early Career of Amos Kendall. The Making of a Jacksonian" (doctoral diss., University of California—Berkeley, 1962), 423–424.

31 *Argus of Western America,* January 16, May 28, October 29, 1828.

32 David Trimble to Clay, October 22, 1828, in *HCP* 7:512–513; Robert P. Letcher to Clay, August 27, 1828, ibid., 441.

33 McCormick, *Second American Party System,* 273–274.

34 Ibid., 277–281; Gerald Leonard, *The Invention of Party Politics: Federalism, Popular Sovereignty, and Constitutional Development in Jacksonian Illinois* (Chapel Hill: University of North Carolina Press, 2002), 1–74.

35 J. Mills Thornton, *Politics and Power in a Slave Society: Alabama, 1800–1860* (Baton Rouge: Louisiana State University Press, 1978), 1–23.

36 Robert E. Shallope, "Jacksonian Politics in Missouri: A Comment on the McCormick Thesis," *Civil War History* 15 (1969): 210–225.

37 William S. Hoffman, *Andrew Jackson and North Carolina Politics* (Chapel Hill: University of North Carolina Press, 1958), 6–25.

38 Harry L. Watson, *Jacksonian Politics and Community Conflict: Cumberland County, North Carolina* (Baton Rouge: Louisiana State University Press, 1981), 49–52, 114.

39 Stanwood, *History of the Presidency,* 136.

40 Mark H. Haller, "The Rise of the Jackson Party in Maryland, 1820–1829," *Journal of Southern History* 28 (1962): 307–326.

41 McCormick, *Second American Party System*, 240.

42 *JQAM* 7:509, 531–534.

43 John R. Commons and associates, *The History of Labour in the United States,* 4 vols. (New York: Macmillan, 1918) 1:185–216; Edward Pessen, "The Workingmen's Party Revisited," *Labor History* 4 (1963): 203–226.

44 William A. Sullivan, "Did Labor Support Andrew Jackson?" *Political Science Quarterly* 62 (1947): 569–580.

45 Commons et al., *History of Labour,* 1:198–199; Sergeant to Clay, October 15, 1828, in *HCP* 7:503; Sullivan, "Did Labor Support Jackson?" 571–572.

46 Donald J. Ratcliffe, *The Politics of Long Division: The Birth of the Second Party System in Ohio, 1818–1828* (Columbus: Ohio State University Press, 2000), 170–173.

47 Clay to Webster, October 24, 1828, in *HCP* 7:515–516.

48 Dixon Ryan Fox, *The Decline of Aristocracy in the Politics of New York 1801–1840,* ed. Robert V. Remini (1919; reprint, New York: Harper, 1965), 341–351; Lee Benson, *The Concept of Jacksonian Democracy: New York as a Test Case* (New York: Atheneum, 1964), 21–30.

49 Donald B. Cole, *Martin Van Buren and the American Political System* (Princeton, N.J.: Princeton University Press, 1984), 170–175.

50 Matthew Warshauer, "Andrew Jackson as a 'Military Chieftain' in the 1824 and 1828 Presidential Elections: The Ramifications of Martial Law on American Republicanism," *Tennessee Historical Quarterly* 57 (1998): 4–23.

51 Mary W. M. Hargreaves, *The Presidency of John Quincy Adams* (Lawrence: University Press of Kansas, 1985), 290–292.

CHAPTER 8 ELECTION DAY

1 Congress did not designate a uniform national voting day for federal office until 1845. I found the dates for the presidential elections in various issues of *Niles' Register*. A convenient table appears in John Bach McMaster, *A History of the People of the United States, from the Revolution to the Civil War,* 7 vols. (New York: D. Appleton, 1907), 5:518.

2 *Niles' Register* 35 (November 8, 15, 1828): 166–167, 177.

3 Green to Jackson, November 12, 1828, in *AJP* 6:531.

4 Robert V. Remini, *The Election of 1828* (Philadelphia: J. B. Lippincott, 1963), 184–186.

5 Sean Wilentz, *The Rise of American Democracy: Jefferson to Lincoln* (New York: Norton, 2005), 308.

6 Thomas H. Baird to Clay, in *HCP* 7:98; *JQAM* 8:78; Margaret Bayard Smith, *The First Forty Years of Washington Society,* ed. Gaillard Hunt (1906; reprint, New York: Frederick Ungar, 1965), 256; Webster to Clay, October 1, 1828, in *DWP* 2:367–368.

7 "One of the People" to Jackson, September 24, 1828, Benjamin McCarty Sr. to Jackson, October 17, 1828, in *AJP* 6:508, 514–515.

8 Jackson to John Coffee, November 11, 1828, Green to Jackson, November 12, 1828, ibid., 529–532.

9 Beecher to Clay, November 6, 1828, in *HCP* 7:530–531.

10 James Parton, *Life of Andrew Jackson*, 3 vols. (New York: Mason Brothers, 1860), 3:150.

11 William Graham Sumner, *Andrew Jackson* (Boston: Houghton, Mifflin, 1882), 129–150.

12 Frederick Jackson Turner, *Rise of the New West 1819–1829* (1935; reprint, New York: Collier Books, 1962), 112; Arthur M. Schlesinger Jr., *The Age of Jackson* (Boston: Little, Brown, 1945).

13 William Nisbet Chambers and Walter Dean Burnham, eds., *The American Party Systems: Stages of Political Development* (New York: Oxford University Press, 1967).

14 Richard Hofstadter, *The American Political Tradition and the Men Who Made It* (New York: Knopf, 1951), 54.

15 Richard P. McCormick, "New Perspectives on Jacksonian Politics," *AHR* 65 (1960): 292.

16 Ibid., 300.

17 Hofstadter, *American Political Tradition*, 44–66; Charles Sellers, *The Market Revolution: Jacksonian America, 1815–1846* (New York: Oxford University Press, 1991); Donald J. Ratcliffe, *The Politics of Long Division: The Birth of the Second Party System in Ohio, 1818–1828* (Columbus: Ohio State University Press, 2000), 233.

18 Edward Channing, *A History of the United States*, 6 vols. (New York: Macmillan, 1921), 5:374–376.

19 Frederick Jackson Turner, *The United States, 1830–1850: The Nation and Its Sections* (New York: Norton, 1935), 35–38.

20 Richard H. Brown, "The Missouri Crisis, Slavery and the Politics of Jacksonianism," *South Atlantic Quarterly* 65 (1966): 55–72.

21 William J. Cooper, *The South and the Politics of Slavery, 1828–1856* (Baton Rouge: Louisiana State University Press, 1978), 5–11.

22 Harry L. Watson, *Jacksonian Politics and Community Conflict, Cumberland County, North Carolina* (Baton Rouge: Louisiana State University Press, 1981), 113–114.

23 Richard R. John, "Affairs of Office: The Executive Departments, the Election of 1828, and the Making of the Democratic Party," in *The Democratic Experiment: New Directions in American Political History*, ed. Julian Zelizer, Meg Jacobs, and William Novak (Princeton, N.J.: Princeton University Press, 2003), 50–85; Robert Pierce Forbes, *The Missouri Compromise and Its Aftermath: Slavery & the Meaning of America* (Chapel Hill: University of North Carolina Press, 2007).

24 For election results, see *New-Hampshire Patriot*, November 10, 1828. Figures on tax apportionment are from *Laws of New Hampshire* 10 (1833): 412–418.

25 For county population figures, see John Hayward, *A Gazetteer of New Hampshire . . .* (Boston: John P. Jewett, 1849), 147–150. In this analysis of county

growth I followed the reasoning of Lynn L. Marshall in "The Genesis of Grass-roots Democracy in Kentucky," *Mid-America* 47 (1965): 277–281.

26 Marshall, "Genesis of Grass-roots Democracy in Kentucky," 273–281.

27 Ratcliffe, *Politics of Long Division*, 166, 270.

28 William G. Shade, *Democratizing the Old Dominion: Virginia and the Second Party System 1824–1861* (Charlottesville: University Press of Virginia, 1996), 89, 237. The election results support Formisano's core-periphery thesis, but in an inverse way. See Ronald P. Formisano, *The Transformation of Political Culture: Massachusetts Parties, 1790s–1840s* (New York: Oxford University Press, 1983), 14–15; Shade, ibid., 70–77.

29 The church statistics are from the *New-Hampshire Annual Register, 1829* (Concord, N.H.: Jacob B. Moore, 1829), 96–103.

30 Lee Benson, *The Concept of Jacksonian Democracy: New York as a Test Case* (New York: Atheneum, 1964), 31–32; Whitney R. Cross, *The Burned-Over District: The Social and Intellectual History of Enthusiastic Religion in Western New York* (Ithaca, N.Y.: Cornell University Press, 1950).

31 For the map and tables on which these patterns of voting in Ohio are based, see Ratcliffe, *Politics of Long Division*, 161, 162, 166–167.

32 Van Buren to Cambreleng, November 7, 1828, Van Buren Papers, LC.

33 For the gubernatorial returns, see *Albany Argus*, December 16, 1828. For the presidential returns, see Svend Petersen, *A Statistical History of American Presidential Elections* (New York: Frederick Ungar, 1963), 19.

34 Remini, *Election of 1828*, 61.

35 The word "improvement" appeared ten times in Adams's first annual message. See James D. Richardson, ed., *A Compilation of the Messages and Papers of the Presidents 1789–1897*, 10 vols. (Washington, D.C.: U.S. Congress, 1897–1899), 2:299–317.

36 William G. Shade, "Political Pluralism and Party Development: The Creation of a Modern Party System," in *The Evolution of American Electoral Systems*, ed. Paul Kleppner et al. (Westport, Conn.: Greenwood Press, 1981), 77–111.

37 Michael F. Holt, *The Rise and Fall of the American Whig Party: Jacksonian Politics and the Onset of the Civil War* (New York: Oxford University Press), 154, 209; McCormick, "New Perspectives on Jacksonian Politics," 300. Not everyone considers the 1830s and 1840s a golden age of American politics. See Glenn C. Altschuler and Stuart M. Blumin, *Rude Republic: Americans and Their Politics in the Nineteenth Century* (Princeton, N.J.: Princeton University Press, 2000), and "Political Engagement and Disengagement in Antebellum America: A Round Table," *Journal of American History* 84 (1997): 823–909.

38 Bruce Ackerman, *The Failure of the Founding Fathers: Jefferson, Marshall and the Rise of Presidential Democracy* (Cambridge, Mass.: Harvard University Press, 2005), 5, 112.

39 Clay to Hammond, November 16, 1827, in *HCP* 6:1269.

40 Lynn L. Marshall, "The Strange Stillbirth of the Whig Party," *AHR* 72

(1967): 452; Kendall to Blair, March 10, 1829, Blair and Lee Family Papers, Manuscripts Division, Department of Rare Books and Special Collections, Princeton University Library, cited in Donald B. Cole, *A Jackson Man: Amos Kendall and the Rise of American Democracy* (Baton Rouge: Louisiana State University Press, 2004), 122; Paul Johnson, "Democrats and the Friends of Adams in New York, 1828: A Study of Local Activists" (unpublished paper, 1970), 1.

41 *United States Telegraph*, November 8, 1828; *Argus of Western America*, October 29, 1828.

42 Porter Clay to Henry Clay, February 22, 1827, Charles Hammond to Clay, October 29, 1827, in *HCP* 6:222–223, 1199; Jeremiah Mason to Daniel Webster, February 20, 1825, in *DWP* 2:28–30; John J. Crittenden to Clay, November 19, 1827, in *HCP* 6:1287n2; Daniel Mallory to Clay, September 28, 1827, in *HCP* 6:1083–1084.

43 Peter P. F. Degrand to Joseph E. Sprague, July 4, 1826, Adams Family Papers, Letters Received, Massachusetts Historical Society, cited in Mary W. M. Hargreaves, *The Presidency of John Quincy Adams* (Lawrence: University Press of Kansas, 1985), 273.

44 Daniel Webster to Ezekiel Webster, January 17, 1829, in *DWP* 2:388. For the inaugural address, see Appendix A.

45 For excerpts from Jackson's first annual message, see Appendix B.

46 Richard R. John, *Spreading the News: The American Postal System from Franklin to Morse* (Cambridge, Mass.: Harvard University Press, 1995), 206–256; Jeffrey L. Pasley, *"The Tyranny of Printers": Newspaper Politics in the Early American Republic* (Charlottesville: University Press of Virginia, 2001), 399.

47 Jeffrey L. Pasley, "Minnows, Spies, and Aristocrats: The Social Crisis of Congress in the Age of Martin Van Buren," *Journal of the Early Republic* 27 (2007): 599–653; Sidney Aronson, *Status and Kinship in the Higher Civil Service, Standards of Selection in the Administrations of John Adams, Thomas Jefferson, and Andrew Jackson* (Cambridge, Mass.: Harvard University Press, 1964); Wilentz, *Rise of American Democracy*, 864n10; McCormick, "New Perspectives on Jacksonian Politics," 292.

BIBLIOGRAPHIC ESSAY

For more than half a century historians of antebellum politics have started their bibliographies with Arthur M. Schlesinger Jr.'s *The Age of Jackson* (Boston: Little, Brown, 1945). Schlesinger's opus remains the classic Progressive statement of the Jacksonian mentality, but it has been superseded by Sean Wilentz, *The Rise of American Democracy: Jefferson to Lincoln* (New York: Norton, 2005). Wilentz's massive defense of Jacksonian democracy is must reading for both general reader and historian, but especially the latter because of its copious footnotes. Also indispensable is Daniel Walker Howe's magisterial *What Hath God Wrought: The Transformation of America, 1815–1848* (New York: Oxford University Press, 2007), which emphasizes the religious, social, and economic revolutions of the era and is less generous toward Jacksonianism.

For the election of 1828 readers have long had the choice of Florence Weston, *The Presidential Election of 1828* (1938; reprint, Philadelphia: Porcupine Press, 1974), or Robert V. Remini, *The Election of Andrew Jackson* (Philadelphia: J. B. Lippincott, 1963), which is more up to date and more fun to read. Remini also wrote a brief account, "Election of 1828," in *History of American Presidential Elections, 1789–1968*, ed. Arthur M. Schlesinger Jr., 4 vols. (New York: Chelsea House, 1971), 1:413–492.

Biographies abound of the main figures in the election. The most scholarly and most sympathetic biography of Andrew Jackson is Robert V. Remini's detailed trilogy, of which the second volume, *Andrew Jackson and the Course of American Freedom, 1822–1833* (New York: Harper & Row, 1981), covers the period of the Old Hero's three presidential campaigns. Another sympathetic treatment of Jackson is Jon Meacham, *American Lion: Andrew Jackson in the White House* (New York: Random House, 2008). More probing and more critical assessments of Jackson's personality and character can be found in Andrew Burstein, *The Passions of Andrew Jackson* (New York: Knopf, 2003), and James C. Curtis, *Andrew Jackson and the Search for Vindication* (Boston: Little, Brown, 1976).

To understand how Jackson was launched into presidential politics in 1824, see Robert P. Hay, "The Case for Andrew Jackson: Eaton's Wyoming Letters," *Tennessee Historical Quarterly* 29 (1970): 139–151. To compare nineteenth- and twentieth-century estimates of Jackson, read James Parton, *Life of Andrew Jackson*, 3 vols. (New York: Mason Brothers, 1860), and John William Ward, *Andrew Jackson: Symbol for an Age* (New York: Oxford University Press, 1955).

After years of dealing with Democrats Remini turned to the other side and produced excellent, well-documented biographies of two Whigs: *Henry Clay: Statesman for the Union* (New York: Norton, 1991) and *Daniel Webster: The Man and His Times* (New York: Norton, 1997). The classic multivolume biographies of John Quincy Adams and John C. Calhoun are still Samuel Flagg Bemis, *John*

Quincy Adams and the Union (New York: Knopf, 1956) and *John Quincy Adams and the Foundations of American Foreign Policy* (New York: Knopf, 1949), and Charles M. Wiltse, *John C. Calhoun,* 3 vols. (Indianapolis: Bobbs-Merrill, 1944–1951). More recent treatments are Paul C. Nagel, *Descent from Glory: Four Generations of the John Adams Family* (New York: Oxford University Press, 1983), and John Niven, *John C. Calhoun and the Price of Union: A Biography* (Baton Rouge: Louisiana State University Press, 1988). For Martin Van Buren, there are Donald B. Cole, *Martin Van Buren and the American Political System* (Princeton, N.J.: Princeton University Press, 1984); John Niven, *Martin Van Buren: The Romantic Age of American Politics* (New York: Oxford University Press, 1983); and the Little Magician's own guarded recollections, John C. Fitzpatrick, ed., "The Autobiography of Martin Van Buren," in *Annual Report of the American Historical Association for the Year 1918,* 2 vols. (Washington, D.C.: Government Printing Office, 1920). Both Cole and Niven present Van Buren as a dedicated party organizer rather than a corrupt politician. Merrill D. Peterson explores the interrelationships of Webster, Clay, and Calhoun in *The Great Triumvirate: Webster, Clay, and Calhoun* (New York: Oxford University Press, 1987).

The six editor-politicians featured in this book have not fared as well. Until recently, only Thurlow Weed had found a modern biographer. Their biographies now number three, along with two autobiographies: Glyndon G. Van Deusen, *Thurlow Weed: Wizard of the Lobby* (1947; reprint, New York: Da Capo Press, 1969); Donald B. Cole, *A Jackson Man: Amos Kendall and the Rise of American Democracy* (Baton Rouge: Louisiana State University Press, 2004); W. Stephen Belko, *The Invincible Duff Green: Whig of the West* (Columbus: University of Missouri Press, 2006); Harriet A. Weed, ed., *Autobiography of Thurlow Weed* (1883; reprint, New York: Da Capo Press, 1970); Amos Kendall, *Autobiography of Amos Kendall,* ed. William Stickney (1872; reprint, New York: Peter Smith, 1949).

Supporting the biographies are the published papers of the major figures. The first to become available were the *Memoirs of John Quincy Adams,* ed. Charles Francis Adams, 12 vols. (Philadelphia: J. B. Lippincott, 1875), and the *Correspondence of Andrew Jackson,* ed. John Spencer Bassett and John Franklin Jameson, 7 vols. (1926–1935; reprint, New York: Krause Reprint Co., 1969). A real breakthrough came in the last few decades with *The Papers of Daniel Webster: Correspondence,* ed. Charles M. Wiltse et al., 7 vols. (Hanover, N.H.: University Press of New England, 1974–1986); *The Papers of Henry Clay,* ed. James F. Hopkins et al., 11 vols. (Lexington: University Press of Kentucky, 1959–1992); and *The Papers of John C. Calhoun,* ed. Robert L. Meriwether, Clyde Wilson, et al., 28 vols. (Columbia: University of South Carolina Press, 1959–2003).

More are yet to come. Editors in Tennessee have published seven volumes of a new edition of the Jackson papers covering the years through 1829: *The Papers of Andrew Jackson,* ed. Harold D. Moser, Daniel Feller, et al., 7 vols. to date (Knoxville: University of Tennessee Press, 1994–). In Boston the staff of the Adams Papers is working on the papers of John Quincy Adams. There is also a microfilm edition of the Martin Van Buren papers: *Papers of Martin Van Buren* (Alexandria, Va.: Chadwyck-Healey, Microfilm, 1987).

To understand the birth of the republic, the reader should start with Gordon Wood's *The Creation of the American Republic: 1776–1787* (Chapel Hill: University of North Carolina Press, 1969) and *The Radicalism of the American Revolution* (New York: Knopf, 1991). To feel the spirit of republicanism, try a chapter or two from Jeremy Belknap, *The History of New Hampshire*, 2d ed., 3 vols. (Boston: Bradford & Read, 1813), and John Taylor, *Construction Construed and Constitutions Vindicated* (1820; reprint, New York: Da Capo Press, 1970). Harry L. Watson describes the assumptions of American republicanism in *Liberty and Power: The Politics of Jacksonian America* (New York: Hill & Wang, 1990). To see how Americans celebrated their fifty-year jubilee, turn to Andrew Burstein, *America's Jubilee: How in 1826 a Generation Remembered Fifty Years of Independence* (New York: Knopf, 2001).

For the economic revolution, the panic of 1819, and the expansion of the Post Office, see George R. Taylor, *The Transportation Revolution, 1815–1860* (New York: Holt, Rinehart & Winston, 1951); Murray N. Rothbard, *The Panic of 1819: Reactions and Policies* (New York: Columbia University Press, 1962); and Richard R. John, *Spreading the News: The American Postal System from Franklin to Morse* (Cambridge, Mass.: Harvard University Press, 1995). Charles Sellers interprets Jacksonian democracy as a negative reaction to dramatic economic changes in *The Market Revolution: Jacksonian America, 1815–1846* (New York: Oxford University Press, 1991). A collection of differing views on this subject can be found in Melvyn Stokes and Stephen Conway, eds., *The Market Revolution in America: Social, Political, and Religious Expressions, 1800–1880* (Charlottesville: University Press of Virginia, 1996). Those interested in the rising labor movement should start with John R. Commons and associates, *The History of Labour in the United States*, 4 vols. (New York: Macmillan, 1918), and Edward Pessen, "The Workingmen's Party Revisited," *Labor History* 4 (1963): 203–226. The best article on the tariff of abominations is Robert V. Remini, "Martin Van Buren and the Tariff of Abominations," *American Historical Review* 63 (1958): 903–917.

There has been steady interest in the grudging acceptance of political parties in America. Richard Hofstadter gives full credit to Martin Van Buren and the Albany Regency, but Jeffrey L. Pasley spreads the credit more widely: see Hofstadter, *The Idea of a Party System: The Rise of Legitimate Opposition in the United States, 1780–1840* (Berkeley: University of California Press, 1969), and Pasley, *"The Tyranny of Printers": Newspaper Politics in the Early American Republic* (Charlottesville: University Press of Virginia, 2001). The most comprehensive treatment of the second party system is Richard P. McCormick, *The Second American Party System: Party Formation in the Jacksonian Era* (Chapel Hill: University of North Carolina Press, 1966). For an influential article on the election of 1828 and the rise of democracy, see Richard P. McCormick, "New Perspectives on Jacksonian Politics," *American Historical Review* 65 (1960): 292.

To understand the transition from the first American party system to the second, start with Shaw Livermore, *The Twilight of Federalism: The Disintegration of the Federalist Party 1815–1830* (Princeton, N.J.: Princeton University Press, 1962), and Norman K. Risjord, *The Old Republicans: Southern Conservatism in the Age of Jefferson* (New York: Columbia University Press, 1965). For the origins of the Democratic party, see Michael F. Holt, "The Democratic Party, 1828–1860," in *The History of U.S. Political Parties,* ed. Arthur M. Schlesinger Jr., 4 vols. (New York: Chelsea House, 1973), and an excellent dissertation by Thomas M. Coens, "The Formation of the Jackson Party, 1822–1825" (Harvard University, 2004). Holt has also written a heavily documented study: *The Rise and Fall of the American Whig Party* (New York: Oxford University Press, 1999).

For the Anti-Masonic party, see Whitney R. Cross, *The Burned-Over District: The Social and Intellectual History of Enthusiastic Religion in Western New York* (Ithaca, N.Y.: Cornell University Press, 1950); Ronald P. Formisano and Kathleen Smith Kutolowski, "Antimasonry and Masonry: The Genesis of Protest, 1826–1827," *American Quarterly* 29 (1977): 139–165; and William P. Vaughan, *The Antimasonic Party in the United States, 1826–1843* (Lexington: University Press of Kentucky, 1983).

The rise of partisan spirit is best seen in the newspapers of the era. A good sampling for the years 1825–1828 includes, on the Jackson side, the *Albany Argus,* the *New-Hampshire Patriot* (Concord), the *United States Telegraph* (Washington, D.C.), the *Richmond Enquirer,* and the *Argus of Western America* (Frankfort, Ky.); on the Adams side, see the *National Advocate* (New York), the *Democratic Press* (Philadelphia), *Niles' Weekly Register* (Baltimore), the *National Intelligencer* (Washington, D.C.), and the *Liberty Hall and Cincinnati Gazette.* In addition to Pasley's *"The Tyranny of Printers,"* the best sources on the press are Culver H. Smith, *The Press, Politics, and Patronage: The American Government's Use of Newspapers, 1789–1875* (Athens: University of Georgia Press, 1977), and Frederic Hudson, *Journalism in the United States from 1690 to 1872* (New York: Harper & Brothers, 1873).

V. O. Key Jr. introduced the concept of political party systems with "A Theory of Critical Elections," *Journal of Politics* 17 (1955): 3–18, which was further developed in William Nisbet Chambers and Walter Dean Burnham, eds., *The American Party Systems: Stages of Political Development* (New York: Oxford University Press, 1967). Ronald P. Formisano dismisses the first party system in his influential article "Federalists and Republicans: Parties, Yes—System, No," in *The Evolution of American Electoral Systems,* ed. Paul Kleppner et al. (Westport, Conn.: Greenwood Press, 1981), 33–76; William G. Shade demonstrates that the second party system started in 1838 in "Political Pluralism and Party Development: The Creation of a Modern Party System," ibid., 77–111. Harry L. Watson defends the idea that there was a golden age of American politics before the Civil War in "Humbug? Bah! Altschuler and Blumin and the Riddle of the Antebellum Electorate," *Journal of American History* 84 (1997): 886–895; Glenn C. Altschuler and Stuart M. Blumin challenge the concept in *Rude Republic: Americans and Their Politics in the Nineteenth Century* (Princeton, N.J.: Princeton University Press, 2000). For a discussion on this subject, see "Public Engagement and Disengagement in Antebellum America: A Round Table," *Journal of American History* 84 (1997): 823–909.

There has been much controversy over the role of slavery and racism in the shaping of antebellum America. In his recent *The Missouri Compromise and Its Aftermath: Slavery and the Meaning of America* (Chapel Hill: University of North Carolina Press, 2007), Robert Pierce Forbes accuses the Jacksonians of racism, a charge that is rejected by Joel H. Silbey, *Martin Van Buren and the Emergence of American Popular Politics* (Lanham, Md.: Rowman & Littlefield, 2002), and Jonathan H. Earle, *Jacksonian Antislavery and the Politics of Free Soil, 1824–1854* (Chapel Hill: University of North Carolina Press, 2004). For books and articles emphasizing the role of slavery and the "slave power" in the election of 1828 and antebellum politics, see Richard H. Brown, "The Missouri Crisis, Slavery, and the Politics of Jacksonianism," *South Atlantic Quarterly* 65 (1966): 55–70; William J. Cooper, *The South and the Politics of Slavery, 1828–1856* (Baton Rouge: Louisiana State University Press, 1978); Richard R. John, "Affairs of Office: The Executive Departments, the Election of 1828, and the Making of the Democratic Party," in *The Democratic Experiment: New Directions in American Political History*, ed. Julian Zelizer, Meg Jacobs, and William Novak (Princeton, N.J.: Princeton University Press, 2003), 50–85; and Leonard L. Richards, *The Slave Power: The Free North and Southern Domination, 1780–1860* (Baton Rouge: Louisiana State University Press, 2000).

On the subject of political patronage during and after the 1828 campaign, see Worthington C. Ford, ed., "Use of Patronage in Elections," *Proceedings of the Massachusetts Historical Society*, 3rd ser., 1 (1908): 359–393, and Carl R. Fish, "Removal of Officials by the Presidents of the United States," in *Annual Report of the American Historical Association for the Year 1899*, 2 vols. (Washington, D.C.: Government Printing Office, 1900), 1:65–86.

The voting results for presidential elections are best found in Svend Petersen, *A Statistical History of American Presidential Elections* (New York: Frederick Ungar, 1963), but Edward Stanwood's *A History of the Presidency* (Boston: Houghton, Mifflin, 1898) is still useful. The results of congressional elections and the names of the candidates are conveniently tabulated in *Congressional Quarterly's Guide to U.S. Elections*, 4th ed., ed. John L. Moore, John P. Preimesberger, and David R. Tarr, 2 vols. (Washington, D.C.: CQ Press, 2001). To find the party affiliation of members of Congress, look in Kenneth C. Martis, *The Historical Atlas of Political Parties in the United States Congress, 1789–1989* (New York: Macmillan, 1989); to find out where they lived in Washington and on what committees they served, turn to Perry M. Goldman and James S. Young, eds., *The United States Congressional Directories, 1789–1840* (New York: Columbia University Press, 1973). For information about the right to vote, see Chilton Williamson, *American Suffrage from Property to Democracy, 1760–1860* (Princeton, N.J.: Princeton University Press, 1960), and Alexander Keyssar, *The Right to Vote: The Contested History of Democracy in the United States* (New York: Basic Books, 2001). Richard Franklin Bensel uses congressional investigations of contested elections to describe behavior at the polling stations, especially violence and coercion, in *The American Ballot Box in the Mid-Nineteenth Century* (Cambridge: Cambridge

University Press, 2004). James Chase describes the rise of political conventions in *Emergence of the Presidential Nominating Convention, 1789–1832* (Urbana: University of Illinois Press, 1973). Bruce Ackerman presents a critical assessment of the founding fathers in *The Failure of the Founding Fathers: Jefferson, Marshall and the Rise of Presidential Democracy* (Cambridge, Mass.: Harvard University Press, 2005).

To trace the rise of political parties at the state level, the best sources of information are state histories and political biographies. For New England, these sources include Thomas L. Gaffney, "Maine's Mr. Smith: A Study of Francis O. Smith, Politician and Entrepreneur" (doctoral diss., University of Maine, 1979); Donald B. Cole, *Jacksonian Democracy in New Hampshire, 1800–1851* (Cambridge, Mass.: Harvard University Press, 1970); Arthur B. Darling, *Political Changes in Massachusetts, 1824–1828* (New Haven, Conn.: Yale University Press, 1925); and Ronald P. Formisano, *The Transformation of Political Culture: Massachusetts Parties, 1790s–1840s* (New York: Oxford University Press, 1983).

There are many histories of New York, but none are very recent: Jabez Hammond, *The History of Political Parties in the State of New-York*, 2 vols. (Albany, N.Y.: C. Van Benthuysen, 1842); De Alva Stanwood Alexander, *A Political History of the State of New York*, 2 vols. (Port Washington, N.Y.: Ira J. Friedman, 1909); Dixon Ryan Fox, *The Decline of Aristocracy in the Politics of New York, 1801–1840*, ed. Robert V. Remini (1919; reprint, New York: Harper, 1965); Robert V. Remini, "The Albany Regency," *New York History* 39 (1958): 341–355; Lee Benson, *The Concept of Jacksonian Democracy: New York as a Test Case* (New York: Atheneum, 1964); Jerome Mushkat, *Tammany: The Evolution of a Political Machine, 1789–1865* (Syracuse, N.Y.: Syracuse University Press, 1971).

Useful sources for the other Middle Atlantic states are Philip S. Klein, *Pennsylvania Politics, 1817–1832: A Game without Rules* (Philadelphia: Historical Society of Pennsylvania, 1940); Philip S. Klein and Ari Hoogenboom, *A History of Pennsylvania* (New York: McGraw-Hill, 1973); Kim T. Phillips, "The Pennsylvania Origins of the Jackson Movement," *Political Science Quarterly* 91 (1976): 489–508; Herbert Ershkowitz, *The Origin of the Whig and Democratic Parties: New Jersey Politics, 1820–1837* (Washington, D.C.: University Press of America, 1982); and Mark H. Haller, "The Rise of the Jackson Party in Maryland, 1820–1829," *Journal of Southern History* 28 (1962): 307–326.

For the South, the best overall treatment of the years down to 1854 is William W. Freehling, *The Road to Disunion*, vol. 1, *Secessionists at Bay, 1776–1854* (New York: Oxford University Press, 1990). Any student of antebellum Virginia must deal with the topics of democracy and the nature of the Richmond Junto, the secret society that dominated politics in the state yet left no records and may not have existed at all. In his *Democratizing the Old Dominion: Virginia and the Second Party System* (Charlottesville: University Press of Virginia, 1996), William G. Shade provides a nuanced analysis of the first topic. Two scholars who believe that the Richmond Junto really existed are Harry Ammon, "The Richmond Junto, 1800–1824," and Joseph H. Harrison Jr., "Oligarchs and Democrats in the Richmond Junto," *Virginia Magazine of History and Biography* 63 (1955):

395–419 and 78 (1970): 184–198. F. Thornton Miller suggests that the junto may have been an imaginary organization created by Ritchie's enemies to discredit him; see "The Richmond Junto: The Secret, All-Powerful Club or Myth," *Virginia Magazine of History and Biography* 99 (1991): 63–80. Charles Henry Ambler's *Thomas Ritchie: A Study in Virginia Politics* (Richmond, Va.: Bell Book & Stationery Company, 1913), is still the only biography of the head of the junto. Robert P. Sutton explains the decline of Virginia in "Nostalgia, Pessimism, and Malaise: The Doomed Aristocrat in Late-Jeffersonian Virginia," *Virginia Magazine of History and Biography* 76 (1968): 41–65.

William S. Hoffman, *Andrew Jackson and North Carolina Politics* (Chapel Hill: University of North Carolina Press, 1958), and Harry L. Watson, *Jacksonian Politics and Community Conflict: Cumberland County, North Carolina* (Baton Rouge: Louisiana State University Press, 1981), offer two different approaches to North Carolina politics.

The best study of a state in the Old Northwest is Donald J. Ratcliffe, *The Politics of Long Division: The Birth of the Second Party System in Ohio, 1818–1828* (Columbus: Ohio State University Press, 2000). Other works to consult are Carlyle Buley, *The Old Northwest: Pioneer Period, 1815–1840*, 2 vols. (Bloomington: Indiana University Press, 1950); Harry R. Stevens, *The Early Jackson Party in Ohio* (Durham, N.C.: Duke University Press, 1957); Donald J. Ratcliffe, "Voter Turnout in Early Ohio," *Journal of the Early Republic* 7 (1987): 223–251; Emil Pocock, "Popular Roots of Jacksonian Democracy: The Case of Dayton, Ohio, 1815–1830," *Journal of the Early Republic* 9 (1989): 489–515; and Gerald Leonard, *The Invention of Party Politics: Federalism, Popular Sovereignty, and Constitutional Development in Jacksonian Illinois* (Chapel Hill: University of North Carolina Press, 2002).

For the Southwest, there are Robert E. Shallope, "Jacksonian Politics in Missouri: A Comment on the McCormick Thesis," *Civil War History* 15 (1969): 210–225; Charles Sellers, "Banking and Politics in Jackson's Tennessee, 1817–1827," *Mississippi Valley Historical Review* 41 (1954): 61–84; Charles Sellers, "Jackson Men with Feet of Clay," *American Historical Review* 42 (1957): 537–551; Jasper B. Shannon and Ruth McQuown, *Presidential Politics in Kentucky, 1824–1848* (Lexington: Bureau of Government Research of the University of Kentucky, 1950), 4–6; Leonard P. Curry, "Election Year—Kentucky, 1828," *Register of the Kentucky State Historical Society* 55 (1957): 196–212; Lynn L. Marshall, "The Genesis of Grass-roots Democracy in Kentucky," *Mid-America* 47 (1965): 269–287; Frank F. Mathias and Jasper B. Shannon, "Gubernatorial Politics in Kentucky, 1820–1851," *Register of the Kentucky State Historical Society* 88 (1990): 253–256; J. Mills Thornton, *Politics and Power in a Slave Society: Alabama, 1800–1860* (Baton Rouge: Louisiana State University Press, 1978); and John M. Sacher, *A Perfect War of Politics: Parties, Politicians, and Democracy in Louisiana, 1824–1861* (Baton Rouge: Louisiana State University Press, 2003).

To understand the election from the point of view of the John Quincy Adams party, Mary W. M. Hargreaves, *The Presidency of John Quincy Adams* (Lawrence: University Press of Kansas, 1985), is indispensable. To understand Adams's dilemma as president, see Stephen Skowronek, *The Politics Presidents Make: Leadership from John Adams to Bill Clinton* (Cambridge, Mass.: Harvard University Press, 1997), which includes a chapter on the failure of the John Quincy Adams administration.

M. J. Heale analyzes the election campaign from the point of view of a British political scientist in *The Making of American Politics, 1750–1850* (London: Longman, 1977); Margaret Bayard Smith offers the perspective of a Washington social leader in *The First Forty Years of Washington Society*, ed. Gaillard Hunt (1906; reprint, New York: Frederick Ungar, 1965). Joel H. Silbey has edited a selection of campaign addresses in *The American Party Battle: Election Campaign Pamphlets, 1828–1876*, 2 vols. (Cambridge, Mass.: Harvard University Press, 1999). There are also a number of useful articles on the campaign: Norma Basch, "Marriage, Morals, and Politics in the Election of 1828," *Journal of American History* 80 (1993): 890–918; Michael Birkner, "The General, the Secretary, and the President: An Episode in the Presidential Campaign of 1828," *Tennessee Historical Quarterly* 42 (1983): 243–253; Anthony M. Brescia, ed., "The Election of 1828: A View from Louisville," *Register of the Kentucky State Historical Society* 74 (1976): 51–57; Edwin A. Miles, "President Adams' Billiard Table," *New England Quarterly* 45 (1972): 31–43; and Matthew Warshauer, "Andrew Jackson as a 'Military Chieftain' in the 1824 and 1828 Presidential Elections: The Ramifications of Martial Law on American Republicanism," *Tennessee Historical Quarterly* 57 (1998): 4–23.

A cottage industry has sprung up around the political tactics, concepts, stories, lore, and artifacts that made the election of 1828 a special one: Arthur M. Schlesinger Jr., ed., *Running for President: The Candidates and Their Images*, 2 vols. (New York: Simon & Schuster, 1944); Jean H. Baker, "The Ceremonies of Politics: Nineteenth-Century Rituals of National Affirmation," in *A Master's Due*, ed. William J. Cooper Jr., Michael F. Holt, and John McCardell (Baton Rouge: Louisiana State University Press, 1985), 161–178; William C. Cook, "Random Jottings of a Collector on the Presidential Election of 1828" (unpublished paper, 2005); William C. Cook, "The Coffin Handbills—America's First Smear Campaign," *Imprint: Journal of the American Historical Print Collectors Society* 27 (2002): 24–25.

To read about the new writing style employed in the election, see Kenneth Cmiel, *Democratic Eloquence: The Fight over Popular Speech in Nineteenth-Century America* (New York: William Morrow, 1990), and Andrew W. Robertson, *The Language of Democracy: Political Rhetoric in the United States and Britain* (Ithaca, N.Y.: Cornell University Press, 1995).

Two studies of the Jackson administration are Donald B. Cole, *The Presidency of Andrew Jackson* (Lawrence: University Press of Kansas, 1993), and Richard B. Latner, *The Presidency of Andrew Jackson: White House Politics, 1829–1837* (Athens: University of Georgia Press, 1979).

For two excellent collections of recent articles on American political history, turn to Byron E. Shafer and Anthony J. Badger, eds., *Contesting Democracy:*

Substance and Structure in American Political History, 1775–2000 (Lawrence: University Press of Kansas, 2001), and Jeffrey L. Pasley, Andrew W. Robertson, and David Waldstreicher, eds., *Beyond the Founders: New Approaches to the Political History of the Early American Republic* (Chapel Hill: University of North Carolina Press, 2004).